Grand Forks

Grand Forks

A History of American Dining in 128 Reviews

MARILYN HAGERTY

AN ANTHONY BOURDAIN BOOK

ecco

FIRST EDITION

Designed by Suet Yee Chong

Library of Congress Cataloging-in-Publication Data has been applied for.

ISBN 978-0-06-222889-5

13 14 15 16 17   OV/RRD   10 9 8 7 6 5 4 3 2 1

This book is dedicated to all the people who have the gumption to work so hard in restaurants across our land.

It is also dedicated to the memory of my daughter Carol Hagerty Werner and in honor of her husband, Curt, along with my daughter Gail Hagerty and her husband, Dale Sandstrom, and my son, James R. "Bob" Hagerty, and his wife, Lorraine. And especially to the eight grandchildren who brightened the last days of Grandpa Jack Hagerty and continue to make my life worthwhile. They are Jack Golden; Carrie and Anne Sandstrom; Curtis, Mariah, and Anna Werner; and James and Carmen Hagerty.

Foreword
by Anthony Bourdain

If you're looking for the kind of rapturous food porn you'd find in a book by M. F. K. Fisher, or lusty descriptions of sizzling kidneys a la Liebling—or even the knife-edged criticism of an A. A. Gill or a Sam Sifton—you will not find it here.

The territory covered here is not New York or Paris or London or San Francisco. And Marilyn Hagerty is none of those people.

For twenty-seven years, Marilyn Hagerty has been covering the restaurant scene in and around the city of Grand Forks, North Dakota, population approximately 55,000. She also, it should be pointed out, writes a total of five columns a week, about history and local personalities and events, in addition to her writing about restaurants and food. As one might expect, she knows many of her subjects personally. Given the size of her territory, it is not unusual for her to write about the same restaurant two or more times in a single year. In short, she is writing about a community that she is very much a part of.

If you knew her name before picking up this book, it was probably because of her infamously guileless Olive Garden review, which went viral and caused a tidal wave of snarky derision, followed by an even stronger antisnark backlash, followed by invitations to appear on Anderson Cooper and the *Today* show, dinner at Le Bernardin, an appearance on *Top Chef,* an Al Neuharth Award, a publishing deal—a sudden and unexpected elevation to media darling.

Why was that?

What is it about the eighty-seven-year-old Ms. Hagerty that inspired such attention and affection?

Why should you read this book?

Of the seven thousand pages of articles and reviews I read while assembling this collection, there is little of what one would call pyrotechnical prose. Ms. Hagerty's choices of food are shockingly consistent: A "clubhouse sandwich," coleslaw, wild rice soup, salads assembled from a salad bar, baked potatoes. She is not what you'd call an adventurous diner, exploring the dark recesses of menus. Far from it. Of one lunch, she writes: "There were signs saying the luncheon special was soup and a Denver sandwich for $2.25. In places where food service is limited, I tend to take the special. I wasn't born yesterday."

She is never mean—even when circumstances would clearly excuse a sharp elbow, a cruel remark. In fact, watching Marilyn struggle to find something nice to say about a place she clearly loathes is part of the fun. She is, unfailingly, a good neighbor and good citizen first—and an entertainer second.

But what she *has* given us, over all these years, is a fascinating picture of dining in America, a gradual, cumulative overview of how we got from there . . . to here.

Grand Forks is not New York City. We forget that—until we read her earlier reviews and remember, some of us, when you'd find a sloppy joe, steak Diane, turkey noodle soup, three-bean salad, red Jell-O in *our* neighborhoods. When the tuft of curly parsley and lemon wedge, or a leaf of lettuce and an orange segment, or three spears of asparagus fashioned into a wagon wheel, were state-of-the-art garnishes. When you could order a half sandwich, a cup of soup. A prehipster world where lefse, potato dumplings, and walleye were far more likely to appear on a menu than pork belly.

Reading these reviews, we can see, we can watch over the course of time, who makes it and who doesn't. Which bold, undercapitalized pioneers survived—and who, no matter how ahead of their time, just couldn't hang on until the neighborhood caught up. You will get to know the names of owners and chefs like Warren LeClerc, whose homey lunch restaurant, The Pantry, turned down the lights to become the sophisticated French restaurant Le Pantre by night. And Chef Nardane of Touch of Magic Ballroom, who, in his 6,200-square-foot space, served cheesecakes inspired by Debbie Reynolds and Elizabeth Taylor and envisioned an exclusive private membership club with frequent celebrity entertainment. And Steve Novak of Beaver's Family Restaurant, who, when Marilyn visited his establishment, spoke of reviving his beaver act, complete with costume, for birthday parties.

And you will understand why the opening of an Olive Garden might be earnestly anticipated as an exciting and much-welcomed event.

Ms. Hagerty is not naive about her work, her newfound fame, or the world. She has traveled widely in her life.

In person, she has a flinty, dry, very sharp sense of humor. She misses nothing.

I would not want to play poker with her for money.

This is a straightforward account of what people have been

eating—still *are* eating—in much of America. As related by a kind, good-hearted reporter looking to pass along as much useful information as she can—while hurting no one.

Anyone who comes away from this work anything less than charmed by Ms. Hagerty—and the places and characters she describes—has a heart of stone.

This book kills snark dead.

Grand Forks

Introduction

When I started writing about restaurants in a weekly column called the Eatbeat, I never dreamed it would catch the attention of Anthony Bourdain or that it would lead to dinner at Le Bernardin in New York City.

All I was thinking was that I write for the *Herald*—the daily newspaper in Grand Forks, North Dakota—and as features editor thirty-some years ago, I wanted to have a restaurant review. After all, I would dine with writers from the Minneapolis *Star Tribune* and the *New York Times* when I attended annual meetings of the Association of Food Journalists. We traveled annually to major cities, to Hawaii, to China. They talked of their restaurant reviews.

My favorite pastime is eating. I know how to cook. Long ago, I memorized *Betty Crocker's Picture Cookbook* and the *Joy of Cooking*. I have edited two cookbooks for my church.

Why not have a restaurant review in Grand Forks? I asked myself. But how could I do it?

We don't have that many restaurants in our city. So I decided it would work if I went to every restaurant in town. That would mean places such as Taco John's, McDonald's, and the truck stops. To me, these places are interesting. And plenty of people eat in them.

To broaden my Eatbeat coverage, I visited neighboring towns. Dinner or lunch and a drive make a nice outing.

Thus began my routine of reviewing restaurants in the circulation area of the Grand Forks Herald. One review led to another. When I traveled in Portugal, Hong Kong, Tokyo, Shanghai, London, and Brussels, I took the Eatbeat with me. Readers told me they enjoyed the travel and dining experiences vicariously. Twice, I have eaten in the White House; once with the American Society of News Editors and once with the Association of Food Journalists.

My goal with the Eatbeat is to tell readers of the *Grand Forks Herald* what is available in restaurants and how much it costs. How clean it is, and how the service is. And yes, the condition of the restroom, because it sends a message. Then when readers come in from around the area they know what to expect.

I write the Eatbeat as a reporter—not as a critic. This is not Los Angeles. It is not New York City. What point, I wonder, is there in tearing down some hardworking restaurant people? Sometimes I point out pluses and minuses. And if a place is just too bad, I move on. I don't write about it.

Some people berate my Eatbeats. Many more tell me they read and enjoy them. Years ago when *Herald* publisher Mike Maidenberg told me he liked what I wrote, I felt I had the green light to keep going.

I go in unannounced, but by now plenty of people know who I am. That just makes it more fun. Since the Eatbeat was my idea and I like to eat anyway, I have always personally paid for my own food at restaurants I review. No expense account. I thank those in restaurants who occasionally offer to give me a free meal. And when I explain why

I cannot accept, they understand and they appreciate my insistence on not being subsidized.

Over the years, restaurants have come and gone. This is a tough business. Here in Grand Forks, there are more chain restaurants now than the home-owned restaurants we used to know. Some longtime residents of Grand Forks may recall the Golden Hour, downtown, where they served heavenly halibut. It's long gone, along with the Ryan Hotel, where they offered lemon pie with mile-high meringue. Gone, too, is Jacoby's Hamburger Heaven, where I would rather go than to a fine dinner. And gone is the A&W Root Beer place where we ate with the kids in the backseat. Only the Kegs Drive-In with its sloppy joes remains from the olden days. The servers used to be on roller skates. People still are drawn back there when they come for high school reunions.

If Food Isn't Right, Diner Should Speak Up—Softly

OCTOBER 7, 1987

To me, it's embarrassing when companions make noisy complaints in restaurants. In fact, I avoid complaining even when asked by the waitress if everything is OK. I usually just nod my head and say everything is fine.

But one of my friends tells me, "You are wrong." She maintains that it helps the restaurant when you let them know what you don't like.

OK. I'll concede you should let them know. But I think you should do it politely.

Recently, a friend complained that the iced tea we were drinking in a local restaurant was so weak it was nothing more than water. She asked the waitress if we could have some fresh iced tea. Within a short time, the waitress came back with iced tea that had some color and flavor. I think the restaurant will serve better tea now that they know the diluted, stale tea they were serving was not acceptable.

The same goes for service. A reader called to tell me she had read a nice write-up about a local restaurant. She said she and her husband had gone there with a reservation. They were left waiting and stranded. They didn't know if they were ignored because they were wearing jeans. But, she said, they wore nice jeans with neat shirts. Still, they had to wait so long after they finally were seated that they got up and left.

"Don't tell me, tell them," I suggested. I encouraged her to tell the manager how they felt and ask if they did something wrong. I think the manager will appreciate it.

This business of rushing diners keeps plaguing me. When I go out to eat, I like to relax and visit with my companions. At some restaurants, the plates are snapped away from us as quickly as we take the last bite—sometimes before we finish.

I know, I know. Waitresses are instructed to remove dirty plates promptly. I think they should wait until everyone at the table is finished.

One day, I was lunching with a friend who had a lot to tell me. I ate my lunch as I listened. By the time she got around to serious eating, the waitress had whipped my plate away. My friend, I could tell, felt uneasy eating alone. So she took a few bites and set her fork down.

To avoid such situations, I now purposely leave a little something on my plate and pretend I am still eating until everyone at the table has finished.

One of my pet peeves about some restaurants is that they serve imitation seafood without acknowledging it. For instance, we were told the special at a Grand Forks dining room was steak and lobster for $8.50. I jumped at the offer, only to find the lobster was some kind of fish reconstituted in the shape of lobster tail. It even had red markings painted on it. Ick.

At another restaurant one evening, a friend ordered a crabmeat salad. When it came, there were little hunks of reconstituted fish in the shape of meat from crab legs. But it clearly was not crab. When we asked the waitress about it, she didn't know. And when we asked her to go and check with the cook, she came back and told us it was not crab.

North Dakota has a truth in menu law that requires food to be represented correctly. If the menu says crab, then it better be crab. If the menu offers buttered toast, then real butter must be used on the toast. The restaurant needn't serve butter on toast. It may serve a substitute. But it must not say that it is butter.

From the other side, I had notes from a waiter, a waitress and a motel maid after I wrote a column with the theme that these people earn every red cent they get. Those waiting tables point out their wages are in the $2.85 range and that they depend on their tips. The waitress said she doesn't mind sharing, or "tipping out," 8 percent to busboys and 5 percent to the bartenders. But she resents being required to tip out to the cooks. She's says it's against federal wage and hour law regulations. But she's afraid to complain because it might bring on retaliation from her employer. In other words, the ax.

Waiters and waitresses work long shifts with no prospects for getting a raise. They work irregular hours. They must handle the heat in the kitchen. The waiter wrote, "So the next time a waitress or waiter leaves your check and tells you to have a good day, remember to tip them well because chances are they're not."

The motel maid said she works for low wages and few—if any—tips. She said, "We have to clean up some of the most revolting messes ever known to man or beast." She says she never realized what a maid has to do until she tried it herself. "You are either bending over a bed or on your hands and knees. By the time you've made 18 to 20 beds, you can't stand straight. You should follow a maid one day, and you'd agree." ❡

Neon Lights, Burgers, Malts Are Topper's Trademarks

OCTOBER 21, 1987

Neon lights announce this is a hamburger grill and malt shop. You swing off North 42nd Street and into a large, paved parking lot. You give your order at the counter. They ask your name. You take a seat. They call your name. You pick up your burger and proceed to an extensive topping bar. There you can put anything your heart desires on your burger.

You take your malt—in the

metal can. You eat your burger, your fries and your malt. Or maybe you prefer a soft drink. You can have free refills from the machine in the dining room.

This is a happy place. This is Topper's.

On our first visit, there were quite a few people. On our second stop last Thursday night, all the tables but one were full. We sat down at the last table and looked around. There was a couple at the next table enjoying each other. As they talked they would put their heads together. Then she spoon-fed him the last of her malt.

Ah, yes. This is the reincarnation of a 1950s malt shop, and it is done well. The walls are white. The accent colors are pink and green. There are neon lights. There is a nickelodeon. On one wall, there are checked running shoes arranged in a trail with a sign saying, "Let's dance." Near the front, there are plastic records in various colors just swinging in the breeze.

The hamburgers are good. They are even better when you add to-mato, lettuce, pickles and onions.

The malts are ample. For $1.85, you get a malt with 15 ounces of ice cream and three ounces of milk. And the ice cream is home-made. There are 16 flavors avail-able, and you can have it in plain or sugar cones. Topper's even has tiny cones that go with the chil-dren's meals, or separately for 27 cents.

Ideas for flavors come from the customers, according to Jane Borman, who, with her husband, John, operates Topper's. She said new flavors are added regularly to the repertoire.

The Bormans are succeeding in a location where several other restaurants have failed. What they did, she says, is to change the image of the place. People seem to like it. And the location close to Crown Colony theaters and UND [University of North Da-kota] seems to help. It's a happy place to be—a good place to go on a cloudy day if you enjoy being around people.

The tables are covered with yellow and white plastic cloths. There are salt and pepper shakers made from canning jars. Plastic containers of mustard and catsup are on each table. And there are little trays of Trivial Pursuit cards, which people seem to enjoy as they wait for their food.

There's no real menu at Topper's. You just read the board above the counter as you come in. You can order burgers, bratwurst, hot dogs, tacos, fish or chicken sandwiches, pita clubs, chili or vegetable soup. You also can get beer or wine at Topper's. In fact, there is one section of the restaurant partitioned off by empty cardboard beer cases.

My idea of fun is eating a hamburger loaded with toppings. I like to go and let my imagination run wild. The french fries look great, but I try not to eat them. My first choice at Topper's is a hamburger and a cone. For variety the other night, I tried a fajita pita, and Constant Companion had a bratwurst. ❡

Topper's succumbed to a fire and the site is now home to a bank.

Mr. Steak Aims to Be the Gathering Place for Birthdays

NOVEMBER 4, 1987

They greet you and seat you promptly at Mr. Steak restaurant. They bring on food a cut above your run-of-the-mill fast food restaurants and a cut in price below your top-drawer restaurants. Mr. Steak has been perking along steadily in Grand Forks for 15 years. On two visits within the past week, they were packing 'em in.

People have come to depend on the restaurant. Senior citizens like the discount. Parents like the attention given their children. People celebrating birthdays go there for a free steak.

We went there Friday night for a quick supper. I was going on to the play at the Fire Hall Theater. You could tell by the green sweaters that many others were going on to the Sioux hockey game. We were seated in a nonsmoking section of booths, and Matt was our waiter. I didn't ask Matt his last name, and he didn't ask me my first or last name. He was a good waiter. Friendly, but impersonal.

I chose chicken strips for $5.99—without the salad bar, which makes it $4.99. That's something I like about Mr. Steak. You can have $1 off if you don't want to go through the salad bar. You still get a nice little loaf of warm whole wheat bread and your choice of potato. And your entree comes with an edible garnish of lettuce and orange slice.

Constant Companion ordered the traditional cut steak, also at $5.99. He elected to forgo the salad, but he requested the "hot, buttery mushrooms." That brought him back up to $5.99. We were well pleased with our food.

We made another swing into Mr. Steak for lunch Sunday. I took a trip through the salad bar and had a cup of soup for $3.99. CC chose the Reuben sandwich, even though he knows every restaurant has its own idea about Reubens. He found Mr. Steak turns out a pretty good version.

Seating is comfortable. In the evening, there's a soft light from the hanging lamps above each table. Plants in wicker baskets and tiny vases of permanent flowers on the tables add to the surroundings. The carpeting softens the slam-banging that goes on in some crowded restaurants.

Among the pluses for Mr. Steak: Large glass glasses of ice water are served promptly; potatoes are extra good; the baked potatoes are reds; the Mr. Steak fries are thick wedges with skin on, done to a deep golden brown; the hostess gives you the precise brand name and cost of wines or beer; and they serve an average of 100 to 110 free birthday steaks every week. ❡

Mr. Steak is no longer in business.

Krumkake Served with Scones at High Tea in Bismarck

DECEMBER 16, 1987

High tea has come to North Dakota, and it is doing very well, thank you.

On the second Monday of each month, between the hours of three and five o'clock, David's Restaurant at Logan and Third Streets in Bismarck holds high tea. Seventy-five to 100 women (and a sprinkling of men) from central North Dakota show up.

They pay $5.25.

In Bismarck's version of the English high tea, guests are welcomed with Concord red grape or cranberry juice in dainty aperitif glasses. They are seated at tables with white crocheted doilies beneath the glass covers. At each table, there are individual tea pots. Many of them are English bone china.

Since Lupe Barbere—who operates the restaurant with her husband, David Barbere—is a tea drinker, she brews the tea herself.

She uses tea balls and only English teas, and she is enthusiastic about the response to the teas, which she has been holding for six months.

"It's time-consuming to make the foods," said Barbere, "but we are getting it down to science now. We serve thinly sliced cucumber and egg slices on little open-face sandwiches. We serve them with English butter with herbs mixed in as spreads. We also have chicken pâté and ham spreads on tiny sandwiches. Last month, we had asparagus spears sliced diagonally on sandwiches. We bake our own scones and serve them with clotted cream and jam. Then we make bars, pinwheels and cookies. And," she continued, "it isn't really English, but we make krumkake and rosettes. The Norwegian people around here like that."

The restaurant makes sure there

are slices of lemon on each table. Four girls in pink pinafores do the serving, and they come around with hot water to add to the tea for those who think it seems too strong.

As high tea progresses, there is usually informal modeling of fashions by one of the Bismarck stores. In December, there was a presentation by Anderson's State Fur. There is piano music in the background.

The teas not only add a touch of glamor to a late afternoon in Bismarck, but they also bring in business at a time of day when the restaurant isn't busy. Lupe Barbere herself has never been to high tea in England, but she knows all about it from reading. And she has had high tea at hotels in San Francisco.

"There," she said, "many guests have brandies with tea. Not many order brandy here in Bismarck. This is a more conservative area." ❡

David's is no longer is business.

The Pantry Brings Blue Plate Back to Grand Forks

DECEMBER 30, 1987

The blue plate special is back. The old-time lunch bargain of the 1940s has returned to Grand Forks with the opening of The Pantry. This is a downtown restaurant at 109 N. Third St., in the building formerly occupied by the Girl Scouts. It's well located for people who work or do business downtown, with a handy back door to accommodate quick entries from the alley.

The blue plate isn't what it used to be. At The Pantry, it's an almost elegant meal of something like three pastas blended with cheeses, or beef stroganoff with a French flair. It is served with vegetables (yes, vegetables are back, too) and wedges of French bread. And it isn't 98 cents. But for these times, The Pantry's blue plate is almost that reasonable at around $3.50 or $3.75.

Since the deli-style restaurant opened here early in December, it has been drawing longer lines for lunch each noon. And customers have started trickling in all afternoon, sometimes just for coffee and dessert. Paul Ringstrom, who operates The Pantry with his uncle Warren LeClerc, says he is looking to expand hours after the New Year.

It seems as though they have a good thing going here. I was attracted to the place even before I got through the front door. I like the blackboard out in front on the sidewalk, where in various colors of chalk, you can read the specials of the day.

Once inside, you queue up. And while you await your turn, you have a chance to look over the foods in the delicatessen case. When you give your order, you get a wooden block—the kind children used to play with—and you take it to your table. Before long, they bring out your order and find you by the letter on your block.

On a recent lunch visit to The Pantry, I ordered a house salad, and added chicken salad for a grand total of $2.97, including the tax. Constant Companion asked for the blue plate special, which was beef stroganoff. It came to $3.97 with tax.

The food is good. So good, in fact, that I went back twice after my initial visit. After lunch one day, I had a chance to visit with Ringstrom, the chef. He told me he has loved baking ever since he helped his grandmother as a child. Ringstrom was born in Devils Lake and grew up in California. He is a graduate of Cornell University, Ithaca, N.Y., where he majored in hotel administration. After graduation, he spent a year in Europe. From the time he bought his first croissant, he has had a passion for French food. So strong, in fact, that he has learned the language, and puts a French twist in almost everything he bakes.

Ringstrom has worked in hotels and restaurants enough to know he wants to help make the decisions. And going into business here with his uncle gives him that opportunity. At 25, he is enthusiastic as he launches into his business. The Pantry will succeed, I predict, if it keeps its quality of food at reasonable prices. What this takes is hard work, and Ringstrom and LeClerc seem ready.

As in all businesses, there are rough spots that need smoothing out. But they are managing to handle unpredictable numbers of customers and stay relatively serene.

My suggestion would be to have the waiters and waitresses slip into aprons and pink pinafores to lend a more professional look. With a little more training, the waitpersons could do a better job in serving and clearing tables.

On the positive side, The Pantry is like a gem. It adds one more option to the variety of eating places in downtown Grand Forks. It will draw me back because of such details as pepper mills on each table, making it possible to help yourself to coarsely ground pepper; slices of lemon in the ice water; wooden boxes in which sandwiches are served; dishes with red and blue designs, which are so much nicer than institutional-type plates, cups and bowls; lace curtains on the windows; and the chance to help yourself to a free mint out of a little machine as you leave. ❡

Gramma Butterwicks Has Soup, Pot Pies Waiting

JANUARY 6, 1988

Grandma puts a little too much salt in her soup, but otherwise it's very good. The beef is plentiful and tender. The vegetables are cut in chunks just the way I like them.

I learned about her vegetable-beef soup when we stopped into Gramma Butterwicks Family Restaurant on South Washington Street on Saturday. When it was first built in 1960s, the restaurant was known as Sambo's. Then it became Seasons. Up until a week or so ago, the place was known as the Crestwood Restaurant. All of a sudden, it sprouted a new sign. "Gramma Butterwicks." It made me curious.

What I found was the same restaurant with a new image and a very appealing menu. It makes you feel good all over when you come to the children's part of the menu marked, "Grandchildren's menu." And then if you're more than 60, you like the next page. It's the seniors' menu, "for Gramma's friends 60 years and over." She likes her senior friends so well, in fact, that "Gramma" offers them free apple pie with dinners served between 4 and 9 P.M. on Sundays.

Actually, there is no "Gramma Butterwick," but it sounds very nice. Kevin Dorman, part-owner and manager, says it's a way of marketing specialties on the family restaurant menu. Dorman is staking his hopes for the success of Gramma Butterwicks on such homey foods as pot pies and apple pie. He's quick to admit that he relies on Charlie's Bakery for his pastries and that there is no grandma in the kitchen.

We were well satisfied with our lunch stop there. With my soup ($1.45), I had the salad bar ($3.25) served with Texas toast. Constant Companion ordered a Philly steak sandwich. The sandwich ($3.99), is made of thin slices of beef with mushrooms, green peppers, onions and Swiss cheese served on a hoagie bun with a small bowl of au jus—or maybe just bouillon. Anyway, he liked it. ❡

Pear Tree Is Place in the Pink for Leisurely Dining

FEBRUARY 10, 1988

It was colder than all get out and I wished Constant Companion would drive our car right into the lobby of the Holiday Inn. As it was he parked as close as he could. And we were all set for lunch in the Pear Tree Restaurant. We went there late for lunch last Tuesday, but there were several tables of people lingering over their coffee.

The luncheon menu is organized neatly. It gives you a list of starters under the heading, "The first move." It lists salads and light meals on one page and sandwiches, "Between the slices," on the next page.

For some reason, the Nutty Bird caught my eye. It's a pumpernickel rye and cream cheese topped with sliced breast of turkey, sprouts and sunflower seeds for $4.35. With the sandwiches, you get fries, onion rings or coleslaw. Constant Companion ordered a Burger Outrageous. This is described as a half pound of choice ground beef, broiled and served on a toasted bun and garnished with "the usual" for $3.25. For 35 cents an item, you can add your choices of cheeses, bacon or barbecue sauce.

CC figured the burger itself would be enough. And when our sandwiches arrived, he was sure of it—although he had a hard time believing it was actually a half pound of beef. My Nutty Bird turned out to be a delightful combination. It's the type of sandwich you eat with a fork. You wipe your chin often with your cloth napkin. And you take your time to savor it.

That's what I like about the Pear Tree. It's a place where you enjoy lingering. The room is done in tones of mauve and gray, with a raised center area for tables surrounded by a brass rail. Around it are large, comfortable booths. The chairs are all upholstered. There are better-than-average goblets and nice tableware along with pink place mats and dainty pink and mauve silk flowers. There are green plants in hanging baskets. And there are accents of light woodwork and latticed windows.

Lunch at the Holiday Inn might cost you a buck or so more than it does when you eat on the run, but it's worth it. You'll spend anywhere from $2.50 for soup and salad to $5.25 for a seafood salad. The food is a grade above what I have come to associate with Holiday Inns in other cities. The salad with my sandwich was crisp and fresh tasting. The sandwich was garnished nicely with a lettuce leaf and orange wedge.

After lunch, I had a chance to visit with Chef Brent Knop, who has been restaurant manager since the first of the year. He formerly worked as assistant director of food service for Southern Illinois University in Carbondale. A 1981 graduate of the Culinary Institute of America in New York City, he's been cooking ever since he was inspired as a youngster by his Lithuanian grandmother. "She never had one meat for a dinner. She had three or four," he said.

Knop likes continental cuisine. He likes dealing with the classics. Recently, he started Saturday evening service of steak Diane, which he prepares tableside. Chef Knop is one of the few professional chefs in Grand Forks. He loves what he does, and that is reflected in the foods he has been turning out. ❡

Chuck House Is Good Place to Be "Out to Lunch"

FEBRUARY 24, 1988

We chose the Chuck House Ranch Restaurant in the Westward Ho Motel when we went out to lunch Feb. 16 because it's steady and reliable. You always can find something unique on the menu.

We found an almost full house when we arrived at 12:30 P.M. We noticed many of the customers were north enders—people from the North Dakota Mill and Elevator and UND, as well as nearby businesses such as Northern Pump and Caterpillar. Intermingled were several lunch customers from downtown. The Chuck House, with its colorful totem poles and rustic decor, always is interesting. The walls are covered with Wild West posters. There are arrows sticking in the walls. The tables are covered with red-checked cloths. The plastic cow cream pitchers on the table are for sale, and customers buy a couple dozen every week.

I like the menu. It's varied. It's clever. And it's easy to read.

Just to be different, I ordered gyros, "a blend of lamb and beef seasoned with herbs, served with Grecian sauce, onions, tomatoes, pita bread and olives." All this for $3.75. Constant Companion ordered barbecued beef served on a sourdough bun with french fries for $3.25. Our waitress allowed him to substitute coleslaw for the fries, and we all were happy. It didn't take her long to motor back with our order. My gyros was topped with eight raw onion rings, so I gave six of them to CC. In turn, he let me finish his coleslaw.

His barbecue meat was lean, and the serving was generous. My meat had a pleasing taste of lamb, and I enjoyed the black olives, lemon and parsley used as garnish. The dressing had a piquant flavor, and I was glad it was on the side. That's where dressing belongs. When I worked my way down to the pita bread, I found it was thick and delicately browned. It tasted maybe like a fat lefse, and it was good.

The Chuck House went an extra mile, with plenty of ice in a nice glass glass of water; a waitress who mercifully asked us only once if everything was all right (six times is too many); and allowed both of us to keep our plates until both of us were finished.

The Chuck House is an anytime-of-the-day place. It flourishes on home cooking with baked goods by Sandy Montgomery.

Breakfasts are big in the Chuck House. It's one of the few places where you can order hash browns and be assured they will be done crisp and brown. It's a popular spot for people who like to eat out on Sunday morning.

In its 17 years, the Chuck House has developed a reputation as a very informal, very casual res-taurant, but owner Don Lindgren takes salads seriously.

"Lately," he said, "we've been paying more attention to salads. We keep our bowls in the refrigerator and serve romaine lettuce. When we hear people comment on the salad they had with a meal, we know it's important to them." ❡

Sonja's Hus Has Cheery Blue and Red Norwegian Décor

APRIL 13, 1988

Sonja's Hus in the Regency Inn, East Grand Forks, is a homey, cheery and rather quiet little place to go for lunch. The wallpaper is bright blue with a white pattern. There are dainty bouquets of permanent daisies on the table. The booths are deep blue with red cushions. The backs of the wooden booths and the valance for the drapes are decorated with rosemaling, a graceful Norwegian style of painting. The walls are decorated with Norwegian art pieces.

The food is reasonable, especially if you choose the specials. Each day, the coffee shop has two lunch choices for $2.29. Last week, I tried the soup, salad bar and sloppy joe combination, offered as a special. Constant Companion asked, as he often does, for a French dip. It was $3.95.

The coffee shop was rather quiet when we came, but it wasn't long before many of the tables were filled. Two waitresses were doing double duty there for a while.

Our waitress was Jane. She didn't have to tell us because she wore a nametag. I thought that was a good idea. She invited me to help myself to the soup and salad bar as she left to put in our order. The salad bar was nice, small but adequate, and all of the items seemed fresh. Sometimes salad bars get so big they are unmanageable. You'll find rubbery vegetables and French dressing slopped across the carrots. Not so at Sonja's Hus. There was one large metal bowl of lettuce mixed with shredded red cabbage and it was replenished. There were several items nearby but not a lot more than would be used.

I started my salad bowl with lettuce on the bottom. I carefully added a couple of broccoli flowerets and three wedges of tomato. Out of respect for my elevated cholesterol count, I used cottage cheese for a topping. I finished it off with a sprinkling of sunflower seeds and grated cheese. Then

I took a cup of beef noodle soup. It was good. The noodles were plentiful and the beef was thinly sliced and lean. The broth was a tad too salty.

It took a while, but my sloppy joe arrived. The meat had a good flavor. I was going to skip the potato chips, but they were better than most chips. So I ate them all and looked out the window to see where my self-control had gone. Meanwhile, CC was examining his French dip, which he said was pretty good. The au jus in which he was to dip his beef sandwich was a little on the oily side.

We had coffee and took our time. Some of the other customers were farmers who had been to a meeting in the Regency Inn. Former UND football coach Jerry Olson was sitting nearby, so I asked, "Would you rather be coaching football or farming?"

Olson grinned and said, "It depends on who's winning." Then he told us he was about to start planting wheat on his farm near Hoople, N.D. I noticed he ordered the other $2.29 special, chicken, potatoes and vegetable.

Before we left, I visited with Kirsten Jones. She is in charge of Sonja's Hus coffee shop and Ferdinand's dining room in the Regency Inn. Her father was born near Erskine, Minn., she said, "and the whole family is Norwegian. So we wanted to use a Norwegian theme in the coffee shop."

Kirsten threw a little Norwegian into the conversation, enough to convince me she is Norwegian. I knew it for sure when she said, "Uff da." ❡

The Regency Inn and Sonja's Hus no longer operate in East Grand Forks.

At the Tomahawk, They Roast the Whole Turkey. People Go to the Highway Cafe for the Kind of Meals They Used to Eat at Home: Meat, Potatoes, Pie.

MAY 4, 1988

"Oh, I see you're out for a home-cooked meal, too," said Roy Bakken as he and his wife, Yvonne, sat down in the booth next to ours in the Tomahawk Cafe one night last week.

"Yes," I said. "This is my idea of a home-cooked meal."

Actually, when you go for a meal at this truck stop cafe near the intersection of U.S. Highway 2 and Interstate 29, you are going back to the basics. There's nothing fast about the food. Nothing fancy, either. If you want pheasant under glass or oysters Rockefeller, you won't find them here. You might, however, find lutefisk and lefse. This is one of those places where they peel a batch of potatoes every morning and make up a big pot of soup. They roast whole turkeys—none of this turkey roll business. People come in here and order meat and potatoes. With it, they get gravy and vegetables. And they get soup and coleslaw.

I heard the Bakkens order roast pork sandwiches. And later on, I heard Roy Bakken say, "Pretty good." That's exactly what Constant Companion says when he is pleased with something. Men don't get exuberant.

I should have settled for a sandwich, but instead I ordered the dinner special: Polish sausage and sauerkraut with hash browns and coleslaw. CC ordered roast pork and dressing.

We started with a cup of navy bean soup, which was good. I mean real good. As we continued on with our meal, we found everything good. The coleslaw was crisp, and the potatoes were fried to a golden brown. The food reminded us of dinners people used to eat at noon. If there was any complaint, it would have been that there was too much food. Some people, we understand, order a half a dinner.

Pies are a specialty at the Tomahawk Cafe. You see them ·when you enter the spacious restaurant. They are going round and round right inside the front door in one of those twirling display cases. Sometimes, I get kind of dizzy watching them. There's a wide choice of homemade pie every day. And they are good. Cream pies are $1.25 a slice and fruit pies are 95 cents. Ask for them a la mode, and it will cost you 30 cents more. But you get Bridgeman's ice cream, which to my mind is about as good as it comes.

The Tomahawk Cafe is one of those places that keeps you coming back. In the first place, it's clean. In the second place, it's homey. The other night, a trucker was sitting at the counter working a crossword puzzle. People were eating their turkey and dressing and Gordon and Colleen Kuklok's children were helping out clearing tables and running the cash register. The children are Heather, 13, Callie, 12, Meaghan, 10, and Eamon, 9.

Business has been good in the two years the Kukloks have been in their new location. Gordon

Kuklok says his philosophy is to serve good food and make it reasonable. They are busiest Sunday, when they serve roast turkey and dressing for $4.25 and hot turkey sandwiches for $3.25. The hours are between 10:30 A.M. and 2 P.M.

Steady customers count on the Tomahawk for soup. They don't need a calendar. They know that if it's pea soup, it's Monday; bean soup, Tuesday; macaroni-tomato, Wednesday; chicken rice, Thursday; old-fashioned tomato, Friday; and vegetable beef, Saturday. ¶

Marilyn says, "Tomahawk has closed down, and there is no new restaurant in its place."

Shore Lunch Adds Another Dimension to Food in Mall

SEPTEMBER 7, 1988

Fish and chips. Clam chowder and hush puppies. That's what you'll find at Shore Lunch, which opened quietly in August in Columbia Mall, right across from John Barleycorn restaurant. With fish as a specialty, Shore Lunch adds another dimension to food in the Mall and to eating out in Grand Forks.

Now that school is back in session and people are home from the lakes, they are beginning to

discover Shore Lunch. You can order a Shore Dinner for $5.75 or a Shore Lunch for $3.75. With each plate, you get coleslaw, hush puppies and your choice of baked or French-fried potato wedges. The difference is in the amount of fish. With the dinner you get two fillets, cut into 10 pieces. With the lunch, you get one fillet, cut into five pieces. They are deep fried to order and have a crunchy brown crust.

Constant Companion ordered the Shore Lunch one night last week. He enjoyed the fish and the fries and the slaw. But he wasn't as crazy about hush puppies as was a young man sitting at a nearby table, whistling them down.

Fried fish and fried potatoes seemed a little much to us. Another time, we decided, it would be wiser to order fish and have slaw and baked potato with it. My order that evening was a fish fillet sandwich for $2.25. You also can get it with fries for $2.75. Or you can get side orders of fish for $2.50, coleslaw for 90 cents, fries for 75 cents, hush puppies for 75 cents, baked potato for 75 cents or onion rings for $1.35.

Owner and manager Eunice Novick told me she is hoping to build up a carryout business. She said she will try to keep the menu simple. The fish, she said, are freshwater white fish from Mississippi. "They're never more than a week away from the water." ❡

Shore Lunch no longer operates in Columbia Mall.

Andrew's Steakhouse Is Gem Along U.S. Highway 2

SEPTEMBER 14, 1988

RUGBY, N.D.—"Now are you sure this is real crab—not just some of that reincarnated stuff restaurants foist off as crab?"

That's exactly what I asked the waitress at Andrew's Steakhouse in Rugby, N.D. She assured me it was for real. So I ordered the special, written in fluorescent letters on one of those shiny blackboards. "Snow King Crab, $9.95." Constant Companion looked over the menu and at length decided to—yep, you guessed it—try the ribs ($7.95).

We were pleasantly surprised when we saw the dining room. It's spacious, colorful and upscale. The red carpeting has a gold-and-blue design. Cloths on the tables are yellow, and there are blue cloth napkins. On each table, there also is a slender vase of yellow or white silk flowers. And there are plastic lace placemats.

We were the first customers into the restaurant, which opens at 5 P.M. Before we finished eating, though, there were seven tables filled, and it still was early. Most people were dressed casually, but this is a place worthy of your good dress or his new necktie.

Our waitress, Lisa, came on with assurance, which I like. She wasn't one of those scared rabbit types. She easily handled all of the tables and was doing a few extra chores on the side. She did two unusual things. First, she took a cloth and wiped the "Snow" off the "Snow King Crab," written on the specials board. Second, she came in with a vodka bottle and watered the plants in the dining room.

Curiosity got the best of me, and I asked her why she changed the special. She said the cook had just told her it should be "snow crab" or "king crab" but not "snow king crab," because there is no such thing. I didn't ask her about the vodka bottle, but I assume it was water she put on the plants.

While we pondered these things, we took a quick walk around the hexagonal-shaped salad bar in the middle of the dining room. This is a rather small salad bar, but those with fewer items usually are fresher. There was some very good garlic bread there, and along with the usual array, I was pleased to find olives.

Our entrees arrived in good time, and they were good. Very, very good. My crab legs were plentiful and were served with real rendered butter with lemon over a tiny flame. CC enjoyed his ribs and was glad to have the sauce on the side so he could see what he was eating.

We wished we had a bone plate. Instead, we used saucers from coffee cups we didn't intend to use. We piled them high with crab shells and rib bones.

When we finished our meal, we had a chance to visit with Terry Atkins, who with his wife, Rhonda, owns and operates Andrew's Steakhouse and the Econo-Lodge. He thinks he draws local people because he is serving food at reasonable prices. And it's working. He must have the same attitude with the 63-room motel operation. He has a sign out in front suggesting, "Spend a night, not a fortune." ❡

Andrew's Steakhouse no longer operates in Rugby.

Royal Fork Serves Sunday Dinners Every Day

SEPTEMBER 21, 1988

It was just after six, and the line for dinner was fairly long at the Royal Fork Buffet in Columbia Mall. My sister, Helen, and brother-in-law, Carl "Bob" Jensen, were interested in it anyway. They were visiting here from Sacramento, Calif., where they have every kind of eating establishment you can imagine, except a Royal Fork Buffet.

As we moved toward the buffet line, we looked over the large color photographs of food along the walls—grapes, carrots, market scenes. They are spectacular. It wasn't long before we picked up our plates and picked our way through the salad bar, which is complete and well-tended. There was one employee just tidying up and wiping up spills.

This is volume business. This is organization, I thought to myself as we approached the vegetables. Then came the hot cinnamon rolls, whipped potatoes and gravy. Since it was Wednesday, there was baked cod, Swiss steak, fried chicken, homemade chicken and dumplings, dressing and blueberry muffins. Enough, already. But it's fun to make the choices.

After we got our beverages, we moved on to the huge dining area. It was busy, all right, but we had no trouble finding places at the end of a table for eight. And shortly after we got seated, a couple from Canada asked if we minded if they sat at the table with us.

"Fine," we said, and they sat down. They were senior citizens—like us—and they told us they come down to Grand Forks often just to have something to do. They always come to the Royal Fork, they said, because they feel it's a good food buy. Also in Grand Forks, they buy cheese for themselves and cigarettes for their son.

We ate, and we talked. My brother-in-law strikes up conversations wherever he goes. He's a big friendly Dane with ocean-blue eyes. He likes his meat and potatoes, and he liked the Royal Fork. The place was bustling with people of all ages—older people, families and groups of guys. Most everyone was serious about their eating.

The Royal Fork, however, is a cut above those places that advertise all you can eat. It's more refined, with its hanging green plants and light oak lattice trim. There are servers who offer more coffee and make sure the tables and booths are clean.

All of the food has a homemade quality. It reminds me of Sunday dinners we had long ago—before people learned about going out for brunch and ordering in pizza. ❡

Frenchy's Cabaret Has New Menu with Combo Options

OCTOBER 19, 1988

"I wonder what they do with the insides they scoop out of these potato shells," Constant Companion said as we were eating dinner at Frenchy's Cabaret last Tuesday evening.

"Dunno," I said, eyeing his cheese-covered potato shells as

I ate a moist, tasty baked potato. CC had ordered a 6-ounce filet mignon that came with sautéed mushrooms for $8.50. I had ordered the 4-ounce top sirloin for $4.50. As a starter, we had a choice of salad, soup, tomato juice or coleslaw. With our entrees, we got our choice of potatoes, and believe it or not—a vegetable. In this case, corn.

We thought it was a pretty good deal since the food turned out to be better than average. I liked the salad because the lettuce was cut finely and so were the tomatoes on top. I liked the red cabbage slivered in with the iceberg lettuce. Instead of salad, CC had dumpling soup. "Tastes good," he commented. "Though a little salty."

Our plan had been to revisit the Cabaret dining room in Frenchy's. We hadn't been there since shortly after it opened four years ago, and we wanted to see how things were going. The dining room looked nice. There is new carpeting and new white and red paper on two walls. White-covered tables all have red napkins and steak sauce on them. On the west wall, there's a mural of cabaret dancers.

But we weren't able to sit in the dining room. It seems there was an emergency when the cook called in sick and one of the waiters wasn't able to make it. Things were at sixes and sevens, so to speak. So we were ushered into the lounge area for dinner.

This was OK. There were several tables of people dining as well as the late afternoon or early evening bar crowd. There was an old movie showing on the big screen, but I don't think anyone was watching it.

Our waitress, in tight-fitting jeans, was businesslike and energetic. She was hopping from one table to another, trying to keep up with everything. Later, I learned she is Lori Hollinger, daughter of Hubert "Frenchy" LaCrosse, the proprietor.

"Frenchy" took time out to answer a few questions when we finished eating. "You picked a fine time to try us," he said, explaining that he fills in at the stove only when the need arises. He also depends on Caryn Swedin to make soups and salad dressings while he does the meat cutting. The kitchen is equipped with a charbroiler, deep fryer, two convection ovens and three microwaves.

LaCrosse went into food service to keep up with the times when the drinking laws were changed. He says that business is pretty good.

"We're still trying to convince people that we're no longer strictly a college place, although we still get some of them," he said. "We are drawing more people from the community. More of a blue-collar and working-class clientele," LaCrosse said. "Two people can come in here and eat and drink for $15."

Before we left, we asked LaCrosse what he does with the insides of the potatoes.

"Oh," he said, "we use them for au gratin potatoes, in potato salad, and in soups." ❡

Hubert "Frenchy" LaCrosse closed Frenchy's Cabaret in the mid-1990s.

Downtown Explorers Discover Dinner in Pantry

NOVEMBER 16, 1988

You should show compassion. You should do anything you can to make him comfortable. But when your Constant Companion has a cold, there's no reason to stay home and listen to him cough.

So, I got in the car and drove down to The Pantry for dinner Saturday evening. When I walked in at 5 P.M., I was the only person in the restaurant. I was pleased the waitress refrained from asking, "Are you alone this evening?" That always bugs me when I happen to be eating by myself. And actually, I sometimes enjoy being alone.

I was comfortable at The Pantry with its red-and-gray decor. There was music playing over a speaker and two ceiling fans turning lazily above the frosted globe lights. Jennifer, the waitress, gave me a menu and also recited the specials for the evening. They were chicken fettuccine ($5.95), lasagne ($4.95), Greek salad ($4.75) and catch of the day, which was orange roughy ($8.45).

After glancing through the menu, I decided to go with orange roughy. And what a good choice it was. It turned out to be one of the nicest meals I have eaten in a local restaurant. In the first place, the tables were set nicely. White cloth napkins. White cloths over the red table covers. A salad of lettuce and red cabbage arrived with two tiny broccoli flowerets, a slice of cucumber and tomato wedge as garnish. With it were two homemade cloverleaf rolls and a small pot of butter, served in a white cloth, inside a box. That made me feel like the kitchen cares, and set the scene for the entree to come.

The orange roughy was poached in white wine and served with a light hollandaise sauce. On the ap-

pealing serving plate, there was a twice-baked potato, a dainty serving of candied carrots with herbs, and two pieces of broccoli. The food was excellent, and I enjoyed it with a glass of Chablis.

When I visited after dinner with the owner, Warren LeClerc, he told me that it was turning out to be the best night he has had. He opened The Pantry for lunches only one year ago—on Dec. 1— with the help of his nephew, Paul Ringstrom. Ringstrom is a graduate of the Cornell University hotel school, and has experience in cooking in France. He was in Grand Forks until October, when he decided it was time to move on. LeClerc said Ringstrom was thinking of starting a restaurant with friends in Barcelona, Spain, when he left.

LeClerc now depends on Roger Leahrman as his chef. And Leahrman supervises the breads and desserts, which are baked on the premises.

It's the attention given to food that makes The Pantry stand out. The desserts and coffee are good enough to bring people in for late afternoon interludes. The Pantry excels in cheesecakes, triple layer carrot cake, pies and rice pudding. It shines with its coffee, which is the best around. That's because the coffee is freshly ground, and brewed in the restaurant. ¶

Dinner and Theater Make "Fantastick" Evening

NOVEMBER 30, 1988

New York City, this isn't. But Grand Forks still has a dinner theater, and the food is very good.

We made our way up the long, wide stairway on a recent Friday evening to the Grand Forks Dinner Theater. We had been hearing about it ever since it opened in July, but never had a chance to go there. It's the kind of place where you go for a special occasion—a birthday or anniversary. It's also the kind of place you go when you have time for a long leisurely dinner. Or when you have guests from out of town.

The current show, *The Fantasticks,* will be continuing Thursday, Friday and Saturday evenings and for Sunday matinees through December and into January. The theater, as most people know, is located above the Windmill Restaurant and Bar, at 213 S. Third Street, which supplies the food served to theater patrons.

Our first impression was favorable, because of the new carpeting in rose and teal tones, and the harmonizing teal paint in the entry and reception areas. A contemporary chandelier at the top of the stairway draws comments and compliments from guests.

The dining room is impressive, with three levels of tables set off by light wood railings. Tables are covered with rose cloths, and there are mauve cloth napkins. Glass-enclosed candles flicker on the tables. This pleasing, warm ambience puts you in the mood for a very special evening.

We went at 5:30 P.M., when dinner service begins. We were offered a choice of walleye primavera, prime rib or chicken teriyaki. We both chose the walleye and ordered a drink as we waited.

First came the salad of greens topped with rings of green pepper and red onion. Our walleye, done in a wine and vegetable sauce, arrived with an attractive garnish of citrus and a welcome serving of carrots on the plate. The baked potato that came with it was a waxy, moist red. It required no butter or sour cream—just a sprinkling of pepper and salt.

For those who want to order wine, the dinner theater has an extensive list of red, sparkling, blush and white in a price range from a moderate $7 to $10—all the way up to $28.50. I figure Constant Companion will order from the top of the line if we make it to our 40th wedding anniversary next summer.

As we finished eating, our waiter told us that the pre-show would be starting soon. Before long, the waiters and waitresses, who were already in theatrical attire, turned into entertainers. They call themselves the "Two-Bit Players," and theirs is a large contribution to the evening of dinner theater. The show itself is performed on a stage that is easy to view from all parts of the house.

The food service doesn't end with dinner. It continues through the show, with desserts and coffee. Desserts include the decadent mud pie, which the Windmill helped establish in this town.

Usually, there is cheesecake, too, with assorted toppings. ❡

Grand Forks Dinner Theater and the Windmill are no longer operating in Grand Forks.

Gordy's Cafe Specializes in Home-Style Cooking

APRIL 19, 1989

Dick King was sitting at the counter eating a pancake when I entered Gordy's Cafe on Gateway Drive Thursday morning. His law office is nearby. King is one of the many regulars who stop in at Gordy's. I sat down beside him while waiting for Constant Companion. We talked about the pancake. King said it was good, but it was too big.

The waitress on duty was Bev Egstad, who has been at Gordy's for three years. She knows most of the customers on a first-name basis. So does the other waitress, Carol Hook, who comes in at 10 A.M.

While Bev took orders and poured coffee, Ruth Jensen was working like a robot at the grill. She would crack eggs, fry hash browns, butter English muffins and toast. She would go back and forth from the kitchen to the cooler. She was in perpetual motion.

Gordy's is a one-of-a-kind place. It's homey, with red-checked cafe curtains on the windows and a row of hanging plants. People park their cars in the unpaved parking lot in a scattered pattern that makes me think of pick-up sticks. The long counter, which seats 16, is covered with pink tile that has splashes of gray and white through it.

I ended up ordering two scrambled eggs and a toasted English muffin. When CC showed up, he ordered the breakfast special of two eggs, toast, hash browns and bacon for $1.99. The coffee was extra.

Everybody seems happy to be at Gordy's in the middle of the morning. The traffic in and out is steady. The waitress knows without asking who wants peanut butter with their toast. She also knows who wants jelly, and what kind they like best.

When Ruth had a break from the grill, I asked her about the business. She said she and her husband, Terry Jensen, have been leasing Gordy's for the past eight years from Gordy Hanson, East Grand Forks. He's retired. The Jensens also operate the coffee shop in the Dacotah Hotel, and last year took on a third operation— the snack bar in the new Home of Economy department store.

Breakfast business is brisk at Gordy's. Then it goes downhill until noon. The restaurant bustles when customers stream in for "dinner." Last Thursday, the choices were a Salisbury steak dinner, $3, soup and a sandwich, $2.50, or chicken strips with fries, coleslaw and a roll for $2.99.

"Just home cooking," Ruth Jensen said. She cracks her own eggs for breakfast, mixes her own pancakes, makes her own soups and peels and mashes potatoes for the dinners and hot sandwiches. When she finishes a day behind the stove, she doesn't feel like cooking at home, she said. She and her husband like to go out to dinner at other Grand Forks restaurants. Rarely do they have time to get out of town.

"Minneapolis is about the farthest we've gone," she said. "Once we rode our motorcycles to Duluth." ❡

Marilyn says, "Gordy's Cafe faded away from Gateway Drive some time ago."
The Jensens continue to operate Gramma Butterwicks.

Gramma Butterwicks Has a Healthy Heart Menu

APRIL 26, 1989

After two visits to Gramma Butterwicks during the past week, I can say I am impressed with the new heart-healthy menu, but I think the restaurant has a way to go. For instance, for breakfast on Thursday, I ordered the heart-healthy scrambled egg and pancakes with coffee for $3.55. When the food arrived, I thought the scrambled eggs made from egg substitute were very good. The pancakes, however, had an off taste that was not pleasing to me. So, I left them on the plate and ate a corner of the regular pancakes Constant Companion ordered.

When I visited with the manager, I asked why they can't just make pancakes without eggs—or use two egg whites to make the equivalent of one whole egg. He said he would be looking into that.

Because I believe consumers need to ask questions—specific questions—I asked him what low-fat and low-cholesterol products the restaurant is using for its heart-healthy menu. He said Eggs Supreme and Promise margarine. He said the broiled skinless chicken breast with rice and vegetables has turned into one of the best items on the healthy heart menu.

While the bulk of the restaurant's business is off the regular menu, the manager said he can tell most people are shunning fat.

He uses less oil for hash browns, for instance. He says decaffeinated coffee makes up about one-third of his coffee business. "There's more requests for it all the time."

Still, the whole world isn't on a diet. The restaurant has a baker, Sherrie Brandell, who turns out caramel rolls as well as oat bran muffins. And this week, there is a new line of Danish pastries for breakfast.

The restaurant soon will be coming up with a 10-minute lunch. If the food isn't delivered in the promised time, the lunch will be free. Apple pie is one of Gramma Butterwicks' specialties. Customers who order a full dinner between 5 and 9 P.M. can get a free piece of pie.

The restaurant is decorated in tones of forest green and beige. There's a counter near the entry and a row of booths that remind me of a railroad diner. This is the smoking area. Farther back, there's a spacious dining room, where smoking is restricted. It's attractive, with healthy-looking plants and North Dakota Centennial prints. ❡

Gramma Butterwicks no longer serves the heart-healthy menu.

Norma's House of Goodies Is Filling Station in the Mall

JUNE 28, 1989

Lunch was $2.60, including tax, and was quick. It was good. And it was eaten in the cool and quiet of Norma's House of Goodies, in City Center Mall.

This is a small cafe that tends to be overlooked unless you regularly travel through the downtown mall. It's worth a stop because it has freshly baked cookies, bars and pies every day. It also has a choice of salads and sandwiches.

I stepped up to the counter last Wednesday and asked for the luncheon combination of a half sandwich and soup. I chose vegetable soup over the cauliflower. And I asked for turkey and Swiss cheese on my sandwich.

The soup was too salty for my taste, but it was pretty good. The chunk of meat I found in it was large. Very large. But it was lean and tender. The sandwich more than made up for any shortcomings of the soup. The turkey was lean and plentiful; the wheat bread was soft and fresh. And there was plenty of lettuce shredded the way I like it on a sandwich.

Norma's House of Goodies is a comfortable stop. There's enough space so that you usually can find a place to sit. The windows have an inviting seasonal theme. Right now, there's a beach with a lawn chair, a beach ball and some ducks.

Norma Kinney, owner and manager, said she likes to do special windows. But mostly she likes to bake. That's why she bought the little cafe last November when she found out Mickey Darbyshire was willing to sell. Darbyshire had opened the House of Goodies in 1985 and established a pretty good reputation for baked goods. She also established the House of Goodies as "the home of the monster cookie." Norma Kenny and her husband, Earl, are carrying on in the same manner.

The Kinneys are on the job early each morning. He helps out as much as he can before he goes to his regular job with Price King Car Rental and Limousine Service. She just keeps baking. Last Wednesday, for instance, she made apple and blueberry and coconut cream and lemon pies and cream puffs before most of us were out of bed. She also baked cookies she had mixed up the day before. On Saturdays, the Kinneys make old-fashioned cut-out doughnuts, which they sell for 15 cents apiece, or two for 25 cents.

Norma got her start in the restaurant business by working as a waitress. She learned a lot about baking from her mother, Geraldine Braaten of Manvel, N.D., who she says is considered a good cook. At least, that's what everyone says.

The Kinneys also make their home in Manvel. They have three children who make quick work of any baking she does at home. At the House of Goodies, she doesn't count the customers. She counts sacks of flour and sugar. She figures she goes through at least 50 pounds of sugar and flour a week. And in the fall, she says, you can double that amount.

About half of her business comes from people who work in the downtown area and stop by for orders they take with them. Although the cafe opens at 8 A.M. she finds she has regulars stopping by before that. They come early for coffee and rolls. ⁋

City Center Mall was destroyed by the Red River flood of 1997.

Bronze Boot Expands Its Dining Area, Shrinks Lounge

JULY 19, 1989

It's business as usual as the Bronze Boot gets a facelift this summer. The supper club on Highway 81-N is getting a new entry, a larger dining area and a smaller lounge. Darcy Fonder, the owner, figures he will have $175,000 into the remodeling by the time it's completed in another week or so. But, he figures, it's a sign of the times. People are drinking less and eating more.

Constant Companion and I went to the Boot for dinner on a Saturday in July with Stan and Gladys Hendrickson (SH and GH), friends who spend more time in Arizona now than they do in Grand Forks. They come back to visit family and friends in the summertime.

SH didn't even have to look at the menu. He said, "I always have walleye when I come to the Boot." I followed suit and asked for broiled walleye, which was perfectly sea-soned and had just enough sliced almonds to give it texture and add interest. It was, indeed, a rare treat.

GH ordered a prime rib sandwich, which she said was delicious. "Just the right amount to eat."

Constant Companion ordered a tenderloin sandwich. His comment: "Very good."

The Bronze Boot is one of those tried and true places you can always depend on. Our waitress was Trudy, who worked 18 years at the Elks Club's restaurant before it closed. Now she loves seeing her friends at the Boot, and she was in an extra-good mood because she was about to embark on a trip with her daughter to her native land of West Germany.

Dinner is rather dressy at the Boot. We had a white cloth on the table, a slice of lemon in our carafe of ice water and the servers were wearing black suits and ties with white blouses or shirts. The ambience is friendly and informal.

Lunch at the Boot is a bargain, and less dressy than dinner. And there's an interesting mix of workmen, farmers, business-people and family groups. You can go through the chuck wagon line between 11:30 A.M. and 1 P.M., for $4, including your beverage. First, there are meats. Last Tuesday, we found lean roast beef, fried chicken, meatballs, mixed vegetables, mashed potatoes and gravy in the hot food sections. We moved on to an array of pasta salads and coleslaw. Beyond that, there was a good selection of fruit and rolls and butter. Iced tea, which is often watery in restaurants, has good personality here.

The Bronze Boot was opened by a group of businessmen and later operated by Leo Wong; Darcy Fonder took over from Wong in 1962. That accounts for the special Cantonese menu at the Bronze Boot, which Fonder said he still makes. ❡

Taco Bell Is Like a Cool Pastel Oasis on a Hot Day

AUGUST 2, 1989

It looked like a traffic accident waiting to happen.

There were too many cars around, and too many people standing in line, the first time we went over to check out the new Taco Bell on South Washington Street. It opened in June, and I waited until things sort of shook down.

Now, it's relatively easy to get into Taco Bell. From the parking lot, you notice the sign, "49 cents original tacos every day." You see an ad for a free Batman cup with purchase of a 32-ounce drink.

The menu board lists tacos and tostadas, fajitas, burritos and enchiladas. Then, there are specialties such as the taco salad ($3.19), nachos belgrande ($2.09), Mexican pizza ($1.99), Kids fiesta meal ($1.69) and Meximelt (99 cents).

The first time I ate at Taco Bell, I had a taco light ($1.49) and a cheese tostado (79 cents). I was with Barbara Lander and her granddaughter. We agreed the restaurant seems like a cool oasis on a hot day. It's decorated in soft pastel tones of peach, lavender, blues and greens. There are artificial cactus and desert flowers and a nice tile floor to carry out the Mexican theme.

On my second visit, with Constant Companion, I asked for the chicken fajita ($1.49) and a bean burrito (79 cents). I liked the fajita and burrito combination better than the taco and cheese tostada. It was more substantial.

I have yet to try the Mexican pizza, but I intend to do that on the recommendation of Marlo Gade. She was eating one the first time I stopped in Taco Bell, and she said it was great. Taco Bell will have a grand opening later on this month, when the drapes are installed.

John Serati, director of franchise operations, is quick to tell you that Taco Bell no longer uses coconut oil for frying. The organization switched to corn oil 18 months ago. He boasts of the real sour cream used at Taco Bell. He said the restaurant "canned" the ranch style dressing that used to add 500 calories to its salads for every three ounces used. And, he says, the restaurants no longer use Yellow Dye 5. ❡

East Side Dairy Queen Offers Soup to Blizzards. Flow of Customers Begins with Early Breakfasts, Ends with Late Evening Snacks.

AUGUST 16, 1989

Can a cholesterol-conscious matron from the west side find happiness at the East Side Dairy Queen?

That was the question on my mind when I drove across the Red River of the North last week.

When I got there, I decided I would first have to find a place in the parking lot before I could find happiness inside. Although it was past 1 o'clock in the afternoon, the place still was surrounded by cars.

Once inside, I waited for Constant Companion. As I did, I could see the East Side Dairy Queen does a good business. Not only is it a Dairy Queen outlet, it also is a family restaurant. Beyond the DQ counter, you find a dining room with booths and tables in dark wood and white walls with brown trim. Desserts and cans of juice twirl around slowly in the display case.

As I waited, I noticed guys with skinny waists drive up in pickup trucks and go away sipping on Dairy Queen treats. There were women and children coming in and out. All sorts of people. When CC arrived, we wondered if we should go up to the counter to order. Then, we could see there were waiters in red vests on duty and menus on each table. We looked over the neat white laminated menu, which has four sections: dinners, sandwiches, breakfasts and Dairy Queen treats.

I ordered a Queen burger ($1.90) and a diet cola, with firm resolve to eat fruit and vegetables the rest of the day. CC ordered the Southern steak sandwich, which is served with mushroom sauce and french fries ($3.30). He doesn't worry about fruits and vegetables, but lately, I have been trying to convince him he should "strive for five." That is, eat five fruits and/or vegetables every day.

Our orders didn't exactly make up a gourmet lunch, but the food was basic and good. While a person doesn't want to eat burgers and fries every day, it's fun once in a while. And the East Side Dairy Queen is a good place to go. It also has a variety of dinner choices for $3.90 to $4.20, as well as buckets of chicken to go. It has sandwiches and salads, too.

Breakfast is a big draw, and manager Jerry Qualley says the restaurant is a gathering place for East Siders. "There's lots of farm trade and lots of business going on here in the mornings," he says. Qualley and other staff members make some of the pies and rolls. And he's proud of the soup, called Chef Francisco, which the restaurant buys from suppliers.

Soup and a sandwich for $2.79 is a luncheon special offered between 11 A.M. and 5 P.M. Monday through Friday. Another feature is the 21-shrimp dinner, which the restaurant serves for $4.20. Qualley says the East Side Dairy Queen is different because it has a restaurant that was grandfathered in before franchise holders were required to stick to Dairy Queen products only.

"You don't find many Dairy Queen restaurants like this," he says.

Qualley says the Blizzard continues to be a big seller in the Dairy Queen end of the restaurant. This year, the version with frozen Reese's Pieces is the No. 1 choice of customers. But he says, they still ask for the Peanut Buster Parfait. It was big before the Blizzards hit. ❡

The East Side Dairy Queen continues to operate the attached family restaurant. Marilyn comments that they have retained a "steady following."

Two Subway Stations Running on Washington Street

SEPTEMBER 6, 1989

Grand Forks has two Subways running along Washington Street, and I decided I should get with it and try them out.

I went into the South Washington Street Subway last Wednesday to check it out. I saw my friend Stephanie Brodeur sitting there with her dad, Dave. Stephanie was starting school this week at Sacred Heart, so after talking about that with her, I moseyed up to the counter. It was then I realized that ordering in the Subway calls for decisions, decisions, decisions. After looking over the list of subway sandwiches, I settled on a super club.

Whole wheat or French bread? Six-inch or foot-long? Mayo or mustard? Extra cheese? Vegetables? You want to eat here or is this to go? It took me a while to get with it. I felt like a klutz. Then I realized that all the fixings are free, and you just move along and tell the attendant what you want

with it: cheese, onion, lettuce, tomatoes, dill pickles, green peppers, black olives, salt, pepper, oil, vinegar, mustard, mayonnaise, creamy Italian.

Whew!

Now that wasn't really so hard. Then, when you order your beverage, you just have to specify whether you want a small, medium or large cup. And you can help yourself. When I got my Diet Pepsi and sandwich and napkins and straw, I sat down in a booth and looked around.

Subway is a cheery, yellow place. The booths and the hanging lamps above them are yellow. Along the walls, there are black-and-white reproductions from the *New York World*, showing scenes from the opening of the New York City subway.

In order to perfect my skill at handling the Subway, I made a second visit on Thursday. This time I went to the Subway at the intersection of North Washington Street and Gateway Drive. Here I found the same decor and the same pattern. I had asked Constant Companion if he wanted to join me, and I felt like an expert as I told him how to order.

After eating a 6-inch sub the first time, I decided to go the salad route Thursday. I ordered a turkey breast salad ($3.39) and CC asked for a 6-inch barbecue beef sub ($2.49). He said it was "kinda good." My salad was fine. I thought I could do as well at home for less. But the point is, I wouldn't. I don't keep shredded lettuce, sliced peppers and tomatoes and black olives all ready to go. Besides, Subway is quick, convenient and fun. It has a following here in Grand Forks. Some customers are card-carrying members of the Subway Sub Club. After they have 11 sandwiches marked off, they are eligible for a free one.

So, who runs Subway anyway, I wondered. I found out the owners are Debbie and Brian Conneran, who are in the process of opening two more Subways in Fargo.

"We're pioneers," Debbie said. "We brought the Subway to North Dakota."

She's from Florida, and she just loves it here. She says she met Brian in a nightclub in Florida on Feb. 16, 1988. "I took one look at him, and that's all she wrote," she says. He is a native of Fishers, Minn., and they were married March 11 of this year in Florida.

"He sent me to Subway School," she says. For two weeks, she attended classes in the Subway Franchise Headquarters in Milford, Conn. "We had classes all day and got on-the-job training at night," she says. "It was tough, but if you don't pass the exam you don't get the franchise."

The first Subway started running in Grand Forks more than a year ago, and the second has been running since February. Business is "fabulous," according to Debbie Conneran. "We couldn't be happier."

They get their bread from the franchise headquarters and bake it up fresh every four hours. "It's always fresh and soft and squishy," Debbie says. ❡

There are currently ten Subway stores operating in Grand Forks.

If It's Thursday, It's German Cuisine at Sanders 1907

SEPTEMBER 20, 1989

Sanders 1907 has turned into a bustling place approaching a bistro atmosphere during the past year under sole ownership of Kim Holmes.

Constant Companion (CC) and I went recently for an early dinner with Fanny Gershman (FG).

Our waiter described the German special ($9.50) as stuffed pork with spaetzle and red cabbage. Both CC and I asked for it. FG asked for the walleye. She always eats walleye at Sanders. We were seated in one of the green booths with high backs. A candle was glowing inside a white holder and there was a lace cloth beneath the glass cover on the table.

First came the bread—the same dense, crusty French bread we look forward to at Sanders. CC ordered a Michelob Dry beer. FG and I each ordered a glass of wine. Mine was Merlot, a wine that's light and a little sweet.

You get a salad with the special dinners at Sanders, whether it's German on Thursday, Italian on Wednesday or French on Tuesday. The house Greek salad is an entity all in itself, the likes of which you rarely find in restaurants around here. It comes spread out on a glass plate and tossed in an oil dressing. There were two or three different greens, fresh mushrooms slices, thin slices of red onion and a spike of cucumber. On top, a generous sprinkling of crumbled feta cheese. On the side, Greek olives.

Actually, I could have gone away happy after the bread, the wine and the salad. But we forged ahead, which was no problem after we saw our entree. Here we had a thick slice of lean, rolled roast pork stuffed with a mixture of apple, spinach and Gruyère cheese. The spaetzle served with it was miniature dumplings, which had been sautéed in butter. Along with the tangy red cabbage, the spaetzle was a perfect accompaniment for the pork.

Our plates were garnished with thick, perky parsley and a large, elaborate radish rose.

While we enjoyed our German fare, FG was focusing her attention on her broiled walleye, new potatoes and broccoli. The walleye was served with a happy face made with a black olive for an eye and thin strips of red pepper for whiskers. These are the kind of special touches that make Sanders a unique place to dine.

We finished our meal by sharing an order of chocolate decadence—one of three glorious desserts on the menu. FG had a cup of Norwegian coffee, which is mixed with a raw egg and poured from a big white enamel "ladies aid" pot. CC and I both asked for cappuccino, because Sanders is one of the rare places where you can find cafe au lait or cappuccino.

We had a chance to visit with Kim Holmes, the owner and head chef, before we hurried away to the preview of *The Octette Bridge Club,* which now is playing in Fire Hall Theatre. Holmes is a gregarious type and he makes a point of greeting and visiting all of the customers. He likes cooking breakfast and is planning to continue his breakfast club one Sunday morning a month. Sunday breakfasts are $10 and include whatever he fixes—usually cheese blintzes, fruit, eggs and home fries. "I like to have people come in with their newspapers and just relax over breakfast," Holmes says. "Really, it's a brunch." ❡

Crisp Fruit Pizza Pies Call You Back to Happy Joe's

NOVEMBER 1, 1989

It was the fruit pizzas that brought me back.

Constant Companion and I visited Happy Joe's Pizza and Ice Cream Parlor one day last week to try their Italian luncheon smorgasbord. We found enough there to keep us interested and eating—and full—for the rest of the day.

You'd think one trip would have held me for a while, but those crisp, crunchy fruit pizzas called me back to Happy Joe's for another go-around the next day. Happy Joe's all-you-can-eat smorgasbord is served from 11 A.M. to 2 P.M. Monday through Saturday for $3.89. Your beverage is extra. So you can kiss a fin (that's what CC and I call $5 bills) goodbye.

I always used to think of smorgasbord as Scandinavian, but the Shangri-La long has had a Chinese smorgasbord. And if Happy Joe's wants to have an Italian smorgasbord, it's OK with me. Uff da.

You enter Happy Joe's spacious dining room through the red-and-white-striped ice-cream parlor. You go clear to the back and pay up. Then, you get a plate, your silverware, a napkin and your beverage. After you have passed go, you proceed to the buffet—or smorgasbord—line. You find first those luscious apple, cherry and blueberry pizzas, and an extra special cinnamon glaze creation.

This may be a little backwards, because next you come to the other pizza—two or three kinds. You take a couple of slices and move on. Next you find three pasta dishes, three soups. Garlic bread. Beyond it, there is a salad bar with the usual assortment.

You do not need or want all this. So, the game is to pick and choose. We found the pizza to be fresh and warm and much to our liking. The pasta, too, is good. We found lasagna, spaghetti and a taco pasta.

There are a few shortcomings. The salad bar needs more tender loving care. Some of the items seemed a little tired. That is, they didn't appear to be fresh. I wondered why places with small staffs don't limit their salad bar offerings to a few items and keep them freshly restocked.

Another disappointment was finding pasta dishes almost empty. They would be far more inviting if they were replenished more often.

The booths at Happy Joe's are as spacious as the dining room, so it's possible to have a rather private conversation over lunch here. I insert this note because a reader recently suggested it is nice to know of places where you can hold a conversation.

Here at Happy Joe's, there is happy music playing in the background. In fact, the ambience is what I would call happy. There are Happy Joe hanging lamps, a big homey fireplace and a deep red carpet. During October, there were pumpkins all over the place.

The service, in general, was adequate. One waiter, Tom Koppenhaver, does an extra nice job of making you feel welcome. He is friendly, but not too friendly.

Happy Joe's has been under new management since Jim and Janice Marter acquired the franchise in September. They are trying to bring back the good old days when you fairly often stood in line to get into Happy Joe's. Among their moves is an Italian night each Wednesday. They are striving for cleanliness and take pride in serving what they call "real food." They say that means fresh pizza dough every day.

With the Marters, Happy Joe's of Grand Forks is beginning a new chapter. The establishment has been a part of the eating scene here since 1977. It is one of the original Happy Joe restaurants. ❡

Happy Joe's Pizza and Ice Cream continues to operate in Grand Forks.

Big Sioux Is Surrounded by Trucks with Engines Idling

DECEMBER 27, 1989

Outside, on a cold day, there may be anywhere from 30 to 70 trucks with motors idling. Inside, there's a faint smell of diesel fuel. If you come during the noon hour, you may have to hunt for a place to sit down in the Big Sioux Truck Stop Cafe.

We chose Big Sioux because I wanted to check out more about the lutefisk dinner for $5.75. It's served from Nov. 15 to Jan. 1. I didn't want to eat it, I just wanted to ask about it. And I learned the cafe sells about 400 pounds of lutefisk each year. It's not the biggest item on the menu, but there are certain people who count on the Big Sioux for their lutefisk each year. They probably are people of Norwegian heritage, with mates of German or Italian background. Our waitress, Mary Jo Carey, says sometimes she'll have six orders during a dinner hour. But, she says, when Southern truck drivers ask about it,

she doesn't encourage them to order it.

We were pleasantly surprised by the quality of food at Big Sioux. I ordered a 7-ounce sirloin steak special ($4.50), which comes with a bowl of soup or fries and toast. Constant Companion ordered the pork dinner special ($3.95). It came with a cup of soup, coleslaw dressing, mashed potatoes, gravy and a dinner roll. That's an amazing amount of food for the price, we thought. Especially since it was excellent food.

The potato soup was thick and hot with nicely diced potatoes. You could tell they were fresh. And the soup did not have the pasty consistency you sometimes get with restaurant soup. Along with potatoes, it had finely diced carrots and ham and snipped parsley in it.

The coleslaw passed the test. It was crisp. The dressing was light and not sloppy. There was a tiny paper cup of applesauce with the pork. Service was prompt and pleasant. No pretenses here. No coming back six times and asking if everything is all right.

The Big Sioux exceeded my expectations with its outward appearance of cleanliness and professionalism. Waitresses wear black-and-white checkered blouses with black vests. Kitchen help, whom you can see through the window, wear clean, white shirts and trousers with blue aprons and red caps. So do those who bus dishes. The caps certainly must impress the city health department inspectors. They have an awful time getting restaurant employees to restrain their hair.

It's fun sitting in a place where truck drivers mingle as they wait for a load of potatoes to carry south, or east. Sometimes, they daydream as they stir their coffee and wait for a page from the message center. Sometimes they swap tales with other drivers. Most of them wear plaid shirts and heavy trousers. They have heavy outer vests and caps. They peel back their outdoor gear as far as they can. ❡

Big Sioux continues to operate in Grand Forks.

VFW Diner Offers Publike Ambience and Basic Menu

JANUARY 10, 1990

We had heard mixed reports on the food served at the VFW Diner in South Forks Plaza. So Thursday, I said to Constant Companion, "There's one way to find out. Let's meet there for lunch."

He was agreeable, and I was glad. I want to make the rounds of the clubs in Grand Forks and East Grand Forks this winter to find out about their food. This gives me a start.

At first, it didn't seem too promising at the VFW Diner, but we found our way into the clubrooms and to a table where we could sit. Nothing fancy, but not bad at all in here. There were signs saying the luncheon special was soup and a Denver sandwich for $2.25. In places where food service is limited, I tend to take the special. I wasn't born yesterday.

CC got a little fancy and asked for the Philly sandwich he saw on the menu. But when he found out they didn't have any roast beef, he settled for the Denver and a Michelob.

The more we looked around the VFW Diner, the more it seemed like a neighborhood pub. Sort of a comfortable, unassuming place to drop in for lunch or dinner. There were several tables of people quietly eating. One gentleman came in and sat in a booth and read while he had a sandwich.

There were a couple of people at the bar cracking jokes and passing the time of day. The lone waitress on duty that day was Kristy Speckman, who was helping out temporarily during the holidays. She was moving around at a steady pace, taking care of everybody but not breaking any speed records. That suited me just fine, because I get dizzy when waiters or waitresses rush the food to me and whisk the plate away before I have time to swallow my last bite.

I chose a golden chowder from four soups offered Thursday. It was thin—the way I like cream soup—with a nice, mild flavor. The Denver sandwiches were just fine. Sort of like you would make them at home. I had plenty of ketchup with mine and enjoyed the dill pickle slices and crisp chips on the plate. The twist of orange slice that garnished the plates sent a message: The cook cares.

All in all, the food was a favorable experience. However, the soiled menus should be replaced.

Quarter-pound hamburgers, which are $1.75 plain, are popular items in the VFW Diner. Weekend specials include a walleye dinner for $5.99 on Fridays. A sign in the entryway says steaks are $1 off on weekends.

The club is open to members of the VFW and those who sign the guest book. Business is bolstered by the Tuesday night bingo games with meat as prizes, a Thursday bingo session for women and a Saturday afternoon bingo game for men. ❡

The VFW continues to serve food in Grand Forks.

Dacotah Passes the Poached Egg Test with Flying Colors

FEBRUARY 14, 1990

John Shaft blew my cover when I sat down for lunch at a table in the Dacotah Restaurant Thursday.

"Here's Marilyn Hagerty," he told the waitress in jest in a loud voice. "Tell Terry not to serve her the same slop you serve everyone else around here." Terry Jensen is the chef and operator of the Dacotah.

Usually, I prefer to be low-key in restaurants I'm reviewing for Eatbeat, but in a city this size, it isn't always possible. So, I just carry on bravely and try to describe each eating place as I find it.

For me, the Dacotah is an institution—a part of my Wednesday morning routine. I go there to have my hair done at Kato's at 9 A.M. Then, I stop in the bank and deposit or extract money for the week. After that, I buy a *USA Today* and go into the Coffee Shop for breakfast. It's the same every week.

My order always is the same. I think the waitress would faint if I varied it. I have a poached egg with whole wheat toast and a cup of coffee. Sometimes, if I haven't had fruit at home, I have a glass of orange juice.

The best thing about it is the Dacotah turns out a perfect

poached egg. There is no other place that I know that does it as well. The egg always is cooked, but not overcooked. I take it from the little dish and put it on top of a half piece of toast. It's a ritual.

But last week was different. I went into the restaurant dining room for lunch and waited for Constant Companion to join me. This is the room that used to be the Dacotah Lounge and it still has the same gorgeous red drapes that went up when the lounge held a grand opening several years ago. The room without the bar is restful and comfortable. There is space between the round, square and oblong tables. The carpet is thicker than that in the Coffee Shop.

Each day, the Dacotah has a luncheon special. These are more like dinners, for less than $4. The dining room no longer serves Mexican food, which was the big feature when it opened after the lounge closed. Now, it serves specials and short orders from a long menu that has a good variety of choices. You find everything from breakfast items to desserts.

CC arrived at 12:15 P.M. and we got down to the serious business of ordering. I asked for a cup of chicken dumpling soup (80 cents) and a monster burger ($2.35). Later, I decided I needed a Diet Coke (50 cents), too, because the chips that came with the burger were salty.

CC started out with only a bowl of chili ($1.25). He had been having some dental work done and chewing wasn't his long suit that day. He nodded and said the chili was the way he likes it—hot and spicy. It also had diced cheddar cheese on top. When he finished, he still was hungry, so he ordered a piece of Dutch apple pie (95 cents) and said it was OK.

My chicken dumpling soup was everything chicken dumpling soup should be. My monster was likewise and I still look to the monster as the Grand Forks version of a hamburger with everything on it but the kitchen sink. The chips were plentiful. Too plentiful. But I ate them all. The little bowl of beans was an unexpected bonus that I had to leave on the plate. After all, you don't ask for a doggie bag to take home a bowl of beans because you're full, do you?

At any rate, our check, with tax came to $6.95. More than reasonable for a lunch for two. CC left an 85-cent tip and took the check.

New restaurants have cropped up to make for stiffer competition downtown, but the Dacotah manages to hang on to its steady customers. These include residents of apartments in the building, now known as Dacotah Place, formerly the Dacotah Hotel. Other constant customers are downtown businessmen, and customers and employees of the Valley Bank located in the Dacotah.

There are many good features about the Dacotah that draw me back to it each week. However, it would be nice to see new tablecloths—maybe be even cloth tablecloths—in the dining room to replace the rather wrinkled plastic covers. And fresh new menus are needed. ❡

Luncheon Buffet Sports Nifty Spaghetti Sauce at Shakey's

MAY 2, 1990

Shakey's was the gathering place when a bunch of us got together for lunch Thursday. We found plenty of food left on the luncheon buffet, even though it was after 1 o'clock and there had been a couple of buses of schoolchildren there.

What we found at Shakey's was a salad bar, pizza, spaghetti and meat sauce, fried chicken, garlic bread, mojo potatoes, soup and dessert pizza. All of this for $3.95. And that includes a beverage.

So, we staked out a table for seven. Then we found our way to the cashier, where you pay first to eat later. We looked over the customary salad bar fare of iceberg lettuce, macaroni ·and potato salad, grated cheese, sunflower seeds, sliced peaches. Well, you know, the usual.

Beyond that, though, we found an assortment of fresh, hot wedges of thin-crust pizza. I took three.

In the next section, I fiddled around trying to get some wiggly spaghetti onto my plate. Just a little, I thought. Enough so I can try the sauce. Then, I saw the mojo potatoes, which are slices of Red River red potatoes breaded and deep-fried. So, I took one. And a half.

It was interesting to see what everyone selected from the buffet. Gerry Vaaler thought the spaghetti sauce was very good. Joyce Pond liked the mojo potatoes. The soup was OK, but no one turned cartwheels over it. Barb Lander thought the garlic bread was good. Donna Gillig, Donna McEnroe and I sampled the blueberry dessert pie with a pizza crust and thought it was quite tasty. The others showed no interest in it.

Along with the Grand Forks Shakey's, Dennis Farley also owns the Shakey's restaurant in Fargo. It is managed by his son, Brian Farley. Shakey's restaurants got their start more than 25 years ago when Shakey Johnson and his partner, Big Ed Plummer, opened the first one in Sacramento, Calif. They wanted a plain old beer joint with something unique. So, they decided to serve pizza and beer and provide live Dixieland music. From those beginnings, Shakey's Pizza grew into family restaurants with a varied menu.

While many pizza restaurants use imitation cheese or cheese substitutes, Shakey's claims to use only real cheese, and lots of it. Recently, Shakey's has added a new hand-tossed "Classic" crust to its lineup of pizza. It's somewhere between a thin and a deep-dish crust. ∫

Shakey's no longer operates in Grand Forks.

Palace Casino Offers Excitement with Burgers and Salads

MAY 9, 1990

It's different, all right. It's alive.

All over the large Palace Casino Sports Bar at the Westward Ho Motel, there are screens—16 of them in all—showing live action. You see tennis, bowling, ball games. The sound was on loud for only the car race on a big screen over the bar when Constant Companion (CC) and I dropped in for lunch Friday.

There were pennants, posters and sports pictures everywhere. The quiet and plushy red velvet Palace dining room, which I considered the nicest dining spot in North Dakota, is gone. It's now a sporty bar and cafe, and it's exciting.

I guess it's an example of the way things change as time marches on. Now, there are teller windows, where you place your bets, and a week's racing program at the end of the bar. The races go on Wednesday, Friday, Saturday and Sunday afternoons. In between, you see sports of all kinds on the screens.

An all-star menu features snack items, Center Court salads, pizza, sandwiches and burgers.

There's a different menu for Sundays, when serving begins at high noon, but the items are pretty much the same.

We noticed a Gino burger in the line-up at the Casino. Anyone who has ever seen a hockey puck knows the burger is named after John "Gino" Gasparini, UND hockey coach and athletic director. It's two quarter-pound cheeseburgers with fried onions and served with french fries and country gravy. Other burgers include a Hail Mary, which is a half-pound burger with mushrooms and Swiss cheese on an onion bun.

My choice was a clubhouse sandwich ($4.25), because the Chuck House coffee shop of the Westward Ho serves one of the best clubs around, and I know that all of the food is served from the same central kitchen. My clubhouse came with a choice of french fries or coleslaw and I chose the latter. It was as good as I had anticipated. It came on toasted wheat bread, as I had asked. The coleslaw was good. That is, it was crisp and not laden down with gloppy dressing. I like the dressing on coleslaw to be inconspicuous.

CC ordered a Philly steak sandwich ($4.75) and found it to be quite tasty, with plenty of fried onions. He likes fried onions a lot.

On a second visit Sunday, I tried one of the Center Court salads—the chef salad ($4.95). It came on a platter big enough to serve three or four people, I think. By the time I was halfway through it, my nose

was wiggling and I felt like a rabbit. I decided I would rather have less salad and have it served with a nice dinner roll.

CC tried a burger with coleslaw and proclaimed the burger VG, or very good. Coleslaw is coleslaw to him, but I keep reminding him he should strive for five fruits and vegetables every day.

Along with the pluses, there were a few minuses at the Casino.

The menu is flawed with misspellings, including "Ceaser," "avacado," "achovie," and "Rueben." We wondered if possibly this could have been done on purpose. Maybe the Casino will set up a contest to win a free meal for finding the most misspellings. ❡

Whitey's Offers Eclectic Menu with Art Deco Ambience

MAY 30, 1990

It smelled good—sort of like a burned toasted cheese sandwich—when I went into Whitey's for lunch Friday. Constant Compan-

ion was there ahead of me and waiting in a booth. And there were a lot of people there, though it was around 1 o'clock.

I like going to Whitey's on Friday because I enjoy the new skewer lunches. They serve an assortment of fresh fruit on a skewer along with a cheese wedge and a hard roll. I asked for the single skewer and soup combo ($2.95) because they serve their wild rice soup on Friday. And it is good. It has a nice flavor and the slivered almonds they use make it crunchy.

CC likes to go there on Friday because stewed chicken and dumplings is one of the specials. That's a whole meal with vegetables, mashed potatoes, gravy and a roll ($3.75).

Our food Friday lived up to our expectations. June Miron, an experienced waitress, served us unobtrusively and efficiently. In other words, she didn't ask us six times if everything was all right. CC enjoyed the dumplings and commented that he really would rather have two dumplings and skip the potatoes. His green peas seemed garden fresh, and were a big improvement over the canned peas of yesteryear.

My skewer held wedges of an orange, honeydew melon, regular watermelon, cantaloupe, fresh pineapple and a big red strawberry with a little dish of 10 red seedless grapes on the side. I got two chunks of cheese and slice of salami. All of this with a sesame seed roll that was very white and very fresh.

It seems as though Whitey's never changes. Actually, the management just makes improvements slowly so the place always seems the same. And that may be why people who have lived here always want to stop at Whitey's when they come back. They may outgrow their college haunts and other places change hands or disappear, but Whitey's is always there, always the same. It's an easy-access place.

Whitey's of 1990 is sort of a monument to Edwin "Whitey" Larson, the former owner who now lives in the Good Samaritan Nursing Center. Whitey started out with a Coney Island stand on a side street in East Grand Forks in 1925 and went on to build the present operation. He sold the business in 1973. Greg Stennes, the general manager, started working for Whitey's as a waiter in 1968. He came back in 1971, after military service, and worked as a bartender. You can tell he loves the place. He discourages the rowdy trade, and takes pride in the menu, which he updates and reprints twice a year. Stennes is a UND graduate with a major in marketing.

Stennes calls steaks and sea- food the mainstay of the business. Some things never change. Mushrooms and asparagus tips on toast has been there forever. And, Stennes says, he will always keep steamed finnan haddie on the menu because "my mother likes that." ¶

No One Goes Away Hungry from New Players Bar & Grill

JUNE 20, 1990

It's busy, busy, busy. And the new Players Sports Grill & Bar on South Washington Street is the talk of the town. I had planned to let things shake down there for a couple more weeks before going out to describe it in Eatbeat. But in almost every place I've been since it opened, I have heard people talking about Players.

So, what the heck. We stopped in Thursday for lunch, and we were delighted with what we saw and what we ate. Not just pleased. I mean delighted. This is a most attractive, upbeat, light and bright place to go. It has had an extensive renovation since the days it was known as CB's and then sat empty. The restaurant opened originally in the early 1970s as the Cape Codder. Then it became Captain's Cove, and later, the Mainstreet.

Generally speaking, it's lighter and brighter now. Specifically, there are more windows. Large screens showing sporting events can be seen from every seat in the grill. The decor is complete with sports pennants and tones of blue, white and green. These are the colors used in uniforms worn by the serving staff. Right now, it's softball jerseys. Later on, the servers will wear uniforms corresponding to the sports in season.

/ The whole idea of the place is to have fun. But it's the homemade pasta that is drawing the most raves. Players has a pasta-making machine, imported from Italy. Into it each day go the eggs and flour and other ingredients for homemade pasta.

I ordered Italian lasagna ($5.95). It's served with a choice of minestrone soup or salad and soft, warm bread sticks, which are lightly flavored with garlic. The lasagna, served on a large platter, was a most generous serving. It was topped with freshly shredded parmesan cheese and surrounded by a classic red sauce, which rates an A-plus in my book. This is a light sauce with a distinctive tomato taste and seasoned with fresh herbs. I learned later that it was developed for Players by chef Kim Holmes, who operates Sanders Restaurant in downtown Grand Forks.

While I ate lasagna, Constant Companion was working his way through a Cajun chicken sandwich and a spinach salad ($5.25). He considered the sandwich very good and said, "The chicken is well cooked." He also enjoyed the Cajun sauce, because it had personality. In other words, fire.

Most salads and sandwiches on the menu are in the $4 to $5 range. Dinners are $6 to $7, but you can go as high as $8.95 for a ribeye steak dinner.

There is one menu at Players, and all the items are served from 11 A.M. until closing time.

Patrons talk about the ample servings.

"No one leaves here hungry, and we send home a lot of doggie bags," owner Jon Borman says. He's been hovering around greeting people, checking the kitchen, reminding busboys to keep the clatter down and not annoy the patrons. Borman constantly studies restaurant and trade magazines and makes frequent checks of the eating scene in Minneapolis. He says the sports grill concept is hot throughout the country. "I wanted to bring it to Grand Forks," he said. ❡

From Pâté to Pears, Dinner at Sanders 1907 Is Unique

OCTOBER 31, 1990

"We don't have anything like this in Bismarck," said some of our guests when we had dinner at Sanders 1907. Seven of us spent a jolly evening during UND homecoming, having dinner in the little cafe on Kittson Avenue that has a built a strong reputation since it opened nine years ago.

Sanders is the sort of place you like to take out-of-town guests. It's also a place where you feel like celebrating birthdays and anniversaries. At the same time, it's the kind of place where you can have ethnic dinner for a moderate price of $10 on Tuesday, Wednesday or Thursday evenings.

Our reservation was for 8:30 P.M., and our table was ready. We were seated in a green high-backed booth. Our guests admired the rosemaling painting on the booths and walls that was done by Linda Evenson when she and her husband, Bob, opened

the cafe. Their stamp remains on Sanders, even though they have moved on to a resort in Minnesota. Sanders is relatively dark and bustling on a Saturday night. You can watch Kim Holmes, the owner, and his sous chef, John Gjovik, at work, framed in the copper-colored tin walls of the open kitchen. Sanders still has the high tin ceiling reminiscent of the era of the building.

The staff is well-trained. Our waiter guided us through our choices of a pâté appetizer, salads, entrees, wines and eventually dessert and coffee. First came the crusty French bread, which is made each day by Holmes and served with unsalted butter. We shared two orders of the pâté, which were presented on a plate garnished with a fat radish on greens, and paired with a hot, spicy cream cheese. With the pâté, there was an assortment of thin crackers. We tried the Caesar salad, although above-average salads are served with the entrees. Then came the main show.

Jean Peterson of Bismarck and I both had salmon, which is flown in fresh and never frozen. It was flaky and moist with a crisp edge that Holmes gets by rubbing the fish in oil, herbs and black pepper and cooking quickly in a hot cast-iron pan. The salmon was topped with a mint pesto sauce. And it was out of this world.

Daughter Carol Hagerty, here on a quick trip from Denver, enjoyed her walleye meunière in a wine butter sauce, although it lacked the fresh quality of the salmon. Constant Companion appreciated the tenderness of his tenderloin steak in green peppercorn sauce.

Tom Golden dug into an order of barbecued short ribs in sweet-and-sour sauce, but it was more than even a growing boy of 13 could handle. So, he took a "doggie bag" home with him.

Bob Peterson of Bismarck had his mind set on the roast caraway duck, but it was not to be. The last duck was sold just before we ordered, and we found out you almost have to call up and reserve the duck ahead of time. It was no big deal, though. He switched his order to prime rib rubbed with herbs and spices, called Swiss Eiger beef on the Sanders menu.

Gail Hagerty Golden ordered crevettes niçoise, or sautéed shrimp, which disappeared quickly when it arrived.

We tried the current "hot" dessert at Sanders. It's a pear filled with cream sauce and drizzled with chocolate fudge sauce and raspberry puree.

Our entire check came to around $185 and with a $25 tip, it was a healthy outlay. But it wasn't outrageous at all when you consider the amount of food and the quality of it. By big city standards, it was a bargain.

Sanders isn't perfect: Caesar salad is misspelled on the menu, and there was a long delay on one of our dinners. But Sanders is awfully good, too. Holmes makes it a point to mingle with patrons, and he combs the markets of Grand Forks to serve the best produce, herbs and fresh fish. Holmes has a flair for turning out dinners with a European flavor. It makes me hope that Sanders will be in business here a long time. ❡

Lumpy's Offers Yet Another Version of the Sub

DECEMBER 5, 1990

The music was rocky at Lumpy's, and loud. There was that usual feeling of disorientation you get when you make your first visit to a fast food place. You have to learn the game plan.

At some submarine shops, it's tough. It wasn't too bad at Lumpy's, because a young woman with an orange Lumpy's T-shirt and a matching cap gave me a little sheet of paper listing all the ingredients in a Lumpy's sub. "All you have to do," she said, "is cross off what you don't want. Then we'll make up your sub the way you want it."

"I like everything." I said. "And I'm hungry."

She said, "OK."

So, I checked wheat bread. I checked small for a $2.39 size sandwich. I could have had a medium for $3.59 a large for $4.79 or a giant for $9.99. But that feeds six people. Then, there's a 3-foot sandwich for $19.99 and a 6-footer for $39.99.

When CC arrived, he ordered the same thing as I had. It's easier that way. We sat down and looked over the place while we waited for our submarine sandwiches. We remembered when the building opened as an Auto Dine in 1966. After that, we remembered it was a Pizza Patrol. It also has been an ice-cream shop. And now we have Lumpy's.

Our sandwiches were ready in a short time. Then we started chewing in earnest. There were thin slices of the meats—pastrami, roast beef, corned beef, turkey, salami, ham and bologna. There was American, Swiss and provolone cheese. Also lettuce, pickles, tomato, onion, mayonnaise, alfalfa sprouts, black olives and Lumpy's special dressing. This is my kind of food.

CC said, "Half of this would have been enough for me."

"Not for me," I said, although I must admit I was almost on full when I finished.

I noticed signs around the place about macaroni and potato salad, taco salad supreme, side salads and chili. A sign said you can buy a Lumpy's T-shirt for $12. Another said you can get a soup and sandwich special every day for $3.50.

Todd Philbrick was cleaning tables and checking supplies. He's the owner of the Lumpy's franchise. Lumpy's is a rather new regional operation, with headquarters in Watertown, S.D. The originator is Jerry Laqua, who started out sell-

ing ham sandwiches in his Teen Center. One thing led to another, and soon he was making submarine sandwiches. So now, Lumpy's is stretching out. There are two in Brookings, S.D., one in Fargo and one in St. Cloud.

Philbrick learned about Lumpy's while working as a route man for Frito-Lay out of Grand Forks. Before that, he had put in six years on a Coca-Cola route here. So, he knows the eating places. He thinks submarines, with their low fat content, are the food of the 90s, and he's proud of the bread, which is baked from the Lumpy's recipe.

He likes the Lumpy's concept of offering everything that goes on a sub instead of offering the basics and charging extra for ingredients.

"Well," I asked, "what do people most usually mark off that they don't want?"

"Provolone cheese," he said. "I don't think they know how good it is. And sprouts. Some people just don't want sprouts." ❡

Marilyn reports that Lumpy's Subs is "long gone from the downtown scene."

Ronald McDonald Is Now at Home in East Grand Forks

JANUARY 9, 1991

John O'Keefe opened Grand Forks' first McDonald's Restaurant on South Washington Street in 1969. O'Keefe's youngest son, Michael, and his wife, Cindy, own the new McDonald's, which opened in December in East Grand Forks. We had been hearing about this new light, bright McDonald's. So, I suggested to Constant Companion we ought to go over there for a bite to eat.

He was agreeable. We put on our woolies, revved up the car and headed across the Red River.

We parked and approached the counter in our usual state of confusion. We looked carefully over the choices in four categories: breakfast items, sandwiches, salads and fries, and beverages and desserts. Feeling rather self-righteous, I ordered a chunky chicken salad for $2.69 and asked for the house dressing. That always seems easier to me than making a decision. This brought me a packet of McDonald's Own Red French reduced calorie dressing.

CC wasn't very adventurous. He asked for a quarter pounder for $1.79. Period. No soft drink. No fries. We sat at one of the tables and looked out through the floor-to-ceiling glass windows. If you're in a good mood, you would feel like you are sitting in a winter wonderland. If you're tired and grouchy and cold, you might feel like you are in Siberia.

I got off to a fast start on my salad because I was hungry. I thought the chicken, mostly on top, was quite tasty. Beneath it, there was a little more chicken and lettuce with bits of red cabbage and green pepper and two nice tomato wedges. CC wondered if his burger was the new low-fat kind. Then he muttered something about liking the fat kind better.

After I finished my salad, I went back for a frozen yogurt cone in a chocolate-vanilla swirl for 59 cents. It tasted more like soft-serve. I bought CC a hot apple pie for 69 cents. He nibbled on it and agreed it had an apple-y flavor, and that it was crunchy.

Servers in the new McDonald's wear maroon and gray striped shirts, and maroon visors. They seem well-trained. Inside the front entryway, there's a big shiny model of Ronald McDonald to greet customers. He's sitting on a recyclable plastic bench.

Michael O'Keefe says the 49-cent and 59-cent hamburgers have been bestsellers in East Grand Forks. They're small hamburgers, calculated at 10 to a pound of ground beef.

Since the first McDonald's opened here 21 years ago, the O'Keefe family has expanded its operation to include three restaurants in Grand Forks, and others in Bemidji, Thief River Falls and Devils Lake. ❡

This franchise continues to operate in East Grand Forks.

Royal Fork in Columbia Mall Has Mammoth Array of Food

MARCH 13, 1991

Canned green beans taste good to me. I've always liked them, so I piled a big helping on my plate, along with some spaghetti. I took a fillet of white fish along with the beans and spaghetti, which was interesting because of the big chunks of sharp-tasting tomato in it. It was 1 o'clock Thursday af-

ternoon when we sat down to eat at the Royal Fork Buffet Restaurant in Columbia Mall. The place was fairly full. You had to scout around to find a table.

I had told a friend that Constant Companion was feeling like breaking out of the house and we had decided to go the Royal Fork.

"Royal Fork?" she asked. "Isn't that kind of a feedlot?"

"Well, yes," I told her, "but the grazing is good. And the price certainly is right." Lunch is $4.35, and dinner is $5.65.

As of late, I've noticed that some people empty their trays, and others eat right off the tray. I like to keep the tray myself. I don't know why.

I was going backwards with this meal. After I finished my entrees, I approached my vegetable soup, which was slightly thick, but clear, with little parsley bits in it. It was better than some restaurant soup, but a tad too salty. Most restaurant soup is.

CC was working his way through a plate of salad. In deference to a low cholesterol diet, he sprinkled it with French dressing rather than the cream dressing. He ate spaghetti, fish and one of those cinnamon rolls that are a trademark of Royal Fork Buffet.

I ate my salad last—European style. It's amazing what you can stack on one small plate if you really set your mind to it. I had lettuce, tomato slices, broccoli, shredded cheese, pickled beets, cottage cheese, sunflower seeds, green peas, grapes and pineapple.

I munched happily along, noticing that CC had finished eating long before me. I encouraged him to graze through the dessert bar. I told him the soft-serve was low-fat even though it is high in sugar. Later, I learned that it is 4 percent milk fat. That's not nearly as high as ice cream.

There's a lot I like about the Royal Fork. The ambience is pleasant and homey. It's a good place for families and for people serious about eating. While it's probably the largest restaurant in Grand Forks, it's relatively quiet and orderly. There is a crew of people keeping the food line clean, clearing trays and even pouring coffee. And the place is attractive. There are large colored photographs of food on the walls. The green carpet has a geometric design. There is a lot of light wood latticework and frosted glass above the row of booths, dividing smoking and nonsmoking sections.

Scott Heilman has been manager for three years. He says volume is the key to keeping the large selection of food at a low cost. And volume he gets: In July and August last year, the Royal Fork served 50,000 people. That's as many as the total population of Grand Forks.

One of the hottest items is the shrimp on Friday nights. Tuesdays are family nights, when children's meals are 10 cents for each year of their age. Once every six weeks, the Royal Fork has a special for senior citizens. It's 50 cents off on a meal.

Heilman's been wearing a happy smile ever since the Sunday opening law was passed. It's been a boon to business, which was slack on Sundays in an empty mall. ⁋

With Lights Down Low, Pantry Turns into Le Pantre for Dinner

APRIL 3, 1991

The lights are turned down low, candles flicker on the tables, and there are folk songs and ballads two evenings each weeks in Le Pantre, in downtown Grand Forks. What's more, reasonably priced dinners are served in this cozy, homey atmosphere.

The Pantry, a good place for lunch, turns into Le Pantre, a dining room with French flavor, at 5 P.M. And the dinners are outstanding.

We were there Friday evening. The orange roughy dinner I ordered was one of the best meals I have had on the Eatbeat for a long time. I was more than pleased. I was impressed.

Orange roughy was one of the Friday specials, for $8.95. The entree was preceded by an iceberg lettuce salad, served nicely on a glass plate with a vinaigrette dressing that was excellent. The orange roughy seemed to be poached with spices. It was soft, tender and tasty, and served with a twice-baked potato. Also on the plate were candied potato strips and broccoli, still green and crisp. There was also a large lemon wedge cut like a flower.

For me, it was a Good Friday blessing to have broccoli that was still vivid green—not overcooked and mushy. The whole wheat buns, still warm from the oven, were an unexpected pleasure. The whole meal was next to perfection.

Where else, except Sanders, I wondered, can you go in the Grand Forks area for a complete top-rate meal like this?

With me were Constant Companion (CC), who ordered lasagna for $5.75, and Daughter Gail (DG). She had just driven in from Bismarck with Little Jack (LJ) and ordered filet mignon ($12.75).

The lasagna is one of five entrees served with a green salad and herbed garlic toast. CC found the meal much to his liking. As DG was eating her filet, she said, "When I do eat beef, I want it to be as good as this."

There were a half dozen other tables occupied while we were in the restaurant. We sat back and enjoyed the singing of Ron Franz, who entertains Friday evenings. On Saturday evenings, there is music by Scott Julin.

Le Pantre features homemade

desserts, which included a gorgeous chocolate layer cake along with several versions of elegant cheesecake. This is extra, of course, and we declined. But the desserts would put a festive cap on a meal here. Or they would be great if you just came in for coffee and a sweet fix while listening to music. Le Pantre is a gem of a restaurant on a street that is quiet in the evenings. How well it will go is still to be seen.

Warren LeClerc, the owner and manager of The Pantry, says dinner business during the week is often nil or next to it. Weekends are better, but not bustling. Still, he takes a positive approach. He has passed the 3½-year mark in business, trying to present an international style of food in Grand Forks. If he can't make things work one way, he tries another.

He reaches out for catering business and has hosted group events in the restaurant. He takes food out. Next week he will face the challenge of serving a dinner to 800 UND students at the Civic Auditorium during Greek Week. On Mother's Day, he will begin serving a Sunday brunch.

Soon, he will be serving sandwiches to downtown business places. He figures if the business doesn't come in to him, he will go out and get it.

Lunch business is good at The Pantry, LeClerc says, but he needs more than one meal to show a profit. The Pantry has distinguished itself with its blue plate specials at noon as well as sandwiches, salads, soups and home-baked items.

CC and I stopped at The Pantry Thursday for lunch. We both ordered fettuccine carbonara, which was the blue plate special for $4.95. It was a hearty main dish, with three cheeses, and flavored with herbs. The noodles were nice, long and al dente. With it, there was garlic bread, much better than the stuff you usually get in cafes.

The Pantry has some shortcomings. With Thursday's lunch, I was served a rather ordinary iceberg lettuce salad with too much creamy dressing on it. At times, the service seems disorganized. On Thursday, there was an unusually long delay in serving one of the two blue plate specials we ordered. But then, in France, things are a bit disorganized and everything always works out. ❡

Marilyn says that The Pantry is
"long gone from the Grand Forks restaurant scene."

Señor Howard's Menu Features Pizza and Mexican Foods

MAY 29, 1991

We drove into the parking lot of Señor Howard's Pizza and Mexican Cantina and Constant Companion said, "They've changed the entryway."

This is the restaurant at 2551

S. Columbia Road that originally was La Farmers Inn. It has been changing its identity from strictly Mexican food to include Howard's Pizza, under the ownership of Frank Basting.

We stepped inside the new side door, which is more convenient. Once inside, we could see that the restaurant has been redesigned with four dining areas. The feeling is cozier. The menu is larger. South-of-the-border music was playing softly in the background and we were seated.

We studied the menu. First page, all pizza. Next page, appetizers and a la carte Mexican selection. Center section, Mexican fare. Next page, sandwiches, side orders, desserts, beverages.

Next page, American dinners, submarines, and buckets of chicken, fish, ribs, shrimp. Last page, spirits and special drinks.

All of this takes a while. Eventually, CC ordered a beef fajitas dinner ($7.95). I ordered a cheese tostada ($2.75) and a beef taco ($1.95) from the a la carte section. With it, I ordered cola. He ordered a beer.

It was just a little after noon on Thursday, and there was a stream of people in and out. This is a relatively peaceful and quiet place to eat. Our booth, with seats covered in orange, was roomy. Dark wood is used in latticework dividers and in the wainscoting. The restaurant still has the colorful hanging lamps and along the wall, the same desert mural.

Our waitress was courteous, but the service was on the slow side. "Maybe," I told CC, "the service is snappier if you order the specials." But our wait wasn't too long. We didn't mind anyway, because we had a big basket of warm chips and nice hot salsa to dip them in.

When the food arrived, CC found the fajitas hard to eat, but the flavor good. I felt the same way about my tostada and taco. The meat was nicely flavored. The cheese had a good sharp taste. It was the lettuce that bothered me. It was shredded in rather large pieces that were hard to eat. What I like with Mexican food is crisp lettuce, finely chopped. (Picky, picky, picky.)

A family nearby ordered the luncheon special, a potato burrito. This is described on the menu as a "gently warmed flour tortilla filled with Red River Valley potatoes and seasoned pure beef, smothered with melted cheese and red gravy. Topped with lettuce and tomatoes." It's regularly $4.25.

With the new menu, owner Frank Basting says business is up 50 percent. He's been holding a grand opening this month. On Thursday, there will be a drawing for prizes. Basting says his menu has almost everything on it, except Chinese food. He's still working with his staff to get used to preparing the varied items, but he believes it's shaping up.

He took over the restaurant in 1988. In February, he added Howard's Pizza. This was a logical step, since he formerly was part of a family operation that sold Howard's Pizza, in Grand Forks. Howard's was the first pizza to come to the Grand Forks area. It was introduced here in 1957 by Howard Guckenberg. The Bastings bought the business in 1975 and continued it here.

Basting is proud of Howard's pizza because, he says, "It's our crust, our sauce. It's all homemade, every ounce. There's no premade sauces."

Along with the restaurant, the establishment has a lounge and casino. This area is set off from the dining rooms and entered through a separate door. ❡

Señor Howard's no longer operates in Grand Forks.

Steak, Lobster Combo Stars in Bronze Boot Repertoire

JUNE 26, 1991

"Where have all of the years gone?" I asked Constant Companion as we settled into a booth in the Bronze Boot to celebrate our 42nd wedding anniversary.

"Dunno," he said.

We got talking about the past 34 years we have spent in Grand Forks. When we came here in 1957, the Bronze Boot was the only supper club. Other choices for dining included the Golden Hour, the Dacotah Hotel and Ryan Hotel dining rooms. And Whitey's, of course.

As times have changed, the Bronze Boot—as well as Whitey's—has remained a constant on the dining scene. You can count on good food and reasonable prices. We felt the Boot was a good choice for an early dinner and a low-key celebration. We were not disappointed.

The Bronze Boot established its reputation as a gathering place for farmers and people from town. Customers come back faithfully to the midday smorgasbord, to the back bar and to the main dining room. You can find good buys on the menu if you want a quick supper before a movie or a game.

In the past two years, the Bronze Boot has taken on a more upscale look, in its effort to shed the western image. It was strictly western decor when it opened in 1957. Inside, it's still dark, but more shiny and plushy. Restroom facilities are vastly improved.

We began our celebration last Wednesday with a toast in the lounge, which is far more attractive than it used to be. In the first place, it's more cozy—not so barny. We moved into the main dining room, which is more upscale, with its mauve and forest green decor. It's nicely arranged on two levels with railing and booths around the edges. Art work in ornate, gold-looking frames is reminiscent of old masters.

Our waitress was Trudy, one of the "pros" who serve food at the Boot. And an experienced waitress makes a difference in how much I enjoy dining out. In the first place, she gave us time to finish our appetizers. CC had wild rice soup, and I had tomato juice.

Then, she brought on the spinach salads. As she did, she lit a flame under the drawn butter that was to go with my lobster and steak special ($12.50). I had heard people talking about this dinner, and I can see now what they mean. It's a real deal. The sirloin steak was juicy and long on flavor. The lobster was fluffy and just the right amount.

CC ordered barbecued loin back pork ribs ($8.75) and found them much to his liking. In the first place, the ribs were very well done. That is, the fat was cooked out of them. And the barbecue sauce was served on the side. My baked potato was great. His hash browns were done to a crispy brown on both sides. Our meal was most satisfying.

Waitresses at the Boot wear black trousers and black vests with black bow ties and white shirts.

We wondered why the cocktail waitress who works in the dining room wore such a brief outfit.

While it might be appropriate in the lounge, it seems a little out of character in the dining room.

We were among the first people in the dining room—after all, we started before six o'clock. We watched the booths and tables fill up. And we watched two chickens turn around above the open pit broiler in the center of the dining room. A friend of mine says she wonders if anyone ever orders those chickens.

Trudy did not push the desserts, but the Bronze Boot has some interesting items. Among them are cheesecakes, and an item called the "Big Blitz," which is patterned after a Snicker's bar. Some people like to round out a celebration with something gooey. Usually CC and I skip dessert out of respect for our cholesterol readings, but I couldn't pass up coffee and a mint at the end of the meal. The coffee was served in the Boot's new clear cups with pedestals. And believe it or not, the coffee does taste better in them. ❡

Inge's Bavarian Cuisine Offers German Specialties

JULY 3, 1991

"Welcome to Inge's Bavarian Cuisine," says the sign out front. Beneath the sign, there are red and white flowers. Above the sign, pink plastic pennants flutter in the breeze.

Grand Forks now has a restaurant with a German accent, so we paid it a visit last week. The building is familiar. It was originally a Country Kitchen, located in the center of a clump of motels in the northwestern corner of the city. It has had a succession of different owners. The latest are Inge and Casper Bartizal. And they hope to make a go of it by specializing in German fare.

It was fairly quiet inside at 6 P.M., June 24, except for the German music that was playing softly. The restaurant is clean. It has lace valances with pink hearts on the windows. There are shiny pink place mats on the tables and dainty baskets of flowers on the walls. A black, red and yellow German flag and the U.S. flag greet you.

The menu is short and sweet and to the point. Since we wanted to try the German food, Constant Companion ordered wiener schnitzel for $7. I ordered a schnitzel sandwich for $3.50 and a cup of pancake soup, 75 cents.

Unfortunately, our waitress didn't tell us about the daily specials, which are printed on a separate sheet. We didn't know about them and we failed to notice the chalkboard announcement on our way in, so we were limited in choice.

My soup was interesting, although it was too salty. The pancake slices were good and not at all soggy from sitting in the soup. Our schnitzels turned out to be breaded and deep-fried pork. With his meal, CC had a salad, which was so-so. And he had German potato salad. The servings were large—more than we could eat.

There is a dainty dessert menu showing Black Forest and Bavarian cheese tortes, strawberry tarts and two other items our waitress couldn't identify. The desserts range in price from $1.50 to $2.

Later, Inge told me that she and her husband have put all the money they could scrape up into the restaurant. They are determined to succeed, even though the credit rating has slipped with a series of changes in ownership. She says they have to pay their bills for supplies as they go. But since opening May 22, she is encouraged. So encouraged, in fact that she has given up her job at

Simplot in order to give her full attention to the restaurant. Her husband, Casper Bartizal, retired from the Air Force, is working for Grand Forks Security Services.

The couple met when he was in Europe with the Air Force. She was born in Portland, but had been living in Bavaria. She worked in the food business in Europe and completed courses in restaurant management there. She has been in this area for the past 10 years and formerly was employed in the bowling lanes at Grand Forks Air Force Base.

Inge is proud of the German pancakes she serves in the morning and the spaetzle noodles she makes daily. She says she works with fresh meats from local suppliers. ❡

Inge's Bavarian Cuisine no longer operates in Grand Forks.

Beaver's Brings Potatoes and Gravy to East Grand Forks

JULY 31, 1991

The prices are moderate. The surroundings are homey. The service is good. On three recent visits to Beaver's Family Restaurant in East Grand Forks, we found the food ranging from so-so to super.

The sign in front of Beaver's boasts the best soup in town. We tried the soup on our first visit to the restaurant July 20, when we ordered the special for $3.75, which was soup and a Denver sandwich. My vegetable-beef soup was very good, loaded with distinguishable chunks of carrots, celery, cabbage and tomatoes. Constant Companion's turkey noodle soup was thick and nice, but far too salty. The Denver sandwiches were extra good. The fluffy scrambled eggs had just the right amount of diced ham and onion for taste.

With those sandwiches in mind, we ordered Denver sandwiches Sunday evening. This time, the sandwiches turned out to be a thin layer of egg wrapped around a dripping collection of ham, pepper, onion and other vegetables. The taste was only OK. The sandwich was messy.

On the other hand, we had a great experience at Beaver's when we ordered the hot beef sandwich special for $3.75 Friday. The meat was lean, tasty and so tender you could cut it with a fork. The mashed potatoes were perfect, and the gravy had a thin consistency and homemade taste. Beaver's boasts of using real potatoes—not flakes—and making its own gravy.

Service is snappy. Waitresses are friendly, nimble and well-trained.

The new beige figured wallpaper and blue valances on the windows create a cozy feeling. The restaurant is spacious, with four or five dining areas. You don't feel squashed in. Booths have glass extensions above them with a pattern of embossed wheat. It's a nice touch and provides a little privacy.

Owner Steve Novak, whose nickname is Beaver, says he listens to people. He likes constructive criticism. He's serious about the customer comment cards on each table. Novak has been operating the restaurant in East Grand Forks since April 1. He says considering the construction work on the highway this summer, things are going well—better than he had projected.

Novak is 26. He got into the restaurant business in Warren, Minn., six years ago because, as he says, "I had a dream." He was working for Marvin Windows, and he has only a high school education. Still, he wanted a business of his own. So, he plunged in and opened a restaurant in Warren. Things went so well that his father, Leonard Novak, is now working for him, running the restaurant with its combined video shop in Warren. That leaves the younger Novak free to concentrate on the East Grand Forks operation.

Beaver has plans for himself as well as his business. He is getting married in September to Melody Olson, who has worked as a waitress for him for five years. He also is planning to revive his Beaver act. In Warren, he dressed up like a beaver for birthday parties in the restaurant. It went over so well in Warren that he is hoping it will also be popular in East Grand Forks. ¶

Beaver's Family Restaurant no longer operates in East Grand Forks.

Tortellini Is Soft, Warm and Like Soul Food at Big Al's

SEPTEMBER 25, 1991

It was darkish inside Big Al's Pasta Parlor, at the Westward Ho Motel. One young man was eating peanuts at a table along the side of the room. The waiter brought us a large laminated menu printed in red and green. In the dimness of the room, we could pick up the green print OK, but the red print was hard to read. The waiter, wearing a sweatshirt with a caricature of Big Al on it, came back to the table and asked, "You guys ready to order?"

"We can't see the menu very well," Constant Companion said.

"OK. I'll be back in a few minutes," the waiter said.

At length, I decided to order tortellini, described as "a blend of beef and Romano cheese, tortellini with butter, spices and heavy cream." CC asked for lasagne, "layered with fresh ricotta, mozzarella and parmesan cheese, seasoned ground beef and red sauce." Both were $6.95, and came with a choice of minestrone soup or salad, and a small loaf of warm bread, served on a board with a knife stuck in it.

The fellow at the other table left. The waiter threw the peanut shells on the floor. Another couple came in and sat down. The piped-in music was metallic, and it kept coming. It had a nice beat. Not too loud.

The bread tasted good. CC said the soup was good, but only lukewarm. My salad was so-so, but nicely seasoned with a fair sprinkling of olive slices and an abundance of croutons. The tortellini was soft and warm and sort of like soul food. The serving was so ample that I could get only halfway through it. CC said the lasagne had a nice, sharp flavor.

We agreed that the quality of Italian food is consistently good at Big Al's, which was the first Italian restaurant in Grand Forks, and continues its exclusively Italian menu after five years. It's fun to eat in the Pasta Parlor, which is also the Peanut Bar, where you can get a beer or a glass of wine with the meal. The same food is available to families who eat in the Chuckhouse Restaurant or patrons of the Casino Sports Bar, also at the Westward Ho Motel.

I liked the shakers of parmesan and hot red pepper on each table. The early evening ambience is right for a quiet, Italian meal. A collection of old chairs and a variety of square, round and oblong tables makes for a casual atmosphere. So does the wooden floor liberally sprinkled with peanut shells. One lethargic fly was driving us crazy. This could happen anywhere at this time of year.

Our service was good. Our waiter delivered us from having to reply 99 times to the question, "How is everything?" He asked only once or twice, and I am convinced that at most restaurants it doesn't really matter anyway.

Our waiter deserves a gold star for telling us, when he delivered the bill, that we should pay it at the bar. He didn't make us play guessing games. He was fairly attentive, but ready to remove the dishes before I was ready to relinquish them. He probably isn't used to people who like to dawdle. When I eat out, I like to take my time.

At 6:20 P.M., a man in a dark jacket came in and was turning the lights up and down. He was puffing on a cigarette.

"Is that Big Al?" I asked the cashier as we were leaving.

"No," he said. "That's Jack Carr. He comes in every night about this time to play the honky-tonk piano for the Peanut Bar." ❡

Big Al's and the other restaurants at the Westward Ho
succumbed to the Red River flood of 1997.

Bit of Norway in City Center Mall Builds a Following

FEBRUARY 5, 1992

The homemade tomato soup was like mothers used to make, when mothers stayed home and made soup for lunch. The potato dumplings were dense and hearty and flavored with bits of ham.

The bread pudding was like something out of the past. It is soul food for children of the Depression.

In the interest of research, we each bought two or three different items when I had lunch Friday with Marijo Shide (MS) and Barbara Lander (BL) at Bit of Norway. Then, one by one, we sampled the food. Before we had time to set our trays aside, we were nodding our approval.

"This is not the kind of food you make by mixing water and stirring," MS said. We laughed because we know that Elizabeth Anderson, who runs the little shop in City Center Mall, is not the quick-mix, fast-food type of person.

Of all the items we sampled,

riskrem was probably the standout. It's a light, fluffy rice pudding with raspberry sauce on top. BL was impressed with the quality of the tomato soup. Coffee, which is good, is 35 cents a cup here.

You place your order at a window when you go to Bit of Norway. Inside, you can see the lineup:

Riskrem, 50 cents. Rommegrot, 50 cents. Bread pudding, 75 cents. Muffin, 30 cents. Caramel roll, 60 cents. Apple pie, $1.50. Soup, $1.25. Lefse, $1 a sheet. Potato dumplings, $1.25.

There are touches that make this food outlet in a mall rather unique. In the first place, it is strictly Norwegian fare. No hamburgers or pizza. In the second place, it has flowers painted on the napkin holders and flowers painted on the listing of items on the wall. And it is clean. Spanking clean.

It's obvious that Bit of Norway has a following already. People seem excited to have a place where they can buy Norwegian food. The Rev. Tim Johnson of United Lutheran Church was there, finishing off a lunch of tomato soup and caramel roll. As he was getting ready to leave, he said, "I will eat caramel rolls wherever and whenever they are served."

Alice Boen was having an afternoon snack and said she stops by often. "I like the vegetable soup when she has it. Her German chocolate cake is out of this world." Another customer, Glenn Rudrud, said he likes the dumplings.

Bit of Norway opened Jan. 8, and so far, so good, Anderson says. For her, it's a new experience to run a food business. She is trying to get better organized. But, she says, "We are busier every day, and that's good."

For Anderson, Bit of Norway is a longtime dream—or at least the beginning of a dream. She would like to have a separate shop, where she could have music from Norway and books about Norway. A native of Beltrami, Minn., she is of mostly Norwegian background. She is active in the Sons of Norway. She feels strongly about preserving Norwegian culture and cuisine in this area where so many Scandinavians settled. ⸿

Gramma Butterwicks Serves Good Food, Nothing Fancy

FEBRUARY 19, 1992

Big chunks of carrot, wide slices of celery and lean, tender meat make up the vegetable beef soup at Gramma Butterwicks Family Restaurant on South Washington Street.

On a scale with 10 at the top, I would say the cup of soup at Butterwicks last Wednesday could rate at least an eight. It was a tad salty, but not nearly as salty as some restaurant soups. The soup came with the club sandwich I ordered, for a total of $4.15. And the triple decker with bacon, lettuce and tomato and my choice of ham or turkey—ham, please—was the best sandwich I have eaten for a while.

But then, I expected it to be as good as the club sandwiches served at the Dacotah Restaurant downtown. After all, Terry and Ruth Jensen operate both places. They also have Gordy's Diner on Gateway Drive.

Constant Companion met me at Butterwicks for lunch and ordered his favorite sandwich—the Philly Steak, for $3.40. This is sliced roast beef on a hoagie bun with mushrooms, onions, Swiss and cream cheese. CC took a couple of bites of his Philly and nodded his approval. "Good," he said.

The nice thing about the menu at Butterwicks is that you can get the sandwich alone at one price.

Or you can make your choice of soup, salad or fries for 85 cents more. Too many restaurants make you buy something with your sandwich whether you want it or not.

With our sandwiches, we drank coffee. It's 65 cents a cup. It's strong. You don't have to worry about it keeping you awake.

Lunching at Gramma Butterwicks is an entirely satisfactory experience. The service is good. The food is basic and wholesome. The management makes no pretext of being fancy. They serve the kind of food that brings you back. Breakfast is served beginning at 5:30 A.M. and you can have breakfast items all day. There are daily luncheon specials, including casseroles. And there are supper specials.

The restaurant has been through a series of managements since it opened here originally as Sambo's in the 1970s. Terry and Ruth Jensen bought Gramma Butterwicks four months ago, and have been putting a lot of energy into running it. All they need, he says, is more hours in a day. "We're happy with the business. It's more than we expected, but we would hope for more."

Terry Jenson started out in the food business at the old Ritz Cafe on Main Street in Fargo. He was chef at the F-M in Moorhead, when it first opened. Then he came to Grand Forks to work for the Westward Ho Motel. Here, he met his wife when she was working at the former A&W Drive In. She has worked as his partner in operating their three restaurants in Grand Forks. ¶

Ruth and Terry Jensen continue to operate Gramma Butterwicks.

Whitey's of East Grand Forks Thrives on Keeping Status Quo

AUGUST 26, 1992

Franchise restaurants may come and go, but Whitey's of East Grand Forks goes on forever. It's a place where people go when they come back to visit this community.

"I think they would be disappointed if we changed too much," says Dave Homstad, an assistant manager. "People seem to like Whitey's the way it is, and I guess we operate on the theory that if it isn't broke, we won't fix it."

This is a great time of year for Whitey's, with the students coming back, the farmers finishing up their work and the people back from the lakes. Whitey's will be swinging into its fall and winter routine, Homstad says. But for a few more weeks, the restaurant will be offering skewer lunches— an assortment of fresh fruit arranged on skewers and served with dip, cheese wedge, smoked sausage slice and a hard roll.

Constant Companion and I have been going there almost every Friday for a single skewer and a cup of wild rice soup for $3.25. That's quite a deal. And it reminds me so much of the pub lunches we enjoyed when we visited London.

We also go regularly to Whitey's when one of our three musketeers comes back for a visit. Usually, they want to see if the steaks are as good as the ones they remember. We went there Friday night with our Bismarck daughter, Gail, and we were not disappointed. She had a 4-ounce beef tenderloin steak ($8.50). Constant Companion tried a half rack of ribs ($8.95), and I settled for a Riverboat sandwich ($4.75). This, to my way of thinking, is a great thing to eat when you don't want to go all out. And it's a great food buy, because it comes in a sourdough bun with a choice of french fries, tossed salad or potato salad.

The dinner items are served with a relish tray, which has become a fairly rare item in restaurants today, and the usual tossed salad, roll and choice of potatoes.

There are pluses and minuses at Whitey's. You get a big, white cloth napkin whether you sit in the dining room or at one of the booths in the lounge. Soups are super. The wild rice on Fridays is a big draw. It's thick, with pieces of carrot and slivers of almond. Chicken and dumplings served on Fridays ($4.25) for lunch are better than your mom used to make, according to Don Anderson, who stopped by our table

recently. Jinny Anderson said it's the walleye that brings her back for more.

On the other hand, some people do not like the laid-back atmosphere in the lounge at Whitey's. They are happier eating at tables in the dining room at the rear.

For the most part, Whitey's staff is experienced and professional, but there are times when you wish some of the waitstaff would spruce up a little and be more concerned about restraining long hair.

Whitey's was established by the late Edwin "Whitey" Larson in 1925 and moved to its present location in 1930. The stainless steel horseshoe bar was the first one built in the United States, and is still referred to as "Whitey's Wonderbar." When a fire damaged the building in 1942, a new front facade was added.

Because it put the emphasis on food, Whitey's is the lone survivor from the days when gambling was rampant in East Grand Forks. In recent years, Whitey's has expanded to include a side bar with pool tables and dart games and a separate back entrance. Thus, the restaurant promotes an atmosphere for everyone.

With its art deco design and American and Canadian flags, Whitey's doesn't change very much. It's a tradition in this community, and thrives on its comfortable mix of clientele and a menu strong on meat and potatoes. But, they have made some concessions to changing tastes, such as adding a taco salad and submarine sandwiches. And, where imported beers used to be displayed, there are now regional beers of America. ¶

County Coffee Court to Feature Soup du Jury, Statute Stew

SEPTEMBER 23, 1992

Where but in Grand Forks could you have a lunch of Norwegian lefse and Chinese chow mein?

I ordered this combination—quite delightful—Thursday at the Courthouse Coffee Shop, which is soon to be known as County Coffee Court. The name change is on a new menu being prepared by Elizabeth Anderson. She took over the coffee shop in September and will run it in conjunction with her Bit of Norway food shop in City Center Mall.

Anderson was in the kitchen, and Bea Jacobson, whom she calls her star waitress, was presiding at the counter of the small lunch room when I stopped in. It's downstairs in the Grand Forks County Courthouse.

Other customers included a county commissioner, an assortment of lawyers and a couple of people in the courthouse on business. And I had noticed the sign pointing down to the coffee shop says, "Public invited."

The menu is short and sweet. In fact, until the new one comes out, it is nonexistent. The new menu says County Coffee Court at the top. It's designed to look like a page from a legal notebook. On the second line, it says: Honorable U.B. the Judge, Presiding.

The menu will feature breakfast items and lunch including, "civil soups" with "writ crackers."

There will be "soup du jury, pea bargain, vegetable brief and statute stew." Pork and beans will be called "habeas porkus leguminus." The "Chief Justice burger" will be "fried speedily and publicly." Prices on the new menu are listed in a column called "out of pocket damages."

The menu closes with the principle that all persons present shall receive their just desserts. These include "unimpeachable pie, oathmeal cookies and tort tarts."

Right now, Anderson is trying to get on track. She says she took on the new venture in order to get a full 40-hour week for her six employees at Bit of Norway. She can use them in both places. She is building a strong reputation for good-quality, authentic Norwegian food, but modesty tends to be a trait of Norwegians.

At the courthouse, she has neat stacks of homemade cookies in plastic containers and freshly fried doughnuts. She has desserts such as bread pudding and apple and pumpkin pie. The luncheon special Thursday was chow mein with rice and a dinner roll for $3. And always, there is lefse. It goes for $1 for a moist, fresh sheet.

I ate lefse, rather than the roll, with my chow mein. The food had a wholesome, homemade quality about it. The serving was ample.

In the background, there was a radio. I could hear Rush Limbaugh spouting about Slick Willie. At the next table, some attorneys were needling me, as attorneys tend to do. One of them said if I used his name, to spell it right. He said it was M-O-R-L-E-Y.

In the kitchen, Anderson was saying she can't turn out lefse fast enough for her two places of business. She says she has a hard time finding people who are willing to help her roll it out.

It was lefse that got her into the food business in the first place.

"I was making it at home and selling it, and you can't do that," she says. "You have to have all that equipment, so I decided to do it somewhere else. After I got started in City Center Mall, I decided I had to offer more than lefse to make a go of it. It takes an awful lot of lefse to make a profit," she muses.

Business has taken off beyond her expectations or dreams. People come in from all over for Norwegian foods, she says. "It's not like with hamburgers. People who buy lefse or rommegrot want to talk about Norway." ❡

Postscript from Marilyn: "The County Coffee Court is long gone from the Grand Forks County Courthouse basement . . . and sadly missed." Owner Elizabeth Anderson died in January 2013.

Red Lobster Offers Seafood in Landlocked North Dakota

NOVEMBER 25, 1992

You get the big welcome and the fond farewell when you visit the new Red Lobster restaurant.

And to visit there is rather special.

In the first place, it's the first strictly seafood restaurant in Grand Forks. In the second place, the restaurant is upscale, with the service well-orchestrated.

On my first trip to Red Lobster, I joined a group of friends for lunch. I ordered grilled sea scallops ($5.99) with a Diet Coke (99 cents).

My check, with tax, was $7.40. By the time I left a 15 percent tip, I was up in the $9 range for lunch. This is more than the average lunch around Grand Forks. But the food was worthy, and the lunch I chose was, indeed, a dinner.

Red Lobster won me over with its warm garlic cheese bread. Then came the cup of smooth clam chowder. My scallops were sweet and meaty, with thin strips of crisp bacon separating them on the skewer and a slice of zucchini at each end. The skewers were served over rice pilaf, and I chose broccoli instead of baked or French-fried potatoes to go with my meal. The broccoli seemed to be steamed gently, and retained its bright green color on the plate, which is garnished with fresh kale and a lemon wedge.

Others around the table tried and enjoyed spicy seafood gumbo with Caesar salad and shrimp Milano. There were no complaints.

On my second visit to Red Lobster, I met Gladys Keig for lunch. We both ordered soup and Caesar salad. The bowl of clam chowder is of a medium-thin consistency, nicely flavored and very filling. The Caesar salad is nicely done with a pleasing dressing and very finely grated white cheese. This is the most inexpensive lunch on the menu. At the same time, it is more than adequate.

The restaurant has a starter menu that includes clam chowder, seafood gumbo, shrimp cocktail, shrimp egg rolls, mozzarella cheese sticks, chicken fingers, fried zucchini, calamari rings, chicken skewers, chilled shrimp in the shell and fried clam strips. The dessert tray of items such as "Fudge Overboard" for $3.35 and "Raspberry Cobbler a la Mode" for $2.35 is trotted out for all diners to see.

Service is impeccable at the Red Lobster. The staff is well-trained and professional in its approach.

Dinner at Red Lobster ranges from $10 to $20, and the waiting line has been long on weekends. People of this region have been welcoming the opportunity to try the lobster, crab, shrimp and scallops. Michael Pauly, an assistant manager, says the restaurant chain has done enough research to believe the honeymoon will end and business will plateau.

The Red Lobster here is the third in North Dakota, with others in Fargo and Bismarck. It is one of more than 550 restaurants in a growing trail across the country. ❡

GF Goodribs Is Warm, Cozy Haven on Cold Winter Night

JANUARY 6, 1993

Oops, I scattered the tossed salad all over the tablecloth and down into my lap. Either the salad tongs are poorly designed, or I am clumsy. Or both. At any rate, I like the idea of serving salad from a large bowl. I managed to scrape things together and continue on with the conversation when Constant Companion (CC) and I had dinner with Jan and Earl Strinden (JS and ES) at GF Goodribs Steakhouse and Lounge.

The date was Dec. 30. We were going to see the UND Sioux women play Portland State, and we got together for dinner before the game. GF Goodribs was a good choice. It has a handy entryway for a cold evening and a nice big cloak area.

Our waiter was Jayson, and he was professional in attire as well as demeanor. JS and I both ordered a crab legs and New York strip steak special ($9.50). CC had baby back pork ribs ($12.95). ES chose Cajun prime ribs ($12.95), his favorite item on the Goodribs menu. He started out with onion soup and ordered a twice-baked potato.

"You have that, too," he suggested to JS. "You like that."

While they ordered potatoes twice-baked, I assured Jayson I wanted mine baked only once.

The restaurant was rather quiet at 5:30 P.M., and we had a chance to visit about Christmas, our families, the Sioux and the world in general. We nibbled on the basket of extra-good garlic toast before our orders arrived. ES asked me to taste his Cajun ribs, and I must say the flavoring was noteworthy. Cajun enough, but not too much.

Once again my dexterity was in question when I approached my crab legs. Goodribs has nice crackers to use and proper forks for digging out crab meat. Still,

I was all thumbs. I kept watching JS because she seemed quite adept.

CC was pleased with his ribs and polished them off in short order.

We had time for coffee after we finished our meal. None of us was hungry enough for dessert, but the tray shown to us by Jayson was appealing. There was a Snickers dessert, chocolate cake and apple crisp—all for $2.50.

Dinner was above average. The price was right.

In order to get a long look at the steakhouse in daylight, I went back alone for a quick lunch Friday, and I found the soup and salad bar for $3.50 a good lunch buy. From it, I chose a bowl of wild rice soup that warmed, filled and satisfied. With it, I had cottage cheese sprinkled with imitation bacon and shredded cheddar cheese. Alongside, I had some raw broccoli, a cherry tomato and a dill pickle spear.

Goodribs also serves Sunday brunch, which is distinguished by its excellent eggs. I don't know what they do, but the cooks keep the eggs fluffy and fresh. You also find ham, sausage and bacon, ribs and potatoes, and fruits, juices, raw vegetables and salad items. At a side table, you find pastries, muffins, cookies and often doughnut holes.

The restaurant has been in operation as GF Goodribs with Paul Waind as owner for seven years. It opened 20 years ago as Desautel's Steak and Stein, and went through a couple of ownership changes. Waind has managed to build up a steady trade specializing in ribs. He has added "steakhouse and lounge" to the name, he says, in order to draw customers from the 700 motel rooms surrounding the supper club. ❡

GF Goodribs no longer operates in Grand Forks.

John Barleycorn Bakes Up Mean Lavosh in Columbia Mall

FEBRUARY 17, 1993

"We'll meet at the Barleycorn," Marilyn Lundberg said. It was her turn to make arrangements for the monthly meeting of friends who used to drink coffee together on Cottonwood Street.

When we got there, the special for the day was Cajun chicken salad, so Marilyn and Ruth Barney went with that. Estelle Graham and Crystal Rice ordered No. 3, which was chicken salad and onion soup. I ordered a Reuben sandwich. And when Geri Ouradnik breezed in, she ordered a half lavosh supreme with mushrooms, green pepper, tomato and red onion.

Then the discussion began. The lavosh, we agreed is the trademark of John Barleycorn. Not everybody likes it, but many do. And many people go to the Barleycorn with lavosh in mind. Lavosh is a thin bread that originated in Armenia.

As always, the service was top-rate. Overall, the food was good. The Cajun chicken salad plate was ample and served with good, warm breadsticks. My Reuben was OK, but a little on the skimpy side, I thought.

We had separate checks, which was no problem. It sure beats a bunch of women digging in their purses and asking who had coffee and who had only water. My check, for the sandwich with fries and a diet cola, came to $6.29 with tax. That's a little heavy for lunch in Grand Forks. But the Barleycorn is a cut above the average eating places in shopping malls. It's been a star performer in the Grand Forks dining scene since 1979.

It's laid out like an old-time town. To the left, there is a livery section with semiprivate nooks and corners for dining. Straight ahead, set off with light wood latticework, you find a gazebo. Surrounding it, on a lower level, you have the park area with green carpeting. At the right, there is a dining room called the general store which can be reserved by larger groups.

Along with its unique design, it has established a reputation for consistently good food. The Barleycorn has long been a popular place to meet for lunch, because it's convenient, and because the staff is accommodating to people who want to linger longer and discuss business or play bridge.

Dinner is a special occasion at the Barleycorn. The filet medallions drew raves recently from a co-worker, Molly Blue. The dinner, for $16.95, features two center cuts of tenderloin with Béarnaise and Hunter mushroom sauce. Blue, a fan of the Barleycorn, also praises the shrimp oreganata ($13.95) from the seafood section.

The new menu, introduced in October, adds pastas and variations of chicken to the offerings. The restaurant also is serving stir-fried vegetables. Mainstays are steaks and seafood. ❡

John Barleycorn no longer operates in Columbia Mall.

Bonzer's on Fourth Still Excites Taste Buds After 10 Years

MARCH 3, 1993

Television sets are running. Music plays from the speaker system. Conversation rises from the high-backed booths. The gentlemen from the Bartles & Jaymes ad jump out from the lighted sign.

Peanut shells are strewn on the terrazzo floor. This is Bonzer's, the nearest thing to a pub in Grand Forks.

From 11 A.M. until 3:30 P.M., Bonzer's is a lunch place. You can get German fare on Thursdays. Late in the afternoon, it turns into a place where people meet for happy hour or a light supper. Or both.

Cindy Bonzer, who operates the pub with her husband, Jon, says, "We're selling more food and less wine and beer now. But I think that's true everywhere."

The Bonzers opened their downtown sandwich pub 10 years ago this week. "We were worried about business when Norby's department store closed early in 1986, but we found more professional people coming in. And we have UND students who live in downtown apartments picking up the slack."

In fact, she says, business has been better for Bonzer's each passing year. "We thought of applying for a liquor license. And then we wondered why, with things going so well just selling wine and beer."

The Bonzers haven't rocked the boat. The walls and shelves are still decorated with the beer memorabilia Jon started collecting in junior high school in California. As a matter of fact, he is a member of the Beer Can Collectors of America. He always is

trading and buying to enhance his collection of trays, cans, bottles, pictures. He proudly displays a Dakota beer can from the short-lived brewery in Bismarck; he says it is one of the most valuable in the nation.

Booths of dark wood provide semi-privacy for patrons. The wooden bar, with 10 high-backed wooden stools, provides a spot for loners or twosomes. A fake tree with forever-autumn leaves stands at the back of the pub. Then, in the corner, there's a private dining area called the Board Room. It can be reserved for groups of around a dozen at no charge.

Constant Companion and I paid a visit to Bonzer's late Thursday afternoon. For some people, it was happy hour. For us, it was supper time. I had a cup of split pea and ham soup and a half of a hot pastrami sandwich ($2.85). CC had a bowl of chili con carne ($1.95) with a Michelob. The chili was hot, hot, hot. The brew was dry.

There's nothing namby-pamby about the food at Bonzer's. It is spiced and flavored enough to make a statement. Soups, which are made by the owners, are thick and hot. Some customers come regularly for soup. Along with soup and a long list of sandwiches, Bonzer's offers an array of mini-salads for $3.25 and large salads for $4.25. The menu is cleverly written and reflects the good humor of the Bonzers. ❡

Bonzer's remains in business in Grand Forks.

Open Kitchen at Sanders 1907 Gives Diners Front-Row Seat

MARCH 24, 1993

Tables are set with crisp white napkins folded into water goblets. Narrow vases on the tables have fresh flowers and tiny branches of trees with spring buds on them. Sanders 1907, with its green tin ceiling and roping painted along the walls, is an inviting setting for dinner. It's a cozy place, narrow and long with three high-backed booths and a series of smaller tables.

At the rear, chef Kim Holmes supervises his crew as another evening of fine dining begins at 312 Kittson Ave. Taped music is playing. The phone keeps ringing.

On Thursday evening, I spent two hours on a bar stool at the counter watching the show—no, make that the three-ring circus—that is Sanders. Presiding at the stove in a small open kitchen was chef John Gjovik. Working with him was sous chef Paul Browning, chopping parsley and arranging antipasto plates.

Three waiters in black shirts, bolo ties and white aprons were doing the side-work. By 6 P.M., the first seating of diners was under way. Sanders 1907 can handle 44 between 5:30 and 7:30 P.M. and another 44 after that.

At 9:30 P.M., it's a free-for-all.

It's what owner Holmes calls "a scene in here." That's when Sanders starts serving off its late-night menu featuring appetizers, salads, buffalo burgers, buffalo lavosh and desserts. Along with this late-night show, there are specialty coffee drinks. For dinner during the week, midweek specials for $11 are offered. On Tuesday, it's Italian food. On Wednesday, it's French food. And Thursday is German night. Last Thursday, the special was pork roast with green caper sauce, German spaetzle and red cabbage.

While diners order the specials, they also favor the fresh fish entrees that are priced according to the market. On Thursday, mahi-mahi was served with fresh asparagus spears artfully arranged on a bed of rice. Plates were garnished with lemon and lime wedges nestled in parsley.

Trademarks of Sanders 1907 include barbecued split beef ribs ($14), roast caraway duck, Czechoslovakian style ($18) and an Italian dinner for two ($50). Swiss Eiger beef ($16) is offered only on Friday and Saturday.

While I watched the activity in the tin-lined kitchen, I nibbled on an antipasto plate ($6.50) and sipped a glass of Chardonnay. The antipasto offering is a meal in itself, when you eat it yourself. Usually, though, two or four people share this positively delightful appetizer while waiting for their entrees. It includes cold rice salad with roasted peppers, barbecued beef, pickled herring in a thick cream sauce, beet and cabbage relish, pickled grapes flavored with cinnamon, clove and onion, and cold duck salad with North Dakota Prairie Juice (a Holmes creation).

The driving force behind Sanders 1907 is Holmes, who drove into Grand Forks in 1985 with all of his belongings in his 1970 van. As he sipped bottled water and reflected on the past eight years, he said he is doing OK. In the next breath, he added, "I have struggled."

He took over full ownership of the cafe in 1989 from Bob and Linda Evenson. They established the restaurant in 1981 in the building her grandfather, Sander Johnson, constructed in 1907. They have since moved on to operating a resort at Lake Winnibigoshish in Minnesota.

Holmes remembers lean times when he was getting started here. Once, on a January night, no one came in the front door. He wondered what he had gotten himself into.

But he didn't wonder long. On many nights, he has to turn away diners who don't have reservations. The small cafe on a downtown side street has established a reputation for exquisite meals. Holmes has drawn on his experience as a restaurant owner in the state of Washington and several years as a chef in Switzerland.

Now he lives upstairs with his wife, the former Beth Hookstra of Northwood, N.D. She helps him with the Sanders line of sauces and marinades, which are marketed with a Pride of Dakota label. Their products include a jerky called "Dakota Jerk." Holmes has developed his own philosophy for operating a cafe.

"You have to be professionally casual," he says. "I hate to hear a waiter say, 'My name is so-and-so, and I'll be your server.' You have to be secure in knowing you give good service and you serve good food. You don't have to go around asking how everything is."

He relies on three regular waiters: Dirk Homeier, Shawn Clapp and Phil Lofthus. His kitchen crew includes Richard West, Dan Slattery and Matt Castle. Becky Rubin does the flowers and upkeep.

As he keeps an eye on the kitchen, Holmes says, "I run this place like a basketball team. Everybody is important. Everybody plays the game."

Each booth and table has a name. When the waiters talk about "Cloud Nine," they mean the booth by the front window. "Cat's Eye" is the booth at the back with lights like the eyes of a cat.

At this point, he doesn't want Sanders 1907 to get any bigger. He just wants it to get better. ❡

Windmill's Sunday Brunch Just About Takes the Cake

APRIL 7, 1993

Poppy-seed bread, breakfast quiche and pull-apart caramel rolls are trademarks of the Sunday champagne brunch served by the Windmill Restaurant. Constant Companion and I went there after church Sunday with Earl and Jan Strinden, and we were able to get a table in the Garden Court atrium. We sat and looked out at the swollen Red River. We watched a big tree bending under the pressure of an ice floe.

The Windmill is an attractive restaurant with a stained glass windmill as the distinguishing feature in the long, maroon-carpeted foyer. There are also curios, such as a cream separator, in the entryway.

On Sunday, we began with juice and champagne. And there was coffee. We moseyed out to the buffet table, where we found a good selection of breads including muffins, bagels, doughnut holes and caramel rolls. There was a tray of fruit, including fresh pineapple, grapes, strawberries, honeydew melon and wedges of watermelon. Beyond that were eggs Benedict, breakfast quiche, pancakes and a white fish in a light sauce.

The Windmill brunch is $7.95. Some people approach it by having breakfast selections first and then going on to lunch items. I sort of cornered the best of both worlds on one plate. With the bread, fruit and fish, I went heavy on the steamed broccoli but skipped the ham.

All four of us made different choices. And we didn't overlook the desserts, which included slices of blueberry pie. Then we sat and visited.

This is what the Windmill is all about, according to owner Tom Potter. "We try to create an atmosphere for relaxed dining," he says. Tom and his wife, Weezie, own the restaurant building at 213 S. Third St. January and February were slow, Potter says, but things are moving faster now. He has plans to feature more dinner theater in the upstairs facility.

He has made arrangements for Fire Hall performances in May, and UND Burtness Theatre productions in July and August. The Rotters also plan to feature Southwest nights in the Garden Court this summer. They also are thinking of country nights, which will include dance lessons.

The Windmill serves lunch and dinners from Tuesday through Saturday. Reuben sandwiches, quiche and pasta are bestsellers at noon. The New York steak and roast ducks are favorites of dinner customers.

Boondocks Lounge, on the lower level, opens at 4:30 P.M. Tuesday through Saturday, featuring different music each night and karaoke on Thursday. ❡

The Windmill is no longer in business.

Even Without Quiche, Lunch at Passages Is Grade A

MAY 5, 1993

"We're out of quiche, our special for today," the waiter said.

"Oh, you're breaking my heart," Vern Sandstrom said.

That set the stage for lunch Friday at Passages in the Radisson Hotel in Fargo. Timothy, the waiter, could appreciate the fact that some men still don't like quiche.

We met Daughter Gail (DG), who was there for a conference, and her new in-laws, Vern and Hildy Sandstrom of Fargo.

Our waiter was the jovial sort. He was patient and sympathetic when Constant Companion (CC) went into a long harangue about how he needs horseradish to go with his bean soup. Timothy brought the horseradish and marveled at the way CC put it in his cup of Knicker-bocker bean soup. With the soup, CC had a half a ham sandwich ($4.25 for the combo).

The Sandstroms ordered turkey sandwiches ($5.25), which were served with potato salad and gar-nished with red onion and tomato on a leaf of lettuce. You get your choice here of white, whole wheat, rye or nine-grain bread.

DG ordered a spinach salad ($6.95), so I did likewise. She usu-ally knows what's good. And it was. There were thick slices of lean, white, smoked turkey on fresh spin-ach leaves. The salad was topped with marinated mushrooms in a warm mustard dressing. It was served with freshly baked minia-ture loaves of French bread. With it, butter, embellished with a sprig of parsley. We had coffee later. It was excellent: strong and hot and served from a small pewter pot.

Passages is one of my favorite spots in North Dakota. I like it be-cause it is upscale—first class.

And sometimes, you feel like being ushered to a table with a sparkling white cloth, ice water in goblets, big cloth napkins, waiters in black and white and soft music in the background.

That's Passages.

It's located on the second floor of the downtown Radisson. There's lots of glass, allowing you to look down to the lobby and over toward the second floor lounge. There are big copper planters holding green vines and small pots with green vines on each table. There is a flo-ral design in the native carpeting and green hanging lamps over some areas.

The restaurant, for this area, tends to be pricey. Sous chef Roger Teegarden says, "We try to make it worthwhile by flying in fresh fish and making special sauces." On Tuesdays and Thursdays, Passages features Atlantic salmon. It's a spe-cialty, along with the grilled New York Sirloin and a barbecued pork tenderloin, guaranteed to melt in your mouth.

The restaurant also has a des-sert menu for those who aren't limited by low-fat diets. You can choose from the likes of chocolate truffle torte, Frangelico cheese-cake and chocolate raspberry dec-adence. ❡

Passages continues to operate at the Radisson in Fargo.

Noel's Spices Up Legion with Indian-Pakistani Fare

AUGUST 11, 1993

Tender tandoori chicken delicately flavored with fresh herbs and spices, vegetable curry and shrimp masala: These are some of the offerings on a special Indian-Pakistani menu featured by Noel's Cuisine in the American Legion Club in East Grand Forks.

The food is so authentic that it is drawing raves from people who have tasted it in the past month.

On Saturday afternoon, I found Chef Noel Singha in the kitchen, wearing a white chef cap and apron. He was getting ready for Saturday night dinners and took time off to talk over a cup of tea.

Singha and his wife, Caryn, leased the dining room from the Legion in April and added the Indian-Pakistani menu four weeks ago. It's an exciting addition to their regular menu.

A native of Pakistan, Singha says he came to Grand Forks a year ago, partly because he has a brother, Dr. Ebenezer Singha, who is associated with the UND Family Practice Center. Singha had extensive experience as a chef in his own country. After leaving Pakistan in 1961, he went to London, where he was manager of Dean's takeout store, which offers Indian fare. In 1981, he came to the United States and operated restaurants in Pittsburgh.

So, it was only natural that he would end up in the restaurant business when he came to Grand Forks. He worked for a while at Perkins before leasing the restaurant from the Legion. The facility has separate doors from the Legion Club and is open to the public.

Some evenings half of the customers in the dining room will ask for Indian food. Other nights, there will be only two or three orders. But people who have a hankering for curry and the bread called naan are finding their way to the restaurant. Some of them are from UND, and others are people of Indian and Pakistani background who live in this area. Others are people who like a switch from the usual salad bar, baked potato and steak when they go out to dinner.

Today, in fact, Noel is making 100 samosas to be served at 3 P.M. Thursday, during the afternoon coffee break at the International Centre at UND. Samosas are pastries stuffed with peas and potatoes.

He uses fresh herbs and spices in his cooking. His peloe rice is made with lamb that is cooked until tender with fresh garlic, ginger and other spices. "Then, we take the lamb out and fry it. We add basmati rice that is aged 10 to 15 years. It is the best in the world," he says.

Preparation of Indian recipes is time-consuming, and Singha has to get some of his ingredients in Winnipeg or Chicago. Both Noel and Caryn do the cooking. With his meals he serves naan bread, made with self-rising flour with some added yeast and shortening.

He says, "Some people have the idea that curry is too hot, but it shouldn't be that way. If you use it carefully, it adds flavor. If you use too much, you don't get the taste."

With that much introduction, we went to dinner Saturday night. I ordered a set meal of rice and chickpea curry, chicken tandoori, a kebab and naan for $7.95. Constant Companion ordered mincemeat curry ($5.50), served with mint sauce, sahita and a choice of peloe rice, paratha or naan.

We needed translation of some of these terms. And even though we didn't understand it all, we enjoyed every bite of the food. In fact, I felt a little sorry for the people who were going to the salad bar and eating the usual Saturday night fare.

This food is worthy of all the accolades it is getting. It is authentic, nicely flavored and filling, and the price is right for such unique food. The service is good and the waitresses are friendly. There is an open kitchen, which, to me, is always reassuring.

It would be better if the foods featured on the special menu came with a description. It would be nice too, if the restaurant had a more cozy feel. As it is, the dining tables are set at the edge of a large dance floor. But then, the glowing candles add warmth. So, too, do the red paper placemats and red napkins.

The very thought of the tandoori chicken makes me want to go back again soon—and often. ⁋

Mexican Village Buffet Is an Adventure in Cuisine

NOVEMBER 3, 1993

Out of a cold, blustery, wet Thursday evening we came into Mexican Village on South Washington Street. It was a good choice. The music was playing, and the salsa that came with the customary chips was nicely flavored.

The carpeting is a deep red and contrasts nicely with white adobe-style walls. There are wrought iron planters on the walls with artificial red flowers in them. Waitresses wear black narrow-legged trousers and black boleros with white shirts. They look professional.

Kristi, our waitress, told us she had been at Mexican Village for four years. We noticed that she was acquainted with most of the customers and was chatting with them as they came in. Mexican

Village is that kind of place. Rather small. Rather quiet. Friendly. In some ways, it is a carefully kept secret.

The Mexican food served here is much to my liking. The prices are most reasonable. There are luncheon specials for $1.95 and $2.95. Evening specials range from $3.95 to $5.95. The beverage is extra.

I like the menu because it is simple, straightforward and well-arranged. You can open it up and see at a glance what the offerings are. You don't have to fight your way through a bunch of cute sayings on five or six pages.

Here, the first page lists customary appetizers: chalupas, tostadas, tacos and enchiladas. The middle part shows dinners, burritos and specialties, including the chimichanga, the chi-chi and the Mexican pizza. There also are submarines, American and seafood choices listed for those who do not want Mexican fare.

The restaurant does some of its best business when it serves a buffet on Saturday evenings. This sampling of Mexican foods gives customers a chance to get acquainted with them and guides them in ordering at other times.

I looked over the menu and was fascinated by the Norwegian taco ($3.25) as well as the Mexican pizza, which I ordered. I asked for the small version ($3.50) and got a crisp flour tortilla, topped with melted cheese, onion, tomatoes, ripe olives and green pepper. It

was good to the last bite and just about the right amount.

Constant Companion ordered an all-meat burrito in the medium size for $3.50. You also can get a small burrito or a large burrito for a dollar less or a dollar more. He could have eaten more, but he was remembering we still had a piece of apple pie at home.

The restaurant deserves pluses for its food, reasonable prices, and good service. The paper napkins are fairly good—a couple of notches better than the skimpy kind. The restrooms are located, as the sign says, out back. But the long hallway is nicely painted with a couple of plants to improve the decor. And when you get there, the facilities are clean and adequate. ❡

Diners Shouldn't Tarry If Going Out to Applebee's

DECEMBER 29, 1993

We were glad we approached Applebee's at 5 P.M. for supper rather than waiting until 6 P.M.

By then it was buzzing, and people were waiting for tables. It's been that way ever since the new restaurant opened in Grand Forks.

We made a second sojourn to Applebee's two days later with Gail, Dale Sandstrom and Little Jack, who were here for Christmas. We went in at 11:30 A.M. to be early for lunch. And again, we were glad we were there before the rush. How long the honeymoon will last is anyone's guess.

On our first visit, we assured our waiter we didn't want any draft beer—even if it was a bargain. What Constant Companion wanted was Canadian and water, and what I wanted was a glass of dry white wine.

Because I had heard people saying how good it is, I ordered the grilled chicken Caesar salad ($5.69). CC ordered a Gyro sandwich (4.99). It's pronounced to sound like "hero," I guess. It's thin slices of meat, and onions, rolled in pita bread with shredded lettuce and tomatoes. Now, CC doesn't exactly like tomatoes, but he wasn't about to pick them out of a pita pocket. So he ate them, and by golly, he pronounced this sandwich "very good."

My salad was excellent. The seasoning was just right, and there was a nice smoky flavor to the slices of char-broiled chicken breast. Served with the salad were two small slices of just-right garlic toast.

This is my kind of place, I told CC. I enjoy going somewhere full of action, where you can order just what you want to eat. I especially like the way sandwiches are offered on the menu with fries for 99 cents extra. All too often, customers are expected to order a sandwich with fries and pay for them whether they want them or not.

On our second visit, CC had a rerun of the Gyro sandwich. I chose chili and a half sub sandwich.

Our Bismarckers went the cheeseburger, fry and salad route. Little Jack had a "girled" cheese sandwich and fries. DS enjoyed a fudge brownie sundae for dessert.

The place itself is inviting, with colorful Tiffany lamps, oak woodwork, brass rails and brick accents. The decor, in tones of cranberry and green, is sporty, with memorabilia from Red River and Central High schools. There's a section devoted to UND athletics and others supporting Minnesota Twins, Vikings and Timberwolves.

There is so much to see at Applebee's. There are railroad crossings, old cars and hubcaps and a section of old movies and movie stars as well as a musical theme in the atrium. It borders on being "busy," but Applebee's wants to have a sporty and casual concept and the feel of a neighborhood place.

Applebee's has 105 full and part-time employees. It's the third and largest Applebee's to open in North Dakota. The others are at Minot and Bismarck. A fourth Applebee's will open in 1994, in Fargo. ∫

Halstad's Kaffe Huset Epitomizes Small-Town Cafes

JULY 27, 1994

HALSTAD, Minn.—The specialty hamburger at the Kaffe Huset in this Minnesota town is called Jotunheimen. It's named after Norway's highest mountain range and described on the menu as "a juicy hamburger topped with a mountain of sautéed mushrooms and onions, melted Swiss cheese served open-faced on a slice of whole wheat bread capped with sour cream."

So I said, "Bring it on. Only hold the sour cream and skip the french fries."

The hamburger was indeed good and indeed juicy, but it came with less than a mountain of mushrooms and onions. With it, I had diet cola and a homemade cookie.

Constant Companion went light. He ordered only a Denver sandwich, which is listed on the new menu that just came out this week as $3.50. My sandwich was $4.25.

We had visited Kaffe Huset three years ago at the suggestion of a reader. It was so good we wanted to go back and see how things are going. We were glad we planned it that way the minute we entered the restaurant. The first thing you see is a case of baked goods, and that puts you in the mood for a meal. The midday special was a roast pork dinner with mashed potatoes and gravy, green beans, soup or salad and a freshly baked dinner roll for $4.25. The cafe also has homemade pie for $1.50 a slice, $1.95 a la mode.

The menu is well-designed, with dark blue print that is easy to read. The children's section is labeled "For Little Ole or Lena." The menu has a sprinkling of Norwegian sayings such as "En kaffe kopp vil friske opp," which means, "A cup of coffee will freshen you." The menu features appetizers, hamburgers, salads. They range in price from $5.45 to $10.95. White curtains on the big front window help create the homey ambiences in Kaffe Huset. Restrooms are spacious and clean.

Mike Cook, who used to be a disc jockey at KYCK in Grand Forks, has a most appropriate name for his current role as cook at the cafe. His wife, Joanne, is a waitress. She also bakes fresh pies—crust and all—and keeps track of how many she sells on the calendar. She says it's about 60 a month. The Cooks took over operation of the cafe two years ago from Joe Noel. He operates Noel's Super Valu across the street and found that handling the cafe and grocery store was too much.

As we drove away from Halstad looking for the right route to Alexandria, Minn., I remembered one of the sayings on the Kaffe Huset menu. "Det kjelper life a skynde seg nor man er pa gal vei." In other words, "It doesn't pay to hurry when you are on the wrong road." ❡

Kaffe Huset no longer operates in Halstad, Minnesota.

Al's Grill Awaits Discovery in Corner of Parrot's Cay

OCTOBER 5, 1994

The sign on the doors says Parrot's Cay, latitude 47 degrees, longitude 97 degrees. Inside, the music of Jimmy Buffett is playing on the jukebox, and a few people are visiting at the wine and beer bar in the center of tavern. Over at the right, in a little alcove, you find Al's Grill. It's been operating for a couple of months, and people seem pleased with themselves for discovering it.

It took me a while to get into the swing of things. I had to learn, in the first place, that a cay is a little island. So this place with parrots all around is supposed to be a little island in the south side of Grand Forks. It's on 36th Avenue South, near Water World. And I suppose I should have guessed that Grand Forks is at a latitude of 47 degrees and longitude 97.

Al's Grill has a short, uncomplicated menu of sandwiches and appetizers. And for lunch, there are salads. Al is Al Decker, who, after 16 years with the telephone company, has teamed up with owner Mark Johnson to provide the food service in the Parrot's Cay.

Al's Grill seems to be taking off. It's another in the lineup of small places with a coffeehouse- or pub-like ambience that are gaining popularity around Grand Forks.

We made two visits to Al's Grill during the past week. The first time in, late one afternoon, I tried the shrimp basket. It includes three hand-breaded jumbo shrimp with onion rings for $4.95. People who say Al has the best onion rings in town might just be right. The onions are covered with a light breading, made to order, and come close to those served at the old A&W. The shrimp, also with light breading, were super. They were enhanced by a sharp cocktail sauce with a tantalizing taste of horseradish. So tantalizing that I want to go back for another round of shrimp.

Constant Companion ordered the Key West, a sandwich in a nice, big bun made with slices of ribeye with green peppers and onions, all covered with Swiss cheese ($2.95). CC nodded his approval of the Key West after his first bite. So that's what we both ordered when we made a return visit to Al's Grill Friday at noon. We split an order of onion rings, and I ordered stuffed jalapeños (you get six for $3.25) from the list of appetizers. Let me tell you, these babies, stuffed with cream cheese and plenty of spice, are hot. Hot, hot, hot. I ate three of them and decided I better lay off. But if I get a cold this winter, I know I will swing by Al's Grill and order some of these jalapeños to clear out my sinuses.

Al's Grill isn't exactly the type of place you'd take your mother-in-law. But then again, you might.

This place appeals to a variety of people. Many of them have one thing in common: They like Jimmy Buffett. In fact, the Grand Forks Jimmy Buffett Fan Club meets at the Parrot's Cay at 7:30 P.M. every Thursday. Last week, 42 of them flew to Denver for the Jimmy Buffett concert. Mark Johnson says the idea of the Cay is to have fun. As long as patrons aren't out of line, he figures they can enjoy themselves at his place. The music has a happy Jamaican beat. Johnson says country western is too depressing.

Decker spends most of his time back in the nice bright kitchen of the Grill. He makes his own hamburger patties and roasts the beef for sandwiches. It's reassuring that he quickly invites you out to see his kitchen. It's that clean.

Al's Grill is the heart of a tavern where people who work hard come in to play hard and enjoy life. It's an upbeat place. ❡

Sanders 1907 Never Lets Its Customers Down

OCTOBER 19, 1994

Gordon and Sandi Schnell of Dickinson, N.D., walked by our table at Sanders 1907 Friday evening with happy—almost smug—smiles on their faces. They had eaten at Sanders, and they were more than pleased with themselves for thinking far enough ahead to make a reservation three months ago.

They knew the past weekend, which was homecoming at UND, would be booked at Sanders. Gordon had eaten the Swiss Eiger beef, Sanders's version of prime rib, and Sandi had enjoyed walleye meunière, with the fish crisply sautéed.

We, too, were complimenting ourselves for having made reservations in August for Sanders. With us were our favorite judges—our son-in-law, Dale Sandstrom, and daughter, Gail Hagerty, from Bismarck.

Constant Companion knit his eyebrows as he studied the description of split beef ribs. He was happy when our waiter announced that the ribs, instead, were pork that night. CC said, "Good, I never order beef ribs."

Ocean scallops were one of the specials, and DS decided to ask for them. For him, it was a tough choice because he has on previous visits enjoyed the Eiger beef. I followed suit with scallops. GH went the Maryland crab cakes route because, as she said, you don't often find them on menus.

After making the tough decisions, we sat back and enjoyed the ambience. There's an intimacy and feeling of friendly camaraderie about the place. The good feeling comes from the anticipation of good food, talk and laughter.

A basket of coarse, crusty bread that is a trademark of Sanders arrived before the salads. We all dug in and commented about the cranberry-pecan bread. It's one of the new creations of Kim Holmes, who is going on 10 years at the helm of the small cafe on Kittson Avenue in downtown Grand Forks.

Then came the salad. I had ordered the Greek version, which I enjoyed to the last piece of crumbled feta cheese. It was a fine salad, with Greek olives, a cucumber spear and a slice of a big, fresh-tasting tomato on greens. DS also had the Greek salad; CC and GH chose the Italian salad.

When our entrees arrived, I was reminded once again that presentation is everything. Our scallops were served on a bed of wild rice with asparagus spears arranged wagon wheel fashion, and a side garnish of lemon and lime wedges. The scallops were just right. Too much heat, and you get rubber. Too little heat, and you get squish-squish. These were done to perfection, and there were at least a dozen of them. They were served with Sanders prairie sauce, described by our waiter as "a little sweet with a lot of heat."

CC was well-pleased with his ribs and rosemary potatoes, although he wasn't able to finish the whole serving. We helped him out by sampling. GH was reinforced in her opinion that Sanders crab cakes with remoulade sauce are the ultimate.

It was enough already. But then came the dessert suggestions. We decided to order just one dessert—the pecan torte—so that we could all take a taste. That was working quite well until I found the dessert so compelling I finished it off while the others were chatting. ❡

Arby's Adds Another Dimension to Fast-Food Scene

FEBRUARY 18, 1995

"This is good roast beef," said Constant Companion as we ate sandwiches for the first time at the new Arby's on South Columbia Road.

I especially liked the bun that

came with my turkey sandwich. The turkey was moist and tasty. We often have visited Arby's on our travels and wished there was one in Grand Forks. Now, it's here, with a convenient parking lot and a light, bright interior. It's decorated in soft shades of blue, green and gray. And there are banners that say, "Go West. It's Better Out Here."

When you call the restaurant, you get the answer, "It's a great day at Arby's."

The western theme, the roast beef, the good cheer. That's Arby's.

I noticed a no-smoking sign on the door as we entered. We stepped up to the counter and concentrated on the reader boards long enough to decide CC wanted a Philly Beef and Swiss sandwich ($2.89), and I wanted a Light Roast Turkey Deluxe ($2.18). I felt self-righteous eating it because it was only 300 calories.

We skipped the sauces at the condiment counter even though there is a sign that says, "Go ahead and add a little kick." You can have Arby's sauce, honey sauce and ketchup. We're not much for sauces on our meat.

Each month, Arby's has a special. We noticed quite a few customers eating the Beef 'n Cheddar sandwiches that are four for $5 through February. Arby's also has four kinds of chicken sandwiches, ham, subs and French dip.

Manager Sharon Becker, who came here from the Bismarck Arby's in Kirkwood Mall, says half of the business here is done inside, and the other half is drive-through. Becker was assistant manager in Bismarck, where she had worked 10 years. Long enough to know that it's fun to work on the sandwich assembly line and not so great on the fry line.

"But then," she says, "someone has to do it."

She says the opening in Grand Forks in December was huge. "People were standing in line outside waiting to get in."

The local Arby's is the sixth in North Dakota. ❡

Noel's Brings the Sweet Smell of Curry to Downtown

JULY 26, 1995

Small cafes such as Noel's Cuisine on Demers make the dining scene in Grand Forks an adventure. We had eaten Noel Singha's Pakistani food a couple of years ago, when he and his wife, Caryn, leased the dining room of the American Legion Club in East Grand Forks. We enjoyed the curry dishes so much at the time that we went back a couple more times. We like to savor the curry and eat the warm bread, called naan.

Noel's has moved to the location that for years was Web's Cafe. We went there Thursday with our houseguest, Fran Froeschle, who used to write food columns for the Detroit Lakes (Minn.) paper when she was managing editor there.

My first surprise—a pleasant one, indeed—was to find the interior changed. Instead of the two horseshoe counters, there are only booths, about 10 of them.

And there is fresh blue paint with homey valances of rose and blue tones on the windows. A cheery decor.

Noel's has a sort of ma-and-pa arrangement. Noel is the chef, but both he and Caryn cook. She was serving the food. The menu lists breakfast and lunch items to suit American tastes. We studied the shorter menu of Pakistani food.

With more than a passing interest in food, Friend Fran (FF) studied the list of appetizers, which includes samosas (pastry stuffed with potatoes, peas and spices for $2.50), and seikh kebab (ground meat and spices for $2.25). Fran ordered aloo tikka (potato cutlet seasoned with spices for $1.75). We all took a taste and found this appetizer to be delightful patties made of potato, onion, green chili and other spices.

Then came the entrees. FF ordered a half tandoori chicken

($6.25), which is marinated in yogurt, lemon juice and spices, roasted and served on top of rice. CC ordered chicken curry ($6.25). After discussing the degree of spiciness with Caryn, he decided to ask for the mild, rather than hot curry. And mild was hot enough.

My choice was lamb biryani. This is a dish made of spring lamb marinated in spices, green chili, coriander, mint, yogurt, fresh-squeezed lemon and served with basmati rice and ghee (clarified butter) with saffron for $8.95.

We all tasted and savored the three dishes and were pleased with the quality of meat and how thoroughly it was cooked and how well it tasted with the flavored rice. "It's interesting," FF said, "how they cut up chicken differently, so you don't know what part it is."

My lamb was tender and tasty. We all agreed it was the dish we would order on another visit to Noel's Cuisine. My serving was so ample that I took half of it home.

I noticed regulars eating vegetarian curry dishes. Noel's serves curries with chickpeas, spinach, potatoes and lentils. The menu also lists Bombay potatoes and okra curry, spiced tea and an Indian dessert. There is a complete list on a reader board of Pakistani foods served for lunch, which are cheaper than dinner prices. This is a good place to stop for a change of pace at noon—a break from the soup and sandwich routine.

Caryn says in their first year, business has been OK. "We have a good following of people who like curry, but we have a problem with some thinking this is only Pakistani food." ❡

Marilyn says, "Noel's restaurant went with the flood of 1997. . . . The owners went back to Pittsburgh, I am told, and he died there. It was a fun little restaurant with a very loyal following."

"Ruth and Cherie Show" Goes On Daily at Dacotah

AUGUST 2, 1995

"Ham dinner and a tuna sandwich with soup," Ruth hollers at the kitchen door.

"More coffee?" Cherie asks a customer, as she pours from a thermal pot.

Ruth stops to play with a baby in a high chair at a long table near the back of the restaurant. Cherie moves over to the cash register as three downtown lawyers get ready to leave. This is the "Ruth and Cherie Show." It goes on every weekday morning at the downtown Dacotah Restaurant. The two waitresses work side by side. Only a few of the customers realize they are mother and daughter.

Ruth Schnebel has been a waitress in Grand Forks for almost 40 years—ever since she started working for Mrs. Oliver, at the Golden Hour, in 1958. From there, she went to the Palace Cafe, the Elks Club and on to Miller's Super Fair on South Washington, where she proudly served up the popular pancakes and homemade syrup.

After a brief interlude at Gordy's on Gateway Drive, Ruth landed at the Dacotah eight years ago.

Here, she is almost an institution. She knows the customers and what they will order. She works well with her daughter, Cherie Kennedy, who started in the restaurant business when she was 14. She washed dishes first at the Palace, and then moved on to be a waitress.

Ruth starts the day at 7 A.M. and finishes at 1:30 P.M. Cherie comes in at 8:30 A.M. and finishes at 2 P.M., in time to rest up for her evening job in maintenance at UND.

Ruth and Cherie are so established and so comfortable in their routine at the Dacotah that work doesn't seem hard to them. Ruth usually presides at the rear of the coffee shop, and Cherie's post is up front. They know their tables and their customers.

"Sometimes, I go back and punch down the toast when I

see certain customers come in," Ruth says. "We know what they will order."

"Most of the time, we just ask if they want the usual," Cherie says. "They say 'the usual,' and it makes it easy."

The regulars who come to the Dacotah have their regular tables. There's a round one toward the front, where you might see John Shaft, Ed Fuehrer or Larry McEnroe. Larry Rux holds down another setting toward the back of the restaurant. Then there's a big round table at the rear, where you find a cross section of Grand Forks men. You might see Dennis Page, Barry Behlhoff, Walt Mikkelson, Tom Jelliff or Jerry Haley. It varies from day to day.

Occasionally, there will a be a woman or two at the round table at the front. The tables at the rear of the restaurant seem to be a male bastion. Always, there is the bantering back and forth with Ruth and Cherie.

"I have to give my customers a bad time," Ruth says. "The customers tell me it's just like home."

Their customers at the Dacotah include downtown residents and people who live in the Dacotah Place apartments. "You miss them if they move away or die," Ruth says.

Cherie is still bummed out over the death of Mabel Jack, who lived downtown and came in for coffee and something chocolate. "If we didn't have chocolate, she would ask for a bowl of soup," Cherie says.

Breakfast items at the Dacotah include a full run of eggs, hash browns, toast, cereal and better-than-average pancakes. Customers help themselves from a pastry bar that features homemade rolls for 95 cents and a wide array of doughnuts, cookies and pie.

Ruth's people order a lot of chef salads ($3.95). Cherie's customers are partial to soup and sandwiches. Each day, the list of noon specials is written on a board. They include items such as a cup of soup and codfish dinner for $4.25. Soup could be old-fashioned tomato or turkey dumpling.

There's usually a footlong hot dog for $1.60. You can get a mini chef salad for $2.95 and a regular chef salad for $3.95. A cup of soup with a tuna salad sandwich and fries is featured at $3.50. You can get a three-piece chicken dinner for $4.25 some days.

Cherie says she and her mother have grown close working together, although she says, "About every seven weeks, we have a little tiff." Working with her mother has given her a chance to see Ruth in a different light than at home.

"She's pretty cool," Cherie says. "I never realized how much fun my mother could be." ❡

The Dacotah succumbed to the Red River flood of 1997. The space has been the home of a number of post-flood businesses, and is currently Shing Ya, a Japanese restaurant.

It's No Bologna—Minto's 10th Annual Sausage-Making Extravaganza That Is Held Each January Is Not Your Average Cooking Contest

JANUARY 24, 1996

MINTO, N.D.—He thought he was going home empty-handed—again. Instead, Merlin Feltman of Grafton, N.D., carried away the first-place trophy from the 10th annual bologna contest here in the Harvey Street Saloon.

This is not your average cooking contest. It is a happening. It draws sausage-makers from two or three counties each January. Last Friday night, there were 66 sausages, or bologna, entered. As teams of judges sampled and savored sausage, parents of Boy and Girl Scouts of Minto were making hay. They served a meal including sausage stew and accepted donations of $1,137 for the Minto Scout programs.

Pickup trucks and vans lined Main Street of this Walsh County community and by 7 P.M., it was getting to be standing room only in the saloon.

Chris Misialek, the barkeeper, presides over the contest with the help of loyal friends. It was 34 degrees below zero outside, but they had to keep opening the doors because it was too warm inside. Around 11 P.M., after a cracker-eating and whistling contest, winners of the bologna competition were announced.

Feltman, a bachelor farmer, was surprised to win after several unsuccessful attempts. Like many competitors, his recipe is a family secret. He will say he uses a 60 percent to 40 percent mix of venison and pork. He flavors his bologna with "garlic and all kinds of stuff." He uses a smokehouse he built on his farm, and his winning ring of sausage was made in a batch of 35 pounds.

Like others, Feltman says he makes sausage to carry on a family tradition. He has a background of Polish and Norwegian grandparents and parents who used to make sausage. After they quit, Feltman took it up.

Joan Slominski, who won last year's contest, made sausage 20 years ago before taking a 10-year break. She restarted when her daughter, Sandy Schrank of Grafton, decided she wants her kids to know how to make sausage.

Slominski says, "We use venison mostly. We have used beef and pork. We like to use the venison. We all hunt long enough to get our sausage meat. We freeze it and use it all year round. We serve it with potatoes, beans or hotdish. I take it out to the workers in the fields. They all like it. If you think you don't have enough food, just throw in a ring of bologna and you're sure you have enough meat."

Suzi Votava Tibert says when you help make bologna, you learn how to do it. And the more people helping, the faster it goes. Tibert is a two-time winner of the classic at Minto. She always hopes for fairly warm weather on sausage-making day. With the right temperature in the smokehouse, she says you get a good, smoky taste and look.

As for the annual contest, Slominski says, "I wouldn't miss this thing. There are people here you might not see the rest of the year." ❡

Red Lobster Reels 'Em In with Seafood, Biscuits

FEBRUARY 28, 1996

The parking lot at the Red Lobster was jammed at noon on Ash Wednesday. And employees look for brisk business on Fridays during Lent. It happens every year.

The restaurant is one of more than 700 Red Lobsters in the United States and Canada, and it has been in operation here for four years. It has a strong following of people who hanker for seafood, and others who say they just go there for the garlic cheese biscuits.

I always welcome a chance for lunch at the Lobster, and I often order the grilled chicken salad ($5.35). That was my choice when four of us met for lunch last Wednesday. Corinne Alphson ordered the same. Donna Gillig settled for New England Clam Chowder ($2.50 a cup and $3.75 a bowl). Irene Fossum chose a seafood Caesar salad with lobster, shrimp and scallops ($5.99).

We meet at the Lobster occasionally during February and March, when the rest of our bridge club is keeping warm in Arizona or Florida. We find it a comfortable place to have lunch, visit and play cards. Staff members at the Red Lobster are cordial and accommodating. They bring us more ice water. They watch over our shoulders as we play.

The chowder is good. And DG says it's plenty. The seafood salad rates at least a B-plus, if not an A. Lunches at the Red Lobster are in the $5.99 to $6.99 range. That is, if you drink water. Coffee or tea is $1.20. Milk is $1.15.

You get the biscuits with the crisp, garlic and cheesy crust with your meal. And if one isn't enough, you can have more. The grilled chicken salad is an ample serving, nicely spiced. It's as much or more than you can eat. I often wonder what the dinner salad is like. If I ever get out at night, I will report on that.

Meanwhile, I have heard glowing testimony about dinners at the Red Lobster. The restaurant introduced a new menu last week, with many of the old favorites and new features. Meal prices range from $9.99 to $18.99. Of course, if you want live Maine lobster dinner, it's more. The price fluctuates, and most recently has been $24.35 for a 1-pound serving. Dinners include the garlic bread, salad and your choice of a potato or vegetable.

I like the Red Lobster menu because it has a symbol for Lighthouse selections that are low-fat. However, I have a hard time finding things on the menu. Maybe it has too many pages. Maybe it's the flaps. Maybe it's the slippery covering. Maybe it's me.

The place has a Cape Cod feel, with banks of big windows framed in rich, dark wood. Tables and captain's chairs are also in wood. Walls are cream-colored and covered with items of interest, including blackboards listing the catch of the day. Restrooms are clean, convenient and roomy. ❡

Red Lobster continues to operate in Grand Forks.

Bit of Norway Fits the Bill for Syttende Mai Meal

MAY 15, 1996

Uff da!

I know it doesn't fit in with light eating, but I ordered meatballs and potato dumplings when I revisited Bit of Norway for lunch in the City Center Mall on Friday.

The visit seemed timely, since Syttende Mai is coming up Friday, and the Norwegians among us will be strutting their stuff. Their stuff is rommegrot, or cream pudding, and riskrem, a rice pudding. It's klotboller meatballs, lapskaus stew and sotsuppe, or fruit soup. Baked goods are rosettes, krumkake, lefse and fattigman.

Bit of Norway lists all of them beside a map of Norway on a big sign at the counter. And Bit of Norway has a wooden-carved gnome, named Ole, perched on the counter with a "velkommen."

The mall seemed fairly quiet around noon Friday, but there was a steady stream of people coming in to order lunch. Specials for the day were turkey hotdish and a hard roll for $2 or a grilled ham and cheese sandwich for $2.50. Usually, there is a soup of the day, too.

The menu lists sandwiches, dinner dishes, salads and soups, desserts, beverages and cookies and pastries. One of the sandwiches is called Roger's special, and is made of hot meatballs with potatoes, gravy, pasta salad and raw veggies. There are homemade doughnuts and cookies available to eat in or take out.

I took my meatballs and gravy and dumplings to a quiet table, where I could read and eat. The gravy was a pleasing, natural gravy that tasted for all the world like that my Danish relatives used to make. The dumplings were filling, and I ate the whole dish of them.

When you order food at the counter of Bit of Norway, you deal with Elizabeth Anderson, the owner-manager, or her assistant, Olga Chikmaverova, who came here as an immigrant from Armenia. Anderson says, "We are turning her into a Norwegian. She is now helping me with the baking, and she does the doughnuts."

Bit of Norway is not one of those quick-serve places. Instead, the service is deliberate, but sure. Even though the foods are served in plastic, the shopkeepers take time to garnish each hot dish with a carrot stick, broccoli floweret or stick of celery—or all three.

Anderson shrugs off any compliments to her cooking by saying, "It's just farm food. It's what I ate when I was growing up." She wishes she could find more help. Her dream would be to have a manager for the kitchen so she could be free to run a little shop in conjunction with Bit of Norway.

Although she is hampered by

arthritis, Anderson is down at Bit of Norway bright and early in the morning. She is ready to serve breakfast if the bus drivers who start out from the mall want it.

She and Olga turn out an array of homemade cookies, bread, doughnuts and caramel rolls in the morning.

Throughout the day, they offer a senior citizen special of cookies and ice cream with coffee for $1.10. Some people come in for a bowl of riskrem—rice cooked in milk and served cold with a bit of whipped cream and a topping of raspberry jam. This is next door to soul food for people who are Scandinavian.

Along with those who come to the mall for a Norwegian fix, there are many more who place special orders for food. On Friday, rommegrot for 70 was going out to United Lutheran Church.

Anderson has been running the business four years. She likes the mall and the people there.

"If I didn't like it so well, I would have quit long ago." ❡

Bit of Norway, along with many other Grand Forks and East Grand Forks businesses, succumbed to the Red River of the North flood in April and May of 1997. Says Marilyn of that time:

There was a period of time when I did not write because of the Flood of 1997. We had to evacuate and went down to Bismarck, where my daughter lives. My husband, retired editor of the *Herald*, died down there after a time in a nursing home.

The *Herald* called and wanted me to write, so I started in. The *Herald* was being published in a school in a small town north of here. There were writers from all over the country in here during the big flood. Still, the *Herald* wanted writing from someone who lives here.

The *Herald*, by the way, won a Pulitzer Prize for flood coverage. I can claim nothing to do with the Pulitzer Prize.

Blarney Mill Would Make Any Irishman Smile

MAY 13, 1998

The opening of the Blarney Mill in East Grand Forks is a cause for celebration on both sides of the Red River. The new Irish pub and grill on DeMers Avenue is receiving a royal welcome in the post-flood recovery era of Greater Grand Forks. The ambience is cheery and lively. The place has been jammed. And the future looks bright.

Usually, I wait for a new restaurant to settle into a groove before I go reviewing, but the idea of an Irish pub right here in the Forks is so appealing I couldn't wait. I went there Saturday night and was joined by Liz Fedor (LF), Scott Hennen (SH), the Rev. William Sherman (FWS) and George and Betty Widman (GW) and (BW).

Since I arrived first, I had a chance to survey the surroundings. There's a fireside room with original brick walls, decorative tin ceiling and a beautiful solid walnut bar handcrafted by Mike

Nigl, a tanker pilot at Grand Forks Air Force Base.

You walk into a setting with lots of greenery and archways made of brick that came off the old Carnegie Library in Grand Forks. It had been on the home of Joan and Jerry Sayler. They operated the Olson Drug Store for years, before the flood, on the corner of DeMers and Third Street, where the Blarney Mill now has taken up residence.

Early in the evening, the interest seems to be on dining. As the night progresses, there's more attention to the bar area, with singing from time to time and sports on television. Saturday evening, a wedding party dropped by for an Irish toast.

It is a happy place. Right now, the Blarney Mill is using a temporary menu with a more permanent menu of Irish entrees, appetizers, soups, salads and sandwiches in the making. Our waitress Saturday evening was Sarah, and she is perfect in an Irish pub. She's friendly, but not too friendly. She's quick on the uptake and equal to all of the bright remarks she hears.

As we gathered, we tried the crab and artichoke dip, made with Parmesan cheese and mayo, and served with fingers of freshly baked bread. This is rich and enticing. And after such a hearty appetizer, I decided to go with a blue cheese shrimp salad ($6.99) for an entree. FWS did likewise. SH ordered the spicy chicken marinara, a dish with fettuccine, sautéed chicken and squash in a spicy marinara sauce (8.99). SH pronounced it good, very good, except that it could have been hotter. LF shied away from the chicken marinara because it was billed as very spicy. She came up with an uninspired order of a Blarney Burger ($5.99). It distinguished itself, however, with caramelized onions and cheddar cheese served on a sourdough bun. And the fries that came with it were nicely done, with skin on.

The Widmans were a little behind us. GW ordered the tur-key club sandwich on rye bread ($5.95). BW was pleased with her choice of a roasted vegetable salad ($5.50) made with mixed greens, red onion and feta cheese. It was tossed with raspberry vinaigrette and topped with roasted red and green peppers.

The feta cheese in the vegetable salad and the blue cheese in the shrimp salad are of good quality and in enough quantity to assert themselves. Usually, I don't care for little shrimp, but the generous serving in the salad I ate were fresh-tasting.

We visited with Manager Jim Schable, who says prices will be competitive at The Blarney Mill. With people waiting up to 30 minutes for a table Saturday, he told us of plans to expand into the building formerly occupied by Frenchy's Jewelry. Irish entrees will include Irish Shepherd's pie, Irish stew, fish and chips, peppercorn salmon, grilled salmon and sausage stuffed pork loin.

While he was at it, he introduced us to Erika Olson, the chef at the Blarney Mill. She has attended cooking schools and has worked in the kitchen of Kincaid's in Minneapolis and the Bistro in Bismarck. She was dressed in white with a blue baseball cap and had a big Norwegian smile.

Where, but in East Grand Forks, I wondered, would you meet a friendly Scandinavian cooking Irish food? ❡

Marilyn says, "The Blarney Mill is also part of the passing scene of restaurants that have closed."

Cozy Millennium Cafe Pays Extra Attention to Presentation

OCTOBER 14, 1998

The specials included halibut filet grilled in a special teriyaki Prairie Sauce and an appetizer of melon wrapped in prosciutto when we dined at Sanders 1997 Millennium Cafe Saturday evening.

I was with daughter Gail Hagerty (GH) and her husband, Dale Sandstrom (DS), and I had made the reservation weeks ago. When they come up from Bismarck, they always enjoy a dinner at this fine, small cafe, relocated since the flood on South Washington Street.

There's something special about Sanders—it's small enough to have a cozy ambience. White tablecloths are covered with glass, and there are crisp, white napkins in the water goblets at each place setting. Our table for three was very near the entry but had very comfortable chairs.

At length, GH chose walleye meunière ($18), which was crisp and not dipped in batter. It had a pleasing touch of lemon sauce. DS asked for pork tenderloin ($16.50), which is served with chipotle sauce that he wisely requested on the side. He enjoyed the tender slices of pork with a touch of the spicy sauce. He said it reminded him of a dish he had at Arthur Bryant's in Kansas City. They had mashed potatoes with a hint of garlic.

My choice was filet mignon ($22). I asked for it medium and topped with Gorgonzola sauce, and I enjoyed every bite of it. I had a baked potato, just the right size. Portions at Sanders are large enough. But Sanders does not go for the oversized portions you sometimes see. Entrees are presented skillfully. Saturday night, there were small asparagus spears fanned out on the potatoes. There were elegant radish roses on the plates and parsley that was thick and crisp.

The meal began with a French bread that had a delightfully crisp crust. Then came the Italian salads—excellent because of the quality of the sliced tomatoes.

It was a tough decision, but DS chose pumpkin cheesecake for dessert and allowed us a taste. Other dessert choices included pecan caramel torte, a caramel custard and chocolate decadence.

Our waiter was watchful, but unobtrusive. He was there when we needed something. And he was there with the check, which I made a feeble effort to take but was outreached.

We had high expectations for our dinner at Sanders, and we were not disappointed. There is no place I would rather have dinner in North Dakota than Sanders. It's a unique restaurant, run by Kim Holmes, who also operates Lola's in downtown Grand Forks. He has been in the restaurant business in Grand Forks since 1985 and is well-known. That's partly because he is willing to pitch in and help with community events.

He lost two restaurants downtown to the flood but kept plugging away until he could reopen Sanders—which he did seven weeks later—on a Friday the 13th. He said he wasn't superstitious. He figured nothing else could go wrong.

And Sanders 1997 has gone right for Holmes. Though business was slow last winter, it picked up and has been going great guns since spring. Sanders 1997 has 20 more seats than Sanders 1907 had downtown. It can handle 60 diners in booths and at tables. The restaurant has an enlarged wine cellar and serves fine wines at correct temperatures.

The most popular entree is Sanders prime rib, called Swiss Eiger beef ($17 and $19). Second in popularity is grilled salmon. The roast caraway duck is another favorite, and some customers insist on grilled lamb served with Sanders apple-apricot chutney. ¶

Red River Cafe Rightly Claims Spot in New Downtown

JANUARY 6, 1999

We went to the Red River Cafe for dinner Saturday night because they would take a reservation. It was wickedly cold and windy, but inside it was cozy, and the menu was outstanding. Saturday night specials included an appetizer of Oysters Rockefeller. The choice of entrees included Roasted Pheasant ($15.99), Salmon Topped with a Riesling Wild Berry Sauce ($15.99), Prime Rib with Lobster ($25) and Hazelnut Crusted Lamb Rack ($18.99).

In addition to Saturday night specials, the regular menu listed a page of starters, a full range of homemade pizza, salads, sandwiches and regular dinner entrees ranging in price from $10.99 to $14.99.

Once we were settled, it was decision time for me and my companion, Fannie Gershman (FG). We both ended up ordering Curried Penne with Shrimp ($12.99). We had a choice of soup or salad and chose salad, which was pretty good. I would put it at 8 on a scale of 10. It had a variety of ingredients, including alfalfa sprouts and round croutons. I counted at least six shrimp in my entree, and FG and I agreed they were done just right. The pasta was tasty, with an extra spicy curry sauce and an interesting texture created by chopped fresh red pepper and onion, Greek olives and scallions.

The pasta was enough to serve a family of three or four, and we left much of it on the plate. That was partly because of the appeal of the good, warm sourdough bread and butter served with the entree.

Then, of course, there was no room for dessert such as Cafe Cheesecake, Chocolate Beyond Reason or Magnificent Seven. The Red River Cafe offers some fascinating desserts, and it makes me think of going there some afternoon for coffee and sweets.

I would give the Red River Cafe high marks for providing a cozy setting, although another time on a cold winter night, I would make sure to find a table away from the door. While our service was good overall, we did have to ask for water and ended up saving our fork from the salad course for the entree.

However, it was an upscale dining experience because of the creative menu and the setting. This included background music—not too loud—of blues and jazz. Our waitress was Anna Bergland, a UND student who was both pleasant and efficient. She was knowledgeable about the menu. She was around when we needed her, but she left us alone to visit without interrupting our conversation to ask if everything was OK.

Julie Conneran opened the restaurant with her brother, Brian Conneran, after the flood. The decor of the Red River Cafe includes used brick wainscoting up to the 54-foot 11-inch level, showing how high the floodwaters rose. There also is a wall of photographs showing how it looked when downtown Grand Forks was submerged in muddy water and ravaged by fire.

Julie says dinner business has become most important since the streets were reopened downtown. When the area was closed off for construction, there were some lean and worrisome times inside the cafe. Time will pass, and our city will heal, it says on the menu, but the strength and courage of its residents will never be forgotten. ❡

Red River Cafe has closed.

Specials Pull In Customers at the 42nd Street Eatery

JULY 7, 1999

Normally, I would think of going to 42nd Street Eatery for the Exploded Pig sandwich. The establishment has a reputation for smoked pork so tender it virtually explodes on a grilled French roll. And it's served with a side of barbecue sauce for $4.99. On Mondays, you can get two of these sandwiches for the price of one. What a deal!

But I went to the restaurant Thursday to try the new Italian meal I had been hearing about. I asked Jan Zahrly (JZ), whom I also call Ms. Manage, to join me. We took a serious look at the offerings on the red Italian menu and noticed they include four appetizers. There is bella Napoli, or Italian nacho chips. There is calamari fritti, otherwise known as breaded squid, deep-fried with spicy marinara sauce. There is breaded ravioli as well as chicken strip Parmigiana.

We asked for none of the above, sensing that we would be more

than sated after eating our entrees. JZ chose tortellini alla prosciutto (Italian ham) ($8.99). This was a cheese tortellini tossed with prosciutto, peas and mushrooms in an asiago cream sauce. I ordered farfalle Milano—butterfly pasta with grilled chicken, sun-dried tomato and mushrooms in a pesto cream sauce ($8.99).

The entrees—a total of 14—are served with an Italian bread that's good and heavy. With the bread, there's a plate of extra-heavy virgin olive oil, and another of olive oil mixed with balsamic vinegar that we found more appealing and lighter eating. The bread was interesting and well-seasoned.

Entrees were enormous, and were presented nicely with a sprinkling of dried parsley flakes. I would have liked at least a small salad or, perhaps, a slice of melon or other fruit with so much pasta. The sauce was appealing, but after eating about halfway through our entrees, we were ready to ask for boxes to take the rest home.

There are three desserts on the menu including spumoni ($1.99), Italian ice cream that, to me, is the perfect ending to an Italian meal—if you save room.

42nd Street Eatery also offers regular specials that seem to draw in diners. Besides the Exploded Pig special on Mondays, there is a $6.99 all-you-can-eat riblet special Tuesdays. On Thursday evenings, customers buy one deep-dish burrito ($6.49 to $7.49) and get a second one for a buck.

With its proximity to UND and its reasonable prices, the restaurant draws students. Clarence and Maxine Thompson, who were sitting at a nearby table eating burritos, said you ought to see the place Sunday evenings, when UND is in session and students swarm 42nd Street Eatery for all-you-can-eat pizza for $5.99. Now on summer evenings, you find young people playing volleyball and using the seating on the deck outside.

Our waitress, Shari Thompson, is a UND student. She seems to have a good time on the job, and her cheery approach adds to the dining experience. ❡

*42nd Street Eatery changed locations and names to become
32nd Street Eatery. It is no longer in operation.*

Lutefisk, Lefse Greet Holiday Diners at the 2-29 Cafe

DECEMBER 8, 1999

The afternoon sun streams into 2-29 Cafe on Gateway Drive and casts a pleasant feeling over the newly refurbished truck stop restaurant. The place is redone in subdued tones of sage green with wainscoting of wood with a reddish cast. There's piped-in music playing, and even in the middle of the afternoon, several tables are occupied. Usually, there are people at the counter.

Because it's open around the clock for truckers and travelers—as well as the local following—2-29 is rarely quiet. It's a good stop in December, when most of us are running around like chickens with their heads cut off. I was there around 3 o'clock one afternoon last week. I was in the middle of a list of errands and not sure whether I was eating a late lunch or an early supper. So, I ordered the Wednesday special: an open-faced sloppy joe for $4.75 with soup or a salad. I also had a glass of milk.

The soup at 2-29 is worth the drive out to the edge of town, where U.S. Highway 2 and Interstate 29 intersect. It was tomato-macaroni the day I was there. The soup with plenty of ground meat was rich and hearty—and the serving was sufficient. It was almost a meal in itself, and they don't scrimp on crackers. They

gave me eight. I really didn't need the cucumber salad I ordered to go with this repast. It had more sour cream dressing than I wanted, although it was nice-tasting, with the addition of dill weed. The cucumbers weren't too crisp. But the parsley that came as garnish on my sloppy joe was good enough to eat.

The 2-29 Cafe on Gateway Drive offers the same menu as its cousin, the I-29 Cafe in the travel center at the intersection of I-29 with South 32nd Street near Columbia Mall. The restaurants are leased by Dean and Vicki Soltis, who got I-29 going again after the flood and gave up temporarily on 2-29, formerly known as the Big Sioux Cafe. However, they have been back in business since April.

"Right now, 2-29 is featuring lutefisk and lefse for the holidays. We get calls from people every year asking about it," Vicki Soltis says. The lutefisk is served with drawn butter, mashed potatoes and choice of lettuce, coleslaw or cucumber salad. The price is $7.95.

On a second visit to 2-29 last week, I took a second look at the surroundings and the menu. The restaurant has two small U-shaped counter areas, but they are a little smoky. Tables closest to the door are set aside for non-smoking. The booths in the cafe have wall phones. Servers in white shirts with black ties look more professional than most servers in overnight cafes.

The menu features 19 different breakfast combinations ranging in price from $2.35 for two eggs and toast or a pancake and egg to $6.85 for a 10-ounce ham steak with two eggs, choice of potatoes and toast. Coffee is extra (75 cents).

There is a full selection of sandwiches and salads at 2–29. Dinners include steaks, walleye, chicken and chops. The truckers 16-ounce T-Bone, topped with onion rings and served with potatoes, salad and bread, is $9.95. One section of the menu offers smaller meals at $2.50 for children and seniors. ⁊

2-29 is now called the Roadhouse Cafe, located with Simonson Station near the intersection of I-29 and 32nd Avenue S. in Grand Forks. The I-29 Cafe is now called the Big Sioux Cafe, located at the intersection of I-29 and 32nd Avenue S.

The Blue Moose Bar and Grill— Little to Criticize, Lots to Love at EGF Restaurant

MARCH 24, 2000

Usually I pay as much attention to the price column as I do to items listed on a menu. But one night in March, I settled into a roomy booth at the Blue Moose in East Grand Forks and decided I would have the most expensive entree on the menu. After all, I had a $25 gift certificate as thanks from people who went on our last Sioux Booster basketball bus. So did Rose Skyberg (RS), who coordinates the bus trips with me, and we were winding up another good winter of basketball.

I ordered five jumbo prawns prepared scampi style ($17.99), and it turned out to be the best dinner I have had in a restaurant all winter. The prawns were huge and broiled with crunchy Japanese bread crumbs as a coating—a unique and most tasty approach. Halfway through the meal, I realized I could have settled for a three-piece order for $11.99.

Meanwhile, RS was enjoying walleye, which is a Blue Moose specialty ($13.99). She said it was excellent. Entrees are served with a choice of soup or salad and bread.

In this case, it is soft French bread, with little pots of butter whipped with garlic.

Because of extra touches, the Blue Moose is easily one of my favorite spots for dinner. The place is arranged in comfortable seating areas. There is a pleasant hum of conversation, but no overbearing music. There is an inviting veranda where you can linger over drinks or have a meal in good weather. You look out over the Red River and Grand Forks.

Sometimes the entryway seems congested, but I find little to criticize and lots of pluses at the Blue Moose. Pluses include the ice water in carafes they leave at tables. I like the way they bring the check in a folder and tell you they will pick it up. And when they return your change, they bring an individually wrapped mint. The Blue Moose definitely is a hot spot on the Grand Forks/East Grand Forks dining scene. ❡

Royal Fork's a Homey Delight—You'll Find Plenty of Old-Fashioned Meat and Potatoes

MAY 19, 2000

Marijo Deitz Whitcomb (MDW) strikes me as a creative person, but I didn't know just how creative she was until I saw her build a dessert at Royal Fork Buffet in Columbia Mall.

MDW calls herself Queen of Desserts, so I asked her to show me what she had. In the first place, she uses a soup mug rather than one of those small dessert dishes. She makes a bottom layer with a chocolate chip cookie if she can find one. She just loves those cookies. Last week, they were all gone, so she made her bottom layer of banana bread. Then she topped it with soft-serve ice cream and used some hot brown Betty dessert and a little cherry cobbler. This was followed by caramel sauce.

"Sometimes," she confided, "I finish it off with sprinkles."

MDW is a woman with a nice figure. I asked how she could eat desserts like that and stay so fit.

Her answer: I walk a lot. Her approach to the Royal Fork Buffet is to start out with a nice big salad. Then she skips the hot tables and goes for the gold—the dessert. She wouldn't eat like that at home, she says.

MDW's approach to the buffet piqued my interest. I wonder what strategy other people have as they approach a buffet. I would like to hear from them by telephone or e-mail.

Outside of MDW and her husband, Kyle Whitcomb (KW), I didn't see anyone I knew at the Royal Fork, except for Chad Mustard, all-American Sioux basketball player. He was quietly filling up and told me he is working hard to make the UND football team this fall. He still could have two years' eligibility, even with basketball behind him.

Royal Fork Buffet has been a popular eating place in the mall for the past 16 years. It's the place to go if you yearn for home cooking. If you remember Sunday dinners with roast beef or pork and mashed potatoes and canned vegetables, you will like this food.

You quickly can get a daily quota of fruits and vegetables at the salad tables. Help yourself to a nice glass salad plate and browse. I found honeydew melon, cantaloupe, green peas, greens, sunflower seeds, sliced black olives. Then I found a table where I could sit.

When I finished, I went back to the hot tables and got a dab of mashed potatoes, brown gravy, green beans and a small slice of ham. You can find all kinds of beverages and ice and water. Just help yourself.

Back at the table, I eavesdropped as three teachers were visiting at the next table. I could tell they were accompanying some students from out of town, who had gone elsewhere for pizza. The teachers grinned and agreed, this is so much better.

Royal Fork Buffet is done in warm tones of green and peach. There are women attendants who wear aprons from home and who come around to pour coffee and remove plates. It's a health department requirement that customers take a clean plate each time they go through the serving lines. Manager Scott Heilman, who has been in his job 13 years, says he doesn't even like to think of how much some people can eat.

Baked and fried chicken moves fast. So does glazed Alaskan pollock and the beef ribs on Thursday. Each day, there is a different menu to help keep the buffet interesting.

The philosophy, Heilman says, is to offer home-style foods in a comfortable and friendly, all-American, apple-pie atmosphere. The restaurant has a couple of party rooms, and promotes its catering services. It's one of four in North Dakota and two more in South Dakota under the same ownership. ❡

After twenty-five years in business, the Royal Fork Buffet closed in 2008.

Twilight Dinners Are a Draw at Ramada—Walleye Is Most Popular Choice off the Menu

JULY 7, 2000

When you find regular customers who come in and joke around with the waitresses, you know you are in a friendly, dependable restaurant. That's the way it seemed the other day when a customer came into the Ramada Restaurant and asked, "What's the special?"

When the waitress said, "Ummmmmmm," the customer said, "Oh, I haven't had any of that for a long time." It was before noon, and she offered to go out to the kitchen to inquire about the special. The customer quipped, "Never mind. It's probably what's left over from yesterday."

In recent weeks, I have had two excellent meals at the Ramada. Last week, I ordered a club sandwich, which comes with soup, salad or fries ($5.95) and a glass of iced tea ($1.15). That is my idea of a perfect summer lunch, and the Ramada serves it well. The chefs have the correct formula for a club sandwich. They serve it on toasted white bread, three slices, with turkey, tomato, lettuce and bacon. They cut the sandwich diagonally twice to make four triangles. And they fasten each section with a toothpick topped with colored cellophane.

Someday, I will find a club sandwich like this with olives on the toothpicks, and my joy will be complete. Nevertheless, the sandwich at the Ramada came as close to being a real club as any I have eaten for a while. The fact that the iced tea was served in a tall, thin glass goblet made it taste even better.

Earlier in June, I had dinner with Stuart and Marceda McDonald (SM and MM), who were visiting here from Denver. With them were their grandson Alex McDonald

(AM) and his friend Jak Kmetz (JK), who are students at UND this summer, and MM's mother, Anna Wright (AW).

We gathered around a table in the restaurant for the twilight dinners served between 5 and 7 P.M., Monday through Friday. These dinners are popular with people who enjoy eating a little earlier and a little less for a little less.

We liked the fact that our waiter, Doug, brought out a basket of garlic toast first. We all were puzzled about where to put the bread. We could have used bread plates. Most of us had soup. SM commented it was good because it had real turkey and not those little cubes. AM, who eats on a student's budget, said, "It's better than ramen."

The salads won our approval because of the variety of greens and presence of red cabbage and carrots. Both AM and I ordered the walleye ($7.25), the reason why many people go to the Ramada. It is excellent, with its crisp covering that includes slivered almonds. The baked potato that came with my dinner was moist and good.

Hot beef with hash browns was the choice of the others, except for SM. He ordered chopped sirloin Sizzler Steak ($7.25) and said it was well cooked. Really good and juicy. With it, there were sautéed onions and mushrooms. More, SM said, than a growing boy should eat. ❡

If It's Monday, It's Chicken Wings at Players

SEPTEMBER 15, 2000

They not only have mustard, they have Grey Poupon at Players Sports Bar and Grill on South Washington Street. But I found out Sunday afternoon you have to ask for it. To me, any self-respecting hamburger or hot dog needs mustard. And I found the hamburger at Players to be respectable. It was good meat. It was moderately sized. The bun was tasty. The coleslaw was at least a B, but the portion was modest. The hamburger and slaw was $5.29, the Diet Pepsi, with free refills, $1.49.

In two visits to Players this past week, I sat in the lounge. Often for lunch at Players, I sit in the lighter and brighter dining room at the south end of the place. There still are tables for dining there, but some of the space has been taken over with a pool table, air hockey, Internet jukebox and a golf game.

Players has in recent years built up a good following for breakfast. There are groups that gather regularly for coffee or the $1.99 Skyscraper Breakfast. That's two eggs, two strips of bacon and all the pancakes you can eat.

Owner-managers Rod and Tammy Oas keep a close watch over their business. When something works, they do it. As he sat in the busy lounge Sunday afternoon, Rod Oas said, "NFL Sunday is huge. Without the screens showing seven football games, you and I might be sitting alone in here."

All around me, people were eating potato skins or burgers and drinking Mountain Dew or lemonade. There were some eating salads served on mammoth platters. And since children eat free on Sundays, there were families seated here and there.

I arrived at Players just after 2 P.M., too late for the Sunday breakfast buffet served from 10 A.M. to 2 P.M. for $5.99. At least 100 people had been there in time for the buffet, though.

Monday Night Football and all-you-can-eat chicken wings brings customers in each week. The wings are served with bleu cheese, dressing and celery. And on a decent Monday night, they go through 300 pounds of wings. Two-for-one burgers are a big draw Tuesday evenings.

There are attractive plaid valances on the windows and on the brass railings that serve as dividers for semi-privacy. Walls are dark green with contrasting light wood wainscoting and parquet floors. Mirrors on posts add an illusion of space.

All of these observations were made with the help of Marge Leigh

(ML) when she and Jim Leigh (JL) and I stopped at Players for the baked potato bar before the Potato Bowl football game. We found the potatoes exceptionally good, al-though they were russets rather than reds. We found the small paper plates inadequate. We needed two or three to hold our potatoes and toppings. ❡

The building that housed Players was found to be not code-compliant, and was razed in the mid-2000s.

Lola's Captures Flavor of Italy

OCTOBER 6, 2000

When I smell the wood fire or see one of the kitchen workers out splitting logs beside Lola's in downtown Grand Forks in the late afternoon, I wish I was going there for supper. It's only occasionally I eat there, so I suggested Lola's when Jan Zahrly (JZ) and I were trying to decide where we should meet and eat.

We met at 6 in front of Lola's and went in together. I had a vague recollection about an ad Lola's has run saying reservations are suggested, but walk-ins always are embraced. I half-expected a hug from the head waiter when we said we had no reservation. In-stead, he gave us a choice of seating. After all, it was early. And it was Monday. Before the evening was over, JZ and I agreed Monday is a fine time to go out to dinner. Things are relatively quiet, and you get all sorts of attention.

We walked past the row of tables near the windows. We passed the tables around the bend. We circled around the glassed-in room where wines are kept at optimum temperatures and went into the lounge area.

We were seated in a booth, near the dark wood bar, which is staffed with friendly university types. Our waiter was Joel Loomis, an airport management major from Minnetonka, Minn. He told us of the Monday $10.25 special. A meatball, he said, but a very large meatball, and spaghetti.

JZ chose Crab Alfredo, an entree made of penne pasta, roasted red peppers, pancetta and Dungeness crab meat tossed in Alfredo sauce ($15.25). I ordered fusilli with scallops (also $15.25). Since I couldn't pronounce *fusilli,* I pointed to it on the menu, and caught on when the waiter said "foosilly." Our entrees were preceded by warm focaccia bread, served with a little pot of butter whipped with sun-dried tomatoes.

Lola's is a special place in downtown Grand Forks. It's open only in the evenings, and it serves such wonderful appetizers that some diners make a meal of them. Appetizers include artichoke dip with grilled Tuscan bread ($7.75) and two crab-stuffed portobello mushroom caps with Dungeness crab and Parmesan cheese ($9.25).

The menu also includes veal dishes and chicken cacciatore. The signature dish is Chianti-roasted duck, served with rosemary potatoes and seasonal vegetables for $19.25. Choices include ribeye, strip loin, grilled rack of lamb, grilled salmon, pizzas and calzones. Last weekend, pheasant was featured. Eighty percent of the food at Lola's is prepared over a wood fire. There is an extensive wine list to complement the food. And the dessert menu is above and beyond, with great endings such as tiramisu, pear pie and chocolate torte.

Lola's has established itself in Grand Forks as a Northern Italian restaurant, and it does a good job of staying with the game plan. It does not try to be everything to everybody. Manager Doug Knoll displays art by local artists, including Diane Rey, Ben Brien and Adam Kemp. He uses live entertainment on weekends to attract a college-age crowd. He encourages sports fans by hosting the Wednesday night coaches show over at KCNN.

The restaurant is artsy and appropriately located in a historic building. The old brick and wooden floors were retained in the decor. Ceilings are high and open. There are white tablecloths under glass and large white cloth napkins.

JZ says she likes the way Lola's keeps tall wooden pepper grinders on each table. That way customers can help themselves when and if they want it—no need for a waiter to go through the charade of "tell me when you have enough." Another plus: good music, played softly. And another plus this time of year: convenient hangers for coats in the entryway. They do away with that awful business of eating a nice meal with your coat or jacket hanging over the back of your chair.

Lola's is marking its fourth anniversary in Grand Forks during October. The Italian restaurant was opened here by Doug and Ralph Knoll and chef Kim Holmes in September 1996. It was closed for three months following the flood. Kim Holmes left Lola's in April in order to devote his full attention to the reopening of his Sanders restaurant. Lola's originally served lunch as well as dinner, but manager Doug Knoll says dinner only works best for his operation at this time. He wants to do well what he can handle, I guess. ❡

Sanders Is Cream of Crop

OCTOBER 13, 2000

We were dawdling over dessert at Sanders and wondering if there is a better restaurant in North Dakota. Daughter Gail (DG) and her husband, Dale Sandstrom (DS), and I had just finished dinner, which has become a traditional outing for us when they come up each October during homecoming at UND.

In Bismarck, they have the Bistro. North of Minot, there's a nice place called Field and Stream. There's an excellent dining room in Prairie Knights Casino near Fort Yates, N.D. The food at the Radisson in Fargo is head and shoulders above other restaurants. And the Fargo Country Club excels—but it is open only to members and has a long waiting list.

All in all, it seems to me that Sanders is the best place for dining in North Dakota, and Grand Forks is fortunate to have it back in business in the heart of a rebounding downtown. Our reservation—which I made a couple of months ago—was for 6:30 P.M. Saturday. We were greeted at the entry and seated in a booth, where I could see the open kitchen with copper kettles hanging above the stoves. DG and DS could see the bar area with its custom woodwork and the booths with Norwegian painting that so long have been a trademark of Sanders.

The whole restaurant has a festive ambience. There is an ornate door from the original Sanders on Kittson Avenue gracing the wine room. Artsy touches include a permanent floral arrangement in the women's restroom. There's an after-dinner room, where you can shoot pool or have a cigar. And it has a special ventilating system to take the smoke right out.

Table settings are upscale, with white cloths under glass and white napkins in goblets. There are proper water glasses. Your waiter arrives with a pitcher of water and a vivid description of the evening specials—usually fresh fish and another choice. Sanders's homemade French bread is served in a basket, with unsalted butter. We found many of the traditional Sanders dinners on the menu. DS remembered well the Swiss Eiger beef and ordered the 12-ounce version ($16). I ordered Grilled Salmon served with Sanders North Dakota prairie sauce ($18).

Entrees are served with vegetables and include salads.

Presentation is a strong point at Sanders. My salmon arrived with creamy mashed potatoes and three spears of fresh asparagus arranged like spokes. Fresh, perky parsley and radish roses are used to carry a message from the kitchen that the chef cares about you.

Sanders has been a part of Grand Forks since it opened at 312 Kittson Ave. in 1982. It was purchased by Kim Holmes in 1985 and developed a strong following up until 1997, when the flood wiped it out with the rest of the downtown. Holmes regrouped and reopened in a strip mall along South Washington Street at 24th Avenue S. He also went into business with Ralph and Doug Noll at Lola's at 124 N. Third St. He left Lola's in April to concentrate on the renewed version of Sanders, which opened in July.

And in the first three months, Holmes says, business has been exceeding expectations. Never did he question whether he should go back downtown with Lola's in the aftermath of the flood. Holmes has a wide acquaintance around Grand Forks and makes it a point to get out and personally greet guests during the evening. That helps create a friendly, intimate atmosphere. His staff includes longtime waiters who also know their customers. His chefs include Paul Browning, who has a four-year degree from Johnson & Wales school of cooking, and Joe Hanson as sous chef.

In his new and larger location, Holmes is reaching out to a more diverse clientele with more variety and a wider range of prices. Dinners from $9 to $12 are specials each evening. His wine list includes 20 bottles for less than $20. He is willing to compete with low prices and happy-hour munchies as well as a late-night menu. It features calamari for $7.50, duck quesadilla for $7, a buffalo burger with fries for $5 and a 16-inch lavosh for $11.

But back to the dessert. Sanders has its traditional Chocolate Decadence at $4. There are cheesecakes made by Beth Holmes. It was the Creme Caramel ($5) that caught the eye of DG and DS. This is a delicately flavored custard served with fresh fruit and real whipped cream.

So much to cheer about with the reopening of Sanders! Not much you can criticize here. However, it seems to me the waiter should tell you how much the specials are after they recite the description. Oh, I know it might not seem genteel, but I like to know the price.

And maybe it's just me, but I would like the waiter to wait until everyone in a small group has finished before removing the plates. When the others' plates are gone and one guest is left eating, it becomes uncomfortable. On the other hand, I know there are people who like their plates removed promptly. ❡

Classics Keep Customers Coming Back to Quizno's

MARCH 23, 2001

"I see you have homemade soup. Is it made here?" I asked as I entered the new Quizno's Subs shop on South Washington Street.

"Well, no," said the attendant at the counter.

"Oh," I said. "Is it made in someone else's kitchen?"

The young man nodded, and I ordered a cup of broccoli cheese soup. Then, never having been to Quizno's before, I tried to figure out what kind of a sandwich I wanted. There are signature subs and classic subs listed on the menu. Under signature subs, I found a turkey-bacon guacamole combination that comes in small ($3.99), regular ($4.99) or large ($6.99). I figured small would do me. I asked for whole wheat bread, rather than white.

This was an excellent sandwich. The bread was toasted and warm. The turkey was very thinly sliced and had a nice smoked flavor. The combination with guacamole and bacon was most tasty. The soup ($1.29) was as thick as porridge. Good enough, but it might not win a blue ribbon at the state fair.

Quizno's is relatively new in Grand Forks, and adds another interesting dimension to the eating-out scene. The company bills itself as an upscale sub shop and is growing rapidly.

Inside all Quizno's shops, the colors are red and green, and the tone is Italian. There are red, green and gold lamps hanging over the counters. When I had lunch there a week ago Thursday, the music was playing, and the pop machine was humming away. My soup came in a paper cup with a plastic spoon. I like the napkins at Quizno's because they are natural-colored and are made from recycled fibers.

My plan was to try a salad or

a classic sub on my second visit to Quizno's. I looked over the hot beefeater, albacore tuna and other sandwiches. But my eye kept straying back to the turkey-bacon-guacamole. I enjoyed it so much I went for a repeat. Thus, I did not taste three other sandwiches that are top choices of Quizno's regulars: classic Italian with salami, pepperoni, ham and cheese; Mesquite chicken with bacon; and Black Angus steak on rosemary parmesan bread.

The cookies are generously sized and $1.09. The lineup includes chocolate chip, oatmeal chocolate chip, oatmeal raisin, peanut but-ter, white chocolate chip, M&M and Reese's Pieces. Dessert choices include a chocolate Bundt cake, carrot Bundt cake, apple cobbler and very berry cobbler. All are $1.69. Coffee and hot tea are 69 cents at Quizno's.

The sandwich I had twice at Quizno's was indeed above average and just a tad pricey. I would go back for it again because I like the way the bread tastes—so fresh and toasted. The bread comes in flash-frozen from Colorado and is baked at the shops. The homemade soup, as it turns out, comes from a grocery supplier. ❡

There are currently two Quizno's restaurants operating in Grand Forks.

Late-Night Grazing Enhances Sanders 1907 Repertoire

SEPTEMBER 5, 2001

At the very mention of Sanders 1907, my mind conjures an evening of fine dining with food and service a cut above anything else around. But the image of Sanders has broadened since it reopened in its larger quarters downtown a year ago.

Sanders, which started as a small cafe that could serve 40, has become a more versatile dining place with an enlarged lounge and pool room. It's a place where you can get late-night fare and listen to music. It can accommodate 100 people without even seeming crowded, since the place flows from the bar area to the dining room with side openings to two semiprivate dining rooms and a pool room. Yes, and a cigar room—carefully cordoned off from the dining areas and equipped with special fans.

The late-night menu has several of the appetizers from Sanders's dinner menu, as well as burgers and fries and such. I tried it out with three *Herald* friends—Jaime DeLage (JD), Tu Uyen Tran (TT) and Rachel Jeffers (RJ).

TT contemplated escargot but decided he would not get enough food for his $8 and opted for a barbecued prime rib sandwich served with fries for $7.50. JD followed suit, and both seemed well satisfied. RJ ordered the duck burrito ($9.50), covered with red sauce, sour cream, corn relish and avocado. It's great if you like a lot of zip.

My choice was smoked salmon Napoleon ($9.50), a delightfully rich combination of smoked salmon, Boursin cheese, and chopped onion, with a nice taste of capers. All of this might have been sort of soggy, had it not been for a built-in crunch of potato chips. It was actually enough for two to share, especially since the late-night fare is preceded by the sourdough French bread and unsalted butter that customers count on.

Buffalo burgers at $6 with fries are a popular late-night choice. So is the lavosh with ground buffalo, tomato, onion, peppers, black olives, mushrooms and Havarti cheese—a 16-inch pie for sharing at $13.

Kim Holmes has a flair both as a chef and as an entrepreneur. He and his wife, Beth, work well as a team. She does much of the bread baking and creates sauces and desserts. We tried a superb creation of white chocolate–orange cheesecake to round out our foray.

One of the strengths of Sanders is the professional staff. Many have been there for several years and have a way of recognizing and giving a friendly welcome to customers.

But, no place is perfect. The second booth in the dining room is squeaky. And avocado is spelled wrong on the late-night menu. ❡

Touch of Magic Caters to Lovers of Cheesecake, Fine Dining

JANUARY 9, 2002

Dennis Narlock, who does business as Chef Nardane, is starting the year 2002 with high expectations for his new Touch of Magic Ballroom in East Grand Forks. He already has hosted a couple of events in the elegant banquet and ballroom overlooking the Red River.

The new ballroom was the scene of a grand bash to thank people who helped build the new facility, and to show it to people of the community who have been supportive of the chef's dreams.

What matters more to Chef Nardane than money, he says, is how guests feel when they reach the top of the wide stairway or come by elevator to this Touch of Magic.

He wants a wow. And that probably is what he will get.

As they arrived, guests were awed by the ballroom that takes up 6,200 square feet of the 10,000 square-foot facility. The rest of the space is devoted to kitchens and offices. The ballroom has paneled windows that provide a panoramic view of the Red River and Grand Forks. There are stone columns with gold gilding at the top. Dark mahogany chairs surround round tables that were set for 350.

Tableware is the large European style, and the gold lines on the china are under a glaze to protect them from wear. Coffee carafes with glass liners were secured by the supplier, Dakota Foods, from

Germany. Russian crystal center-pieces, designed in Poland, have a Star of David on top.

Chef Nardane says that his family is just one generation away from Poland. He is one of six children of Dan and Yvonne Narlock. And he says all the jobs he hated to do in the kitchen as a child when his mother was sick gradually have become an asset.

He has developed a specialty of cheesecakes named after celebrities—or, as he calls them, the icons in his lifetime. The dessert table at his opening party included Debbie Reynolds crème caramel cheesecake, chocolate strawberries and pineapple, His Holiness Pope John Paul II pierogi cheesecake, Dame Elizabeth Taylor's Beverly Hills cheesecake, and mountain cake.

The menu for his first party began with liver pâté and garlic cheese served with crackers and breads at the round tables. The salad course served at the tables was mixed greens topped with raspberry vinaigrette. The main course buffet featured creamed salmon, rack of lamb with raspberry mustard sauce, prime rib, garlic mashed potatoes and asparagus with toasted cashews.

A buffet, Chef Nardane says, offers a choice of tastes for the guests. The Touch of Magic dinner plates make plenty of room for tasting, too, since they are 11 inches in diameter.

As he was preparing for a wedding reception Dec. 29, Chef Nardane was working with a staff of four in the kitchen and planned to have six or seven servers. Usually, he figures on one server per 50 guests. The dinner was to be served buffet style, with servers available to assist any guests who find a line difficult.

Chef Nardane, at 36, is a man who dares to dream. He was operating Touch of Magic in the Comfort Inn of East Grand Forks until the motel was closed because of the flood. He was about to leave the area before he found the place to follow his dreams.

With the help of Mayor Lynn Stauss of East Grand Forks, he was able to get a low-interest loan to develop the vacant area above Applebee's. And arrangements were made to work with the new Cuckoo's Nest lounge owner, Kyle Gregoire, for service of wine, beer, champagnes and liquor.

Now, he envisions a private membership club in his new Touch of Magic Ballroom. He hopes to start in the coming years a club that would provide celebrity entertainment and fine meals to members.

The chef told guests at his opening party he is grateful for a family that taught him to believe nothing in life is impossible if you have a vision. ❡

After nine years of business, Nardane closed Touch of Magic and began selling off his assets. On June 12, 2011, the Grand Forks Herald *reported that Nardane intended to join a recently established Catholic religious order in the Diocese of Fargo.*

Diners Can Tee Off on Good Food at Eagle's Crest Grill

FEBRUARY 27, 2002

The opening of Eagle's Crest Grill at King's Walk Golf Course seems to summon a new era in Grand Forks. Since its opening Feb. 4, Eagle's Crest Grill has been trying to get acquainted with people of the area. Special rates and discounts have helped encourage diners to come out. Sunday brunch has been drawing crowds.

The place is appealing, with a huge fieldstone fireplace in the center and its high vaulted ceiling that rises to 37 feet at its peak. The place has a sporty ambience, with deep green and burgundy plaid carpeting. Golf clubs and golf photos are used on the walls.

The setting is, indeed, ideal. There was a fire glowing in the fireplace when I went to Eagle's Crest Grill with a couple of friends

Feb. 13. We went early in order to avoid any dinner hour crush. We ordered the dinner special—crab-stuffed walleye with bay shrimp in a seafood sauce and flavored with Parmesan cheese and cracked peppercorns ($12.95). We could get a view of the cooks in the kitchen from the open window beyond the bar.

Our salad was nice and not too large, with a variety of greens. I enjoyed mine with vinegar and oil. Dinners are served with baked potato or rice pilaf, house salad and rolls.

Other entrees include chicken cordon bleu ($11.99), filet mignon champignon (8 ounces, $16.99 and 6 ounces, $14.99), sirloin (10 ounces $13.99), grilled halibut (8 ounces $15.99), walleye northern lights (8-ounce serving, $12.99) and stuffed shrimp scampi (five Gulf shrimp stuffed with crab meat and oven-broiled, $14.99). There are four children's items on the menu, along with three pasta choices, burgers, appetizers and homemade soups and salads.

Our entree was garnished with orange and tomato slices. The walleye was delicious with its well-flavored sauce and stuffing. It was more like a feast.

On the plus side: Dinner rolls are above average. Service is top-notch. Our waiter was Derek Ebertowski.

On the minus side: It would be better if place settings included two forks. We had to save our forks from our salad for our entree. The onion rings atop the salad were white, not red as indicated on the menu. No need during golfing season, but it would be nice if there was a place for diners to hang their coats, rather than on the back of their chairs.

All in all, it was a delightful experience dining at Eagle's Crest. The staff seems young and energetic and are appropriately dressed in polo shirts with Eagle's Crest logo and dress shoes. Right now, there are five assisting cooks in the kitchen, four bartenders and a half dozen on the waitstaff. Chef Dan Horski says it is his goal to keep the place busy and full. ❡

Eagle's Crest Grill continues to operate as a restaurant and catering venue.

Dinner at Lola's: Everything from Polenta to Fried Leeks

MARCH 27, 2002

The smell of the wood-fired ovens, a view of chefs in the open kitchen, tables close together and soft lighting—that's Lola's Northern Italian Restaurant in downtown Grand Forks. And since it opened here five years ago, Lola's has established itself as one of the best bets for dinner.

Lola's is a unique restaurant set in an old warehouse building. With its old wooden floors, high ceiling and brick walls, it is a delightful setting. It's a place where you can focus on appetizers and wine, choose pizza or pasta or find an excellent dinner of salmon, lamb, veal or roast duck.

It was the perfect setting for a birthday dinner for my daughter earlier this month. I was glad I had made a reservation for five well in advance, because Lola's was almost full when we arrived at 6:30 P.M.

Our table was off to the side, near the wine room. Our waitress was with us as we were seated, aptly describing the specials for the evening—a venison dinner and a pasta with shrimp and chicken. She gave us the prices of around $20 and $14, which is helpful.

Then, as we turned our attention to the menu, she described the wines. We ended up with a bottle of Clos du Bois Merlot ($29), and we got serious about our dinner selections. Mary Golden (MG) knew what she wanted immediately: the eggplant parmesan ($15.50), which she thoroughly enjoyed. Al Golden (AG) chose grilled Italian sausage served with polenta, marsala sauce, roasted red pepper and wild mushrooms. He said the polenta was especially good. My son-in-law, Dale Sandstrom (DS), ordered butternut squash ravioli served in a nutmeg cream sauce ($14.25) and a salad ($2). Daughter Gail Hagerty (GH) ordered grilled salmon with a honey and mustard glaze and fried leeks ($19.50). So I said, "Likewise." She studies food and knows what to order, so I often just ask for the same. And this was a marvelous dinner, served with asparagus and rosemary roasted potatoes. The fried leeks added another taste and crisp texture to the meal.

It was an excellent meal, preceded with warm focaccia bread in baskets and an accompanying spread of butter flavored with sun-dried tomatoes. With a meal such as that, none of us would have wanted appetizers. However, I couldn't resist ordering a tiramisu dessert ($5.50) to celebrate the birthday of GH. Our waitress was most willing to bring extra plates and forks so that we could all taste it. And this is a specialty at Lola's: delicate and sweet, but not too sweet. In a word, excellent.

Lola's was a perfect choice for this kind of a dinner party. The place was almost crowded on a busy Saturday night, and that made for a festive feeling. Lola's is slightly upscale, but still down-to-earth with its white paper tablecloths. The restaurant has appeal to a wide clientele. Owner Doug Noll says he is trying to make the restaurant affordable to college students, and caters to them with pizza and tap beer for $5 after 9:30 P.M. The restaurant also features pasta dishes in the $6 and $7 range early in the week. Students are an important part of the business, he says. Maybe 35 percent.

The staff at Lola's seems to be well-trained. Noll says he holds regular sessions to keep waiters knowledgeable about the wines. He wants his servers to be accommodating and never say no to a customer. If they have special requests, he says, Lola's will meet them. ❡

Take In Dinner, Play at Starlites

JUNE 5, 2002

You have a choice of four entrees when you do dinner at the new Starlites Dinner Theatre in the Grand Cities Mall. I contemplated the choices of stuffed chicken breast, pork tenderloin, sirloin medallions and vegetarian lasagna. Then, I ordered up two pork tenderloin dinners and hoped my friend Barbara Lander (BL) would like that.

She did. We found the pork tender and tasty with its Grand Marnier sauce. But first came the salad with parmesan, and croutons that were soft enough to eat. When I get little bullets for croutons, I just pile them up at the edge of my salad plate. The pork tenderloins were accompanied by a baked potato and green peas in the pod. Dinner rolls were a cut above some you get with a meal.

Starlites Dinner Theatre has finished its run of *Lend Me a Tenor* and is starting *Singin' in the Rain* on June 12. After that, it's a mystery, *The Hound of the Baskervilles*,

from July 24 through Aug. 25. You can make reservations by calling the theater number below. Prices for the show and dinner range from $35 to $47, depending on whether you are a student, a senior, a regular feller or a group, and whether you attend on a weekend, choose a matinee or go in the evening.

Although the newly renovated theater has a kitchen, the managers have found it more feasible to have the food catered. The contract presently is with GF Goodribs. All entrees are served with a salad, rolls, vegetables and a nonalcoholic beverage. We chose coffee, although there was a wide range of soft drinks available. Appetizers, desserts and drinks from the bar are served at an additional cost. Dessert selections include Snickers or caramel-apple cheesecake ($4.75).

It was amazing to see how the former movie theater has been transformed—at an outlay of $120,000—into a pleasant dinner theater. You feel welcome from the time you enter the theater area in the mall with its blue neon lights. We were greeted by Dan Eggen and his wife, Marla Kalin, who operate the nonprofit professional theater. At this time, one of the former twin theaters is being used. There are plans to have two of them up and running.

The dining area is spacious and attractive, with several levels of tables with white cloths and blue-cloth dinner napkins. We enjoyed the soft music during the leisurely dinner. The theater allows an hour and a half for serving before the 7:30 P.M. shows. Some people come only for the show.

We had a five-minute warning before the show started. And then a one-minute notice. We sat back and thoroughly enjoyed the show, which in itself is cleverly written and was done exceedingly well by the Starlites cast of actors.

The food, along with the friendly ambience and high-quality show, was good enough to set the scene for a pleasant evening. The audience was thin, but management of Starlites is optimistic. They hope to build audiences as new shows come up every six weeks. ❡

Starlites was evicted from Grand Cities Mall in August 2002 for nonpayment of its rent.

Sachi Serves Sushi at Kon Nechi Wa's in Grand Cities Mall

JULY 3, 2002

Sachi MacGregor thinks retirement is the time to do something for which you have a passion. Her passion is preparing Japanese food, and she has opened a small cafe in Grand Cities Mall, where she sells teriyaki meals and sushi. Going into her third month, she couldn't be happier. Along with her love of cooking, she enjoys her customers.

Her partner in the business is her husband, Lester MacGregor, a retired U.S. Postal Service employee. But he says it's Sachi's business and that he is just the chief bottle washer. Others on the staff are two women who come in to make up everything fresh each morning—Chika Price, who originally came from Japan, and Harumi Pavlicek, a native of Okinawa.

Sachi was born in Japan and met her husband in Okinawa when he was there in the U.S. Marine Corps. The couple has five grown children and six grandchildren.

You get a warm welcome from the MacGregors when you go to Kon Nechi Wa's at the front of Grand Cities Mall. The location formerly was occupied by Antonio's Pizza, and by Figaro's before that. The MacGregors explain that *kon nechi wa* means "good afternoon."

They have a special every day for $4.95 and teriyaki meals ranging in price from $6.95 to $9. They serve three kinds of sushi, and it is made up to order. Their aim is to get orders out within four to five minutes, but they can't always meet their self-imposed deadline.

Sushi is described in my guide from the Association of Food Journalists as "Japanese; various combinations of seasoned rice, vegetables, raw fish (sashimi), wasabi, seaweed (nori)."

My first visit to Kon Nechi Wa's was with Barbara Lander (BL) late in June. BL tried the beef stir-fry with noodles and found it very good. I went for the daily special of fried rice with chicken and vegetables, an egg roll and beverage. I found it to be a tasty and satisfying meal. On a second visit, I had another special of stir-fried rice topped with pea pods, carrot slivers and onion, accompanied by a crisp egg roll and choice of soda or tea.

I visited with Tammy Tanke (TT), who had come in to pick up sushi on her way home from work. TT said she does this often and enjoys it. She chose Inari Sushi with seaweed wrap, seasoning, sushi rice, daikon-sweet pickle and ginger ($4.50). TT appreciates the fresh ginger. The wasabi, she says, has a good bite.

You get a little container of wasabi with your sushi, and Sachi recommends mixing it with soy sauce.

Other choices of sushi are crab roll, made with crab meat, sushi rice, seaweed wrap, egg, cucumber, ginger and wasabi ($4.50). Then, there's my favorite, California Wrap Sushi, with rice, crab meat, egg, avocado, ginger and wasabi ($4.50).

Customers enjoy watching from behind the glassed-in work area as Sachi makes up the sushi. And Sachi is living out a dream in her cafe. For 25 years, she sold cosmetics and jewelry and managed the department for J.C. Penney Co. "Basically," she says with a smile, "I was married to J.C. Penney. It's a wonderful feeling

now to be retired and have a second chance."

She started out in the food business with a small cafe on wheels, taking her Japanese foods to events in the summertime. She is a charter member of the Farmers Market on Saturdays in Grand Forks. She will be at the Fourth of July celebration at University Park and Catfish Days in East Grand Forks. Meanwhile, she wears a happy smile behind the cheery counter of Kon Nechi Wa's.

She makes the sweet-and-sour sauce and hot sauce that are on each table. She orders ingredients from Winnipeg, Minneapolis and Fargo. Regularly, she makes up a fresh batch of Japanese doughnuts (50 cents) that she keeps in a jar on the counter.

"In my mother's generation," she says, "if you can't make these doughnuts, you are not ready to get married." ❡

Irishman's Shanty—Far More than a Supper Club

OCTOBER 23, 2002

The Irishman's Shanty, nestled among commercial buildings in the south end of Crookston, is a place where you can find a top-grade steak for a moderate price. And you can enjoy it in cozy, unpretentious surroundings.

As we drove away from the supper club on a recent Saturday evening, I said, "I would sure go back."

My friend, Barbara Lander (BL), said, "I would, too."

The dinner special was 9-ounce Cajun prime rib for $11.25, and we thought about that. But since I rarely have steak, I decided to order filet mignon wrapped in bacon ($12.75). BL ordered a combination plate with two jumbo shrimp and a half rack of ribs ($13.75). Our dinners included the salad bar, a mini loaf of sourdough bread and choice of potato or wild rice. The salad bar offered choices of several salads and an excellent homemade Minnesota cheese soup. Salad greens were crisp and inviting. The cottage cheese was fresh.

I ordered my steak medium well because I can't stand the sight of blood. It was top-notch. BL found the shrimp and ribs to her liking, but she mentioned she would like it better with the barbecue sauce on the side rather than slathered all over the ribs. Her half portion was so large she took part of it home in a little plastic box.

We were too full for dessert, but I noticed the Shanty specialties include Irish Cream Pie, Caramel Apple and Snicker Pie as well as Turtle Cheesecake.

Irishman's Shanty is sort of a square, one-story building with a lot of shamrocks on it. Inside, the decor is Irish, of course. The bar sports, in the ceiling, what might be the world's largest shamrock made of wire mesh.

The menu is great because it isn't

too complicated and is easy to read. It's complete with steaks, chicken, ham, fish, seafood. Entrees include liver with onions and bacon. And there is a section for the lighter appetite at lighter prices.

Owner Paul Gregg says he realizes many people don't want to eat large portions. Thus, the light choices. And, he says, the Shanty is perfectly willing to serve half-orders or split orders for people. On the other hand, he says, many of his customers are active blue-collar workers who want to fill up. The half-pound hamburger is the signature item for Irishman's Shanty.

The Irishman's Shanty is far more than a supper club. It serves an early morning breakfast that draws a small but steady following. When it's finished, a second round of area farmers come in for coffee and shake the dice to see who pays. And then there's lunch. ❡

Stormy Sledster's Makes a Lively Addition to the Downtown Scene

MAY 7, 2003

Ever since it opened downtown in February, Stormy Sledster's has been a busy place—especially at mealtimes and after work. The place is sort of dark and funky and has a publike feel about it. Still, it attracts people of all ages and has specials for children and seniors on its menu.

The place is operated by Norman Braaten, who is known as "Stormy" to his partner, Jeff Spicer. Braaten is a somewhat modest man who wouldn't want to name a restaurant after himself. So, he chose the name Stormy Sledster's and uses sleds as his decor. Braaten has collected old sleds, skis and snowshoes. He says sleds usually bring happy memories to people, and he likes to display them.

On four visits to Stormy Sledster's, I have found the food to be above average. The prices are moderate. Service is good.

On my first visit, before an event in the downtown Empire Arts Center, I tried the sirloin special. This was a good meal with a salad and baked potato. My only mistake was asking for the steak medium. I should have said medium rare. I shared an appetizer of chili con queso with Katie Mullen (KM), and we agreed that almost could be a meal in itself. KM, who professes to be a cheese freak, ordered the bleu cheese burger ($5.49) and gave it a thumbs-up. Jamey David (JD) ordered baked rigato ($7.99), which turned out to be a tasty and hearty dish. The serving was so large he couldn't finish it. With this entree you get spicy Italian sausage or chicken tossed with mushrooms, rigato pasta and sun-dried tomato sauce baked with mozzarella cheese.

On another visit, KM ordered a chimichanga ($6.99) and rated it "really, really good." Barbara Lander (BL) was pleased enough with a turkey bacon melt sandwich ($6.79) to want to go back to Sledster's again. The sandwich is served on grilled potato bread and comes with fries that get high marks.

The soups at Stormy Sledster's are good. For light lunches, I have tried the tortilla and vegetable beef. And before the Shrine Circus, we found the place works well for children, too. The three grandsons of Joyce Pond (JP) and Bill Pond (BP) were pleased with the lemonade (since they aren't allowed to drink pop). They liked the pizza and grilled cheese sandwiches. JP ordered taco salad ($5.79 when served with beef and $6.79 with spicy chicken). BP chose a Reuben sandwich special.

The dinner section of the menu includes walleye ($9.99), a 10-ounce ribeye ($10.99) and an 8-ounce filet mignon ($13.99). With its eclectic menu and its varied clientele, Stormy Sledster's seems to have a good future downtown. Braaten and his staff obviously are hardworking. He also has been operating the Fireside Grill in Thompson, N.D., for the past four years. It is the only restaurant in Thompson and has built a following of customers from nearby towns.

There are plenty of pluses at Stormy Sledster's. The women's restroom is large and attractive, but it's a one-at-a-time kind of place. Servers wear coordinated uniforms and look professional.

On the minus side, although the smoking area is toward the back, it is not separated from the non-smoking area in the front. Unless you ask, it might take a while to get your check. The menu says soup is served with a breadstick, but on one occasion I got crackers. ❡

Flashy Cooks, 13 Sauces Await Mongolian Grill Diners

OCTOBER 15, 2003

Sheila Jerik (SJ) and her daughter April Wicks (AW) invited me to join them for lunch when I was standing in line in the new Mongolian Grill near Super One—at 2791 32nd Ave. S. We had our choice of three sizes of bowls called Little Khan ($4.75), Mighty Khan ($5.75) and Barbarian ($6.75). There's also a Kid's Khan for children younger than 10 ($2.75).

Then we moved down a line of pea pods and freshly cut vegetables such as cabbage, broccoli, cauliflower, peppers. There were noodles, seafood and thinly sliced chicken, beef and pork. I noticed peanuts, water chestnuts, pine-apple, celery, carrots, zucchini, onion greens, tomato, hot peppers. So many choices.

After all of the choices, you find 13 sauces and select what you want to enhance your food when it goes on the grill. You can choose curry, garlic, oyster, Mongolian, barbecue, sweet and sour, lemon, orange, hot red. If you need help, you can follow one of the Mongolian Grill recipes.

Then the fun begins. You watch the chefs cook your meal on the large, gas-fired grill. There are three or four chefs on duty at mealtimes wearing dark green shirts that say "Wok this way" on the back. The chefs use long sticks to stir your meal and cook it for you. And they do it with a flourish as they fill a bowl half full and raise it behind them and then flip all around without spilling a dab. Then they finish filling the bowl.

You take your bowl to your booth or table, where you find a soup of the day and a bowl of rice. Beverages are extra, but SJ and AW and I found a glass of ice water awaiting us. SJ and AW asked for chopsticks, so I followed suit. I like to try to eat with chopsticks.

As we ate, AW commented on the nice presentation by the chefs. SJ called the Mongolian Grill meal "satisfying food." I agreed. I had selected the vegetables and meat I wanted and was enjoying it. I also enjoyed the rice and the egg flower soup.

Later, I visited with owner Namtrung Nguyen, who came here from Montana to open the Mongolian Grill. After the first three weeks of business, he said it was not going as well here as in the six similar restaurants he owns in Boise, Idaho, and Billings, Mont. However, there seemed to be enthusiasm for the different-style Asian restaurant among the people who were coming in. And they were going out and spreading the word. Nguyen said he came here because he was encouraged by people from this area to open a business here. He wants people to come in and appreciate the open kitchen and the smell of fresh food that is cut twice daily.

His philosophy is that the customer pays only for what he eats by choosing from three different-sized bowls. Boxes are available to take leftovers home. The soup is different from day to day. It may be egg flower, Mongolian rice, seafood, hot and sour or vegetable noodle.

I like the Mongolian Grill because it is possible to pick up a healthful meal. The customer is in charge of what is going into the bowl. There is no monosodium glutamate used, Nguyen said. The only drawback is that it is confusing to understand what you are doing the first time through. The second trip is probably a breeze. You can follow the recommendations for sauces to create hot, medium or mild food. ❡

"Expect Something Different" When You Go to Mamaz

DECEMBER 31, 2003

Count me among the curious who have gone to Mamaz on Demers Avenue in East Grand Forks to see what it's like. After all, it's a new restaurant in a familiar location, and it has a motto, "Expect something different."

The evening meal I had there with Katy Mullen (KM) on Dec. 18 was different, all right. On the advice of Maria, the waitress wearing a Santa Claus hat, we ordered the special of the day— Indian Taco ($6.99).

"We sell a lot of these," said Maria, as she brought us each a huge plate with mounds of chopped lettuce. She told us that Thursday was the day for Native American specials. Our entree was grounded with fry bread. On top of it, there was ground beef, diced tomato, onion and chili and grated cheese. To go on top, Maria left little packets of sour cream and taco sauce.

It was good eating and provided a lot of chewing, which I like. I was full by the time I got to the fry bread. But I tasted the fry bread and enjoyed it.

We looked around the restaurant that was formerly an Irish pub and before that an Italian restaurant. Now the decor centers on huge prints along the walls of wolves, panthers, cougars, zebras, leopards. That's because Rachelle Weiss, the owner of Mamaz, likes wildlife. The restaurant has red, white and blue hanging lamps. It is divided into different areas for smoking and nonsmoking guests. Some of the divisions are created with brick archways and brick walls that seem appropriate for the theme of Mamaz. This is a place where you can buy dream catchers and earrings.

The Indian taco was different and good enough, but it would not draw me back. However, we returned to the restaurant for brunch on a Saturday in December, and I left with a feeling I would go back for breakfast—which is served all day. I ordered the first item on the breakfast menu—three pieces of bacon, two eggs and toast ($4.25). Coffee, which was good, is $1.25. The bacon was thick and done to perfection. It was crisp and free of grease. The toast was good.

I asked for my eggs scrambled. And scrambled they were—to perfection. All too often in restaurants, I am disappointed when I order scrambled eggs and get an egg pancake made from eggs that are mixed up ahead of time and waiting in a pitcher to be poured out and fried. You could tell these eggs were scrambled to order. They were fluffy and hot from the stove.

I was so intent on eating my scrambled eggs it took me a while to notice the breakfast pizza KM had ordered. This is a delightful concoction of eggs and nice melted cheese with a choice of sausage, ham or bacon—or all three—all on a crispy tortilla base. The breakfast pizza was nicely served on a plate with a twisted slice of orange as an ap-pealing garnish. The pizza comes with another plate of hash browns and toast. All in all, a meal huge enough to satisfy your hunger for a week.

Mamaz has a complete breakfast menu and a lunch menu with burgers and sandwiches. The prices include french fries or potato chips. The dinner menu ranges from ribeye and sirloin steaks at $10.99 and $11.99, respectively, to chicken drummies for $6.75. Barbecued ribs are $8.99 and pork chop dinner is $8.25.

Weiss, the owner of Mamaz, has been asking opinions of her customers since opening her restaurant in November in East Grand Forks. She grew up near Mahnomen, Minn., and has had restaurant experience in Las Vegas. She promises there will be surprises as Mamaz gets established.

She has applied for a liquor and wine license. And she said Dec. 20 she was in the process of getting the paperwork taken care of and that she believed the license would help sales.

Besides the Native American foods on special Thursday, Mamaz features American, Mexican and Italian foods on other days. Weiss says she has Native American people who make the fry bread for her Thursdays, and people asking for it every day. ❡

Mamaz is no longer in business.

Sarello's Calls with Curried Sea Scallops, Lobster Ravioli

NOVEMBER 10, 2004

We ordered curried sea scallops for an appetizer, and they were the best I ever have eaten. We were in Sarello's Restaurant and Wine Lounge, which seems cleverly hidden at 28 Center Mall Ave., in Moorhead. That's right near Herberger's in the Moorhead Mall.

The sea scallops were very white, very moist and very tender. They came in a spicy red curry broth with fresh basil and broccolini. My daughter Gail (DG) and I split the appetizer ($9), and our waitress, Tara, brought two serving plates without being asked.

I had a feeling of accomplishment as we settled into a table covered with a white cloth and large crisp white napkins on a recent Saturday evening. I had heard of Sarello's and been told it had the best food in Fargo-Moorhead. You have to reserve early. They serve dinner from 5 to 10 P.M., but they serve lunch only once a week, on Fridays.

Our reservation was for 6:30 P.M. We were served in the main dining room, which is small and intimate and rather quiet. There is enough space between the tables so that you can carry on a private conversation. Although it has an Italian flavor, the restaurant describes itself as "Contemporary Dining" on the front window. The place is rather understated. It's nice without chandeliers and brass railings. It has a wine wall in the dining room. It is my kind of place!

The menu is a la carte. We skipped soup and salad, intending to concentrate on our entrees. DG ordered grilled salmon fillet with a honey soy beurre blanc sauce, Asian noodles and sugar snap peas ($17). She found the peas were crisp and nicely flavored. I ordered lobster ravioli with asparagus and shiitake mushrooms ($17). Every bite was tantalizing. Portions are adequate, not enormous. There are 10 entrees on the menu ranging in price from $16 for peppercorn pork chop with potatoes au gratin and asparagus to $28 for filet mignon with whipped potatoes and asparagus.

Service was impeccable. Tara told us in detail about the menu. I appreciated the fact that she also told us the cost of each entree she described. She was professional, pleasant, and not intrusive by repeatedly asking, "How is everything?" She just made sure everything was right.

I noticed Tony Sarello, the owner, around the rooms all of the time. And I thought how impor-tant it is to have the proprietor on the premises and visible. He, too, was friendly and professional in a business suit. There seemed to be a rapport between the staff and customers and several of the customers knew each other.

Anthony "Tony" Sarello told me later in a phone conversation that he originally was from Toronto. He and his wife, Sarah, met while working on a cruise ship. That also is where they met their chef, Christian D'Agostino. Since Sarah originally was from Fargo, they decided to open their restaurant in the area four years ago in December.

Sarello's desserts are flourless chocolate torte, banana chocolate chunk bread pudding, gelato, sorbetto, vanilla bean crème brûlée and dolci del giorni (the daily specials). DG ordered a trio of brûlées: vanilla bean, chocolate and caramel—that came in three small custard dishes. Again, Tara brought an extra plate and dessert spoon knowing full well I would be tasting. We finished with coffee.

Our check came to $69.01, and that included two glasses of wine. ❡

Sarello's is still in business.

Whitey's Continues to Offer a Fine Dining Experience

NOVEMBER 24, 2004

At the grand old age of 79, Whitey's of East Grand Forks is easily the oldest restaurant in the Grand Forks area. It is, in fact, an institution, having survived since the days of the 1930s, when East Grand Forks was a mecca for bars and nightclubs, and the Flood of 1997, to flourish in the aftermath.

These days, the post-flood Whitey's sits up the block from its former building but retains most of its distinguishing qualities. The horseshoe bar, built in 1933, was saved from the floodwaters. The glass blocks are there. The very feel of Whitey's is there.

And lately, longtime staff members are wearing smiles. They say business has been good, and the Canadians are coming back again. They get calls for reservations when there are hockey games on weekends. They run a bus to Ralph Engelstad Arena.

The carefree ambience of Whitey's continues along with a couple of old trademarks on the menu—although the restaurant adds items right along to keep up with the times.

I made a lunch visit there on a Tuesday in November, since pan-fried chicken livers ($6.29) are one of the features on Whitey's luncheon menu. I can think back 30 or 40 years and remember ordering chicken livers when we would go out to dinner at Whitey's. And they are as good as ever, whether you eat them at noon or in the evening from the dinner menu ($8.99).

The chicken livers, which are marinated in a butter-wine sauce before being pan-fried, are plentiful. With them, at lunchtime, you get a very good, fresh poppy-seed hard roll and butter and your choice of potatoes or vegetables. Mine was an attractive plate of vegetables. I ended up taking half of the liver home for a second meal.

I went back on a Sunday to try another Whitey's classic—

mushrooms and asparagus tips over toast topped with melted Swiss cheese. This was $6.99 on the Sunday brunch menu. With it, I had a choice of soup or salad and took the ham and bean soup. I was brunching with Katie Mullen David (KMD), and I think she made an even better choice of French onion soup and a half of a fried Canadian walleye sandwich ($5.49). For some reason, I always think the people I am eating with make better choices.

KMD noticed an interesting wrap sandwich on the menu, but dismissed it saying, "You can get wraps anywhere. The walleye is good in Whitey's."

And it's true. When you are in Whitey's, it is well to "do" the Whitey's specials. June Miron, who served my chicken livers, says, "Whitey's has the best shrimp, prime rib and steak in town." She also is proud of the chicken liver pâté. June is one of the core members of the staff who have spent decades working at Whitey's. Lolly Metcalf has been there even longer.

June started in the 1960s, and has been there off and on ever

since. She remembers giving the late Whitey Larson rides home. And she helped train Greg Stennes, who now is general manager and owner along with Lyle Gerzewski and Alice Davis.

With its longevity, Whitey's has the distinction of being a meeting place for people who come back to town. In its recreation, Whitey's is a sports bar where people gather.

Among the things I like about Whitey's is the Canadian flag that hangs behind the bar. I like the nicely starched, brilliantly white napkins. I like the narrow shape and the thin glass in the drinking glasses. I like the fact that the staff wears white and black. Usually, the service is good. Sometimes, it is slow—as it was on a recent Sunday. But the staff always is courteous.

You can still walk into Whitey's and circle the bar to find your friends. The booths around the perimeter provide a bit of privacy. The dining room with a wall of windows looking out on DeMers Avenue usually is filled first, and it is a pleasant area for lunch or dinner. ❡

City's Only Japanese Restaurant Doubles Size in New Site

DECEMBER 8, 2004

A cheery waitress, Christian Baker, welcomed me to Kon Nechi Wa's in its new location, near Menards, on a recent Sunday afternoon. As I puzzled over the menu, she explained that sushi is the rice, sashimi is raw fish and calamari is squid.

This I know, but this I forget. It isn't often I visit a Japanese restaurant.

It's pleasing to see this one faring well in a new location that has double the space of its former location, in the Grand Cities Mall. Kon Nechi Wa's (which means good afternoon) is a unique, appealing place. It now has three small rooms, in traditional Japanese style, that are semiprivate, with half-length curtains. Instead of seating on the floor with space for feet in a pit below, Kon Nechi Wa's has tatami mat seats of regular chair height for Westerners, with cushions for comfort. It provides an opportunity to experience fairly authentic Japanese dining.

The menu features a daily special of chicken or beef fried rice, an egg roll and beverage ($4.95). There are appetizers, teriyaki stir-fried meals ranging from $6.95 to $9. Soups, fried rice and sushi are offered in a variety of combinations. The rice is prepared each day, and sushi is made to order. Some customers ask for no monosodium glutamate. Others ask for ingredients in a wheat-free diet. Sachi MacGregor, owner and head chef, is willing and eager to accommodate.

My choice was a skewer of five coconut-breaded shrimp ($3.75) and a pork egg roll ($2) from the appetizer menu. That tasted so good, I asked for an order of smoked salmon sushi to take home ($8). It came with a touch of wasabi (you have to go easy on that green hot horseradish) and some ginger. The food, especially the sushi, was excellent and a pleasing departure from the routine. It was well presented and inviting. It left me thinking I ought to pick this up more often.

I like the freshly prepared food in Kon Nechi Wa's and the variety of choices. I like the fish-shaped pottery plate on which the shrimp was served and the matching plate for the egg roll. I don't care much for the plastic glasses that say Coca-Cola, but they are new and shiny.

It's also nice that there are disposable chopsticks on each table, as well as sweet-and-sour sauce in mild and sharp versions. Somehow, Japanese food tastes better to me if I use chopsticks—albeit clumsily.

Soft background music would be nice. As it was, there was only the sound of a compressor while I was eating. ❡

Great Wall Offers More than 100 Choices on a Vast Buffet

MAY 11, 2005

A dab of fried rice, a piece of salmon, an egg roll. Skip the chicken on a stick. Take some lo mein (soft noodles). Take some mixed vegetables with garlic sauce. Oh, oops, here are some American foods. I can't pass up green olives. Oh my, here is some imitation crab salad. I need a little of that. And maybe a little vegetable egg foo yong.

I have twice eaten lunch at the Great Wall Buffet, which opened April 20 at 3555 Gateway Drive, a location that had been empty since a similar restaurant was closed several months ago. Now, under a new lease and ownership, the restaurant is busy, and its huge buffet table offers more than 100 choices.

The staff is attentive, friendly and accommodating. They welcome you and seat you promptly and offer you a cup of tea or other beverage, which is included in the cost of the buffet.

I joined Ruth Holweger (RH) for lunch on my first visit to the Great Wall. We sipped tea and chatted before going around the buffet. We marveled at the array of food available and agreed it was more of a Chinese-American buffet. You find such things as pizza rolls here.

RH was saying the choices were "incredible," and she especially liked the crab salad. We went back and selected some fruit for dessert, and I had the obligatory almond cookie to end a Chinese meal. I noticed there were six kinds of ice cream along with Jell-O, tapioca pudding and other desserts.

You get an amazing amount of food for $5.95 during the lunch hours, from 11 A.M. to 4 P.M. And there is a 15 percent discount for senior citizens and disabled people (but I notice you have to ask for it). The dinner cost is $8.25 for adults. Children age 6 to 10 pay $4.75 and from ages 3 to 5, it's $3.50.

The Great Wall Buffet is well-arranged, with a series of four dining areas set off by glass divid-ers with etchings of animals, fish, flamingos and flowers. The buffet table in the center is well tended, and a wall mirror gives the illu-sion of a large space. There are new chairs and tables with laminated light wood tops. Windows on three sides of the building make the restaurant bright.

Great Wall was just as busy on my second visit for lunch as it was the first. On that day, I found some stuffed mushrooms that were deli-cious. I noticed a lot of heavy-duty eaters go there. It's too bad that some people take food they don't eat and leave it on their plates. In all fairness, they should take only what they can eat, since they are free to go back for more. Some cus-tomers prefer to come in and fill a box to take out.

The restaurant says it special-izes in Cantonese, Szechuan and Hunan cuisine, though that might be a stretch. There is no distinct style of Chinese cuisine to the buf-fet. Customers seem to favor the sesame chicken, honey chicken and sweet-and-sour chicken. I es-pecially liked the sliced strawber-ries in a light sauce.

Some customers like to use the

wooden chopsticks and ask the staff how to go about it. I like to try. Most use the eating utensils that come wrapped in small, light-weight napkins. These napkins, of course, are too small to be much good. I noticed one man with the napkin tucked into his shirt collar like a bib.

Linda Chan, who is listed as owner on the restaurant's license, originally is from mainland China and came here from New York, where she attended a two-month business school in Chinatown. She has taken over ownership, succeeding Hong Peng, who was forced to close the restaurant last year after charges of hiring illegal aliens.

Chan, whose Chinese name is Wen Yu, says she has eight on the staff, all with American citizen-ship or American green cards and proper documentation for work-ing here. ❡

Great Wall continues to operate at this location in Grand Forks.

Paradiso Completes Expansion, Almost Doubling in Size

MAY 18, 2005

With its ongoing remodeling project, Paradiso Mexican Restau-rant on South Washington Street now has seating for 350. And that makes it one of the largest restau-rants in Grand Forks. The restau-rant is planning a grand reopening and has a new menu coming out in June.

Paradiso has a new recep-tion area and additional dining rooms. I was seated in a new din-ing area with nicely tiled wain-scoting when I went there for lunch the other day. The booths have high backs, and the place has new leaded-glass windows, new lamps and new artwork.

I ordered the Luncheon Taco Platter ($4.39), a large corn tortilla filled with seasoned beef and served with lettuce, Spanish rice and refried beans. This was plenty to eat and good enough to order again. The tortilla was crisp and thin. The meat within was lean and well-seasoned. The Spanish rice has a nice tomato taste with a touch of garlic. Even the refried beans were tasty—and I am not a big fan of most refried beans.

Sia Anvarina, the general manager, invited me on a tour of the kitchen when I interviewed him after lunch. It is huge, and well-arranged with four different entryways. In the back, Michael Briones was tending a huge vat of Spanish rice and keeping check on chicken cooking in another enormous pot. Briones has been with Paradiso 11 years.

Most people who go often to Paradiso have their own preferences for enchiladas, burritos and tacos. Fajitas are far and away the bestsellers, with 900 to 1,400 going out the kitchen each day. When Anvarina eats in one of the Paradiso restaurants in North Dakota, he orders the Santa Fe Salad. It's made with char-broiled mesquite chicken breast with greens, Mandarin oranges and red onion rings and poppy-seed dressing ($7.99).

Paradiso started in Grand Forks in 1975 and first was known as La Campana. Anvarina has been associated with the Mexican restaurant for 25 years. He also is general manager for the Paradiso restaurants in Fargo, Bismarck, Jamestown and Minot. With its renovation, Paradiso almost has doubled in size from 3,000 square feet to 5,500 square feet. There is space for parking in two lots. The restaurant has 140 full- and part-time employees. As many as 40 to 50 people show up every day to get a free dinner on their birthdays with proper identification. ¶

Paradiso's four North Dakota locations, including the one in Grand Forks, continue to operate.

3rd Street Slowly Builds Up Clientele

SEPTEMBER 7, 2005

In November, the 3rd Street Cafe will mark its first year of business. It's been a godsend to people working downtown who want a place to grab breakfast, and a convenience for people who like to meet for lunch or coffee downtown.

The cafe is in the location occupied, in pre-flood days, by the Dacotah, which had been a gathering place. Laurie Bergman, who owns and operates the 3rd Street Cafe, is excited about the way her business slowly is building.

Before she went full-time into the cafe business, she had worked 10 years as a car saleswoman. She knows it will take time and effort to keep building on volume. She offers breakfast specials between 7 and 9 A.M. during the week. She gives one free lunch a week in a drawing from business cards left by customers.

Improvements have been slow and steady. When it opened, for instance, Laurie had a friend use water paint to put the name of the cafe on the window, and it kept washing or fading off. Now, there is a permanent painting on the window and on the door. When it opened, there were wooden booths and tables. Now, there is a second row of booths that are soft and comfortable. Now, the tables have real cloths on them. There is a valance across the bottom of the front window. It has taken on the look of a place where you can find home cooking.

When I went in recently around noon, I ordered two scrambled eggs and an English muffin. The waitress said, "Sorry, we don't serve breakfast after eleven."

"OK," I said. "I'll have a cup of chicken dumpling soup and a half of a ham on rye sandwich" ($3.79). This actually was a better choice, anyway. The sandwich was small, but great. So was the spear of dill pickle that came with it. The chicken dumpling soup was Grade A, except that it was not hot enough. I found out later I really could have had breakfast. The waitress was new and didn't know.

I stopped in again for breakfast on my way to the Farmers Market on a Saturday. I knew 3rd Street Cafe serves breakfast until 2 P.M. on weekends. So I ordered two scrambled eggs, sausage and an English muffin. The waitress said, "Actually, we are out of English muffins." I said, "Fine. I will have wheat toast." The breakfast was good.

The cafe bakes its own pastries, and is proud of its pie, made by Laurie's mother, Marlene Hanson. The lemon pie, though, is a specialty prepared by Jenny Brandon of the waitstaff. Laurie also is enlisting her father, Duane Hanson, for soup making. With her brother and sister, Rick and Becky Hanson, Laurie has operated the Kegs Drive-In for the past four years.

Lunch or "dinner" specials are featured on weekdays in 3rd Street Cafe. Recent offerings have been hamburger macaroni hotdish with Jell-O and a roll ($4.89) and roast pork with applesauce and mashed potatoes and gravy, vegetable and roll ($6.49). With cooler weather, chili will be offered every day.

Dinner choices include chicken, walleye, shrimp, hamburger steak, liver and onions and chicken strips. Prices range from $6.19 to $6.49. And there are burgers and sandwiches.

Pluses include nice-quality napkins, nice table settings with underlining plates, and generous servings of vegetables and coleslaw. There are very nice large salt and pepper shakers made of glass with chrome tops. Service is not swift, but then, this is not fast food. Sometimes, food listed on the menu is not available. ❡

3rd Street Cafe closed and was replaced by
an Italian restaurant, Bella Vino.

Panda Buffet Features Unique Mongolian Stir-Fry

NOVEMBER 9, 2005

"Hi, how many?" asked the waitress at Panda Buffet on Columbia Road. It was a day in late October, and I was meeting Marge Leigh (ML) for lunch at this popular restaurant.

"Two," I said, as I sat down on one of six straight chairs to wait near the entry. Although the place was fairly full during the noon hour, it was relatively quiet. You could hear some music, probably Chinese, in the background.

ML arrived, and we had a table by the windows on the north side of the restaurant. We formed a game plan. I decided to go for the Mongolian stir-fry, which comes with the price of lunch ($6.49). ML said she would just pick and choose from the extensive buffet.

I waited briefly while the chef took ingredients selected by a customer ahead of me and fried them up on the stir-fry grill. The choices for combinations include lo mein noodles, bean sprouts, shredded cabbage, onion, pineapple, peppers, broccoli, crab meat, water chestnuts, squid, pea pods, tiny corn cobs and tofu. I chose greens, water chestnuts, pea pods, tofu and thinly sliced beef. Then, I watched the chef whip and turn and flip my selection onto a plate. He does it with flair.

You can choose your style of Mongolian dish, too. You can specify 1, 2 or 3 to tell the chef whether you want to go light, medium or strong on garlic, teriyaki and Mongolian sauce.

The chef at the stir-fry grill was kept busy with customers' orders. The average time to cook stir-fry for a customer is a minute and a half, according to John Chang, manager of Panda Buffet. Chang was born in mainland China but grew up in Virginia and New York. He has been in Grand Forks for two years. He enjoys his job, but he finds Grand Forks a "quiet place."

Most of the 10 employees in Panda Buffet are from China. Chang says, "Everyone here has legal status." And he notes that officers from the Border Patrol sometimes come in to eat.

Along with the stir-fry, I picked up some favorite foods from the buffet. There is a vast choice here of noodles, meatballs, vegetables, pickles, olives and mushrooms. You find pizza, french fries and wings, which ML said were very good. The layout is described as "International Super Buffet" and includes Chinese, American, Italian, Japanese and Mongolian barbecue.

Before we even started eating, we asked for extra napkins. Although Panda Buffet has moderately strong napkins, it takes more than one when you are into this heavy-duty eating. We ate; we tasted; we talked. And we went back for more. You can do that at buffets. You should take all you want, but eat all you take. There's no point in wasting food.

It's hard to resist one last trip to check out the dessert area. There, you find a little of everything: pie, bars, puddings, gelatin, cream

puffs, éclairs, macaroons, crescent moon and almond cookies. I took two of the almond cookies. They are slightly sweet sugar cookies with an almond on top.

Panda Buffet includes all-you-can-eat lobster for $9.99 on its buffet from 4 to 10 P.M. Friday and Saturday. The lunch buffet is served daily between 11 A.M. and 4 P.M. at $6.49 for adults and 40 cents a year for children younger than 12. The dinner buffet runs from 4 to 10 P.M., for $8.99 and 50 cents per year for children 12 and younger.

The pluses at Panda Buffet include the wide array of food and the option of having stir-fry prepared as you watch. You can select a healthful meal, and you also can indulge in some favorite foods. Service is quite good. It's an everyday kind of place. Also on the plus side, I was asked only twice on a second visit to Panda Buffet if everything was OK. The servers seem energetic and friendly. They look good in white shirts with black vests and trousers.

On the minus side, the restaurant seems a little untidy. There are weeds growing alongside the building. Inside, near the entry, there is a station for collecting dirty dishes, and here you see cleaning supplies and rags that could better be kept out of sight. And in the women's restroom, there are more cleaning supplies sitting around. It would be better to keep them in a closet or cupboard.

While there is a fork and spoon wrapped up in a napkin for each customer, there are no knives. And a knife would be handy for some of the items, such as the long green beans that are too crisp to cut with a fork. True, there are chopsticks in a container. And some day, I am going to master the fine art of using them. ¶

Panda International Super Buffet continues to operate in Grand Forks.

Suite 49 Establishes Itself as a Force in Less than a Year

NOVEMBER 23, 2005

If memory serves, the halibut served by the Golden Hour, a popular downtown restaurant that closed years ago, had a crunchy golden crust. And the Golden Hour halibut that now appears on the dinner menu in Suite 49 in Grand Forks is pretty close to that prepared by Mrs. Oliver long ago.

I couldn't resist ordering the halibut ($14.95) when I went to dinner at Suite 49 earlier in No-

vember. I was with Donna McEnroe (DM), who had a half-order of crab legs ($18), and Eleanore McEnroe (EM), who ordered shrimp alla diavolo ($14.95). The entree is a new item among the 15 choices for pasta.

Dinner at Suite 49 is an upscale experience because of the full menu of unique offerings. With dinner entrees, you get a choice of soup or salad, a vegetable and your choice of roasted herb, horseradish mashed or baked potato.

The strength of this dinner is that the salad is excellent, and the vegetable of the day is prepared to order. The bread that comes with it is toasted and thinly sliced focaccia. And the potatoes are above average. I once tried to eat a couple bites of the horseradish mashed potatoes and couldn't resist finishing the whole serving.

It's actually hard to decide what to order because the menu is inviting, with clever—but not too clever—names for various items. Chef Nathan Sheppard offers, for example, Drunken Rooster, Pork Chop Carambola and a New Walleye Scampi. There's an 8-ounce filet and a 16-ounce ribeye, too, and steaks have been a popular choice of Suite 49 customers.

Suite 49 is sleek and streamlined-looking, with 18 flat-screen plasma televisions. There are big, roomy black booths and tables. When it opened a year ago in December, Suite 49 was projecting a sports bar image. But it has developed as more of a dining and entertainment center, according to Eric Martz, general manager.

Suite 49 is open Tuesday through Saturday. There also is a private dining room. Proximity to Ralph Engelstad Arena means there is a ready-made crowd whenever there are special events or games.

In its first year, Suite 49 has established itself as a place for lunch, dinner and evening entertainment. There are people who go for lunch of the white chili, which always is on the menu, and a salad. Lunch fare includes a new Thai chicken salad, blue chip taco salad and a new salmon and avocado salad. Beef or bison burgers are offered in various forms. Blueberry bread pudding and Sailor Jerry spiced rum apple crisp are among the dessert offerings.

The ready welcome you get in the entry is another strength of Suite 49. Along with all the pluses, though, there are minuses. While we enjoyed our waiter, Bobby, there was some confusion about our orders. This was not his fault. It happens because the waiter takes the order you give him on an electronic gadget and it goes right into the kitchen. This is good. It saves time. It was a problem, though, because a different server delivers the order.

DM had asked if her crab could be removed from the shells, and Bobby said yes. When the order arrived, the server was not aware of the earlier conversation. I had asked if I could substitute soup for a potato and was told I could. When I got home and re-read my bill, I could see I paid extra for it.

No big deal. Still, it was a little disconcerting. Also, I felt a tad rushed. When I go out to a full dinner, I like to take my time and pace the meal. I like to wait until everyone is finished before the plates are cleared. And yes, I realize there are some people who want them whisked away.

I will go back to Suite 49 as soon as a friend suggests it because overall I like the unique menu that an independent restaurant offers. All in all, Suite 49 offers an above-average eating experience. ❡

Boot Marches Through 52 Years of Business in Grand Forks

JANUARY 25, 2006

It was 6:30 P.M. on a Friday evening in January, and I was meeting some friends at the Bronze Boot. We were taking our chances at seating. The Boot doesn't take reservations, except for groups of six or more. Fortunately, it didn't take long until we had a table near the open-pit broiler.

The fact that the Bronze Boot is packed on weekends is a testimony to the steaks and seafood it serves. The supper club with a boot on the top was established in 1954, and it has been in business longer than any other restaurant in Grand Forks. It has become a legend, like Whitey's of East Grand Forks, which is the granddaddy of all area restaurants.

Service was quick, but we weren't rushed. Our waitress, Roxi, gave us a chance to visit and study the menu. There was fresh Atlantic salmon, halibut, jumbo shrimp, shrimp David, walleye pike, jumbo sea scallops and Alaska king crab. A section of "Stage Coach Specialties" included center-cut pork chops, pork ribs, teriyaki chicken, tom turkey dinner, ground sirloin steak, veal cutlet, fried chicken and vegetable lasagna.

Plenty of choices, but my mind was made up before I sat down. I had eyes only for the steaks, and I knew I wanted the 4-ounce tenderloin, which I have eaten before at the Boot. All the steaks are cut in-house. I ordered it medium, and it was excellent, as always. The dinner ($14.25) includes a choice of tomato juice or soup and salad. I had tomato juice and a spinach salad.

I was eating with Jan and Earl Strinden (JS and ES) and Vonnie Goodman (VG). JS and VG also had the 4-ounce tenderloin, and ES had center-cut pork chops served with applesauce (12.95).

We enjoyed the bread basket that came soon after we were seated. We dug under the big white buns on top to get the thin, toasted garlic bread below. We were well pleased with the quality of the food. I thought the spinach salad was especially good with its light dressing that included bacon bits. We reminisced about the early years of the Bronze Boot in Grand Forks. ES was saying, "This is still such a good place to go. The soup is good. The pork chops are good."

The Boot is one of my favorite places for dinner because of the steak and seafood. You get a complete meal—and a nutritious meal. I like the cheery ambience and the hustle and bustle on weekends. I also like having a quick burger in the lounge before a hockey game.

The Boot still serves Pete's Special, named after the late Pete Smith. It's a half-pound bacon cheeseburger with fries, soup or salad ($6.75).

Besides dinners, the Bronze Boot serves a smorgasbord-style lunch on weekdays. Those who want the full buffet with three entrees pay $6.25, and those who want only one entree or meat pay $5.55.

The Bronze Boot has an area for hanging coats—so important in this climate—and a waiting area at the entryway. Some patrons wait in the lounge, where they also can order food. The place has a classic look and is decorated in tones of deep green and mauve. ¶

The Bronze Boot closed in May 2012, after Don Shields, director of the Grand Forks Public Health Department, discovered water leaking in several areas of the restaurant. At that time, Shields told the Grand Forks Herald *that he hoped the restaurant would be able to reopen. "It's a long-term Grand Forks institution," said Shields. "The steaks are great."*

Capone's Puts the G in G-Man

FEBRUARY 1, 2006

When I went to Capone's for lunch with Vonnie Goodman (VG), we were greeted at the door by a "G-Man," and welcomed inside Capone's new restaurant on Gateway Drive by another gunman. By the time we were seated by a young woman wearing flapper dress and lots of beads, we knew we were having fun.

Capone's opened on the birthday of Al Capone—Jan. 17—and is currently serving only lunch, with plans to serve multi-course dinners soon.

I ordered what is called Uncle Bit's Favorite Italian Beef Sandwich ($8.99), a generous serving of beef cut thin and piled high on Italian bread. It was nicely garnished and finished off with a spring onion on top—a trademark of Chef Liz Stempinski. And since soup is one of her specialties, I ordered a cup of white chili soup and found it up to expectations.

VG ordered an Italian Trio Salad ($12.99) that came with beef, sausage, green peppers, onions, mushrooms, black olives and parmesan cheese. With it, she had a raspberry vinaigrette that was especially piquant and thicker than most vinaigrettes. This is one of Capone's signature dishes.

Lunch choices include pastas and salads. Since we were exploring the menu, we went for desserts, including a mango cheesecake and spumoni.

Our service was good and fast. VG commented on the food being piping hot. All the while, we were enjoying the music in the background that helped set the scene of a place full of Chicago gunmen.

Capone's reflects the thought that has gone into every phase of the ambience and the menu. The restaurant is decorated with authentic family photos, including some of Stempinski's grandfather, who was a chef in Chicago. On one wall at the rear of the dining room there is a collection of sheet music from the 1920s and 1930s.

It adds up to an atmosphere conducive for having fun and eating Italian food.

The entrees include king crab served with drawn lemon butter on the side ($36.99) and another called Pretty Boy's Porterhouse, which is a 24-ounce version with crispy roasted red potatoes ($36.99). Then there's Lucky Luciano's Chicken, served with asparagus and hollandaise sauce ($29.99). Scallop cakes and pork tenderloin dinners are also on the menu ($32.99). Other entrees are baby back ribs and seafood pasta parmesano ($36.99).

The restaurant is planning a Valentine dinner, by reservation only, that will feature a reenactment of the St. Valentine's Day Massacre in Chicago. ❡

Sirloin Tips Top Menu at Al's Grill

MARCH 1, 2006

People tend to visit with other people at nearby tables in Al's Grill on South Washington Street. Herb Seaver of Larimore, N.D., told me he likes everything on

the menu—especially the deluxe sirloin tips. Seaver and his wife, Clara Lou, stop in Al's often, and she orders broiled walleye.

Al's Grill is a friendly sort of

place that in a year and a half since opening has become a popular spot to eat for people who want good food and no frills at reasonable prices.

My most recent visit to Al's Grill was on a Saturday, when I had lunch with Donna McEnroe (DM), Ellen McKinnon (EM) and Donna Gillig (DG). DM ordered a broiled walleye platter ($10.95), which comes with choice of potato, coleslaw and a roll. EM ordered a cup of wild rice soup ($2.25) and a hard roll (35 cents). DG ordered a taco salad ($6.50), and I chose a half Reuben sandwich ($4) with a cup of wild rice soup.

Our service was good. The food came to the table as it was ready, not all at once, which often means some is cold. The walleye is excellent at Al's, and DM had a unique serving of whole red potatoes in a white cream sauce. With it, coleslaw with a vinaigrette dressing. That is the way coleslaw should be made.

When EM's soup arrived, we found out the hard roll is really soft. It has a quality of the brown-and-serve rolls we used to make at home, but bigger and better. DG's taco salad was served on a plate big enough to be a platter and was presented with plenty of eye appeal and tostado chips arranged around the edge.

The Reuben sandwich was one of the best I have eaten in a restaurant. No, make that the best. The corned beef was lean and of good quality, and it was piled thick with just the right amount of sauerkraut. The bread was toasted and had a nice taste of caraway.

Al's Grill is basic and unpretentious but still inviting. Among the pluses are the napkins of fairly good quality, the coleslaw and the casual ambience. Among the minuses: It can be cold sitting near the entryway. The silverware is minimal. When I made that comment, one of my friends said, "At least it isn't plastic." ❡

Al's Grill continues to operate in Grand Forks at 3615 Gateway Drive.

Toasted Frog Takes Its Place in Downtown

JUNE 7, 2006

We ordered a side of fiddlehead fern and a side of garlic wasabi mashed potatoes along with a pheasant lavosh. Then, we sat back and studied the Toasted Frog, which has been open slightly more than a month in downtown Grand Forks.

I was eating out with Katie David (KD), and we agreed the Toasted Frog is indeed a unique place for casual dining—a notch or two above the same old places. It is unique because of the menu that suits the customer who wants a beer and wings as well as those who want a full dinner. And it's unique because of the artsy, trendy decor.

And yes, there are frog legs on the menu. They are served with buffalo sauce ($10). There are also sautéed clams, fried oysters and shrimp skewers.

The fiddleheads, not usually found on menus in this area, were excellent. So, too, the mashed potatoes. The pheasant lavosh ($15) with its light cracker crust was delicious. The tender pheasant was enhanced with red onion and roasted red peppers in a light cheese topping. The serving was enough for KD and me, with the leftover portion going home in a takeout box.

The Toasted Frog also has an open-faced pheasant melt ($10) sandwich. All sandwiches are served with french fries or sweet potato fries. Seven wood-fired pizzas are on the menu, including a Rome Dakota version with olive oil, garlic, basil, artichoke hearts, sun-dried tomatoes and marinated pheasant.

The menu, with a frog watermark on each of the two pages, lists fish tacos, lobster tail, walleye fingers, Angus burgers and buffalo wings. It's not redundant or complicated, and that's a plus.

Our server, Laura Holt, made the outing pleasant with her good humor and helpfulness. The staff of 16 seems friendly. They wear khaki trousers and black shirts with Toasted Frog insignias beneath long black aprons tied at the waist. The music was not too loud, but it was enough to mute conversations at nearby tables.

It seemed the opening of the Toasted Frog was a long time coming. It is good to have the corner of Second Avenue North and North Third Street, which used to house Lola's, open and busy again. Those who enjoyed Lola's are finding their way back to the Frog.

The Toasted Frog retains some of the best features of Lola's. The bar, designed by David Badman, now is in the rear and faces the open kitchen, where patrons can watch the chefs in white at work. The private dining room still is there. So, too, is the room-sized wine cellar. The bar along the side and the private booths are there. Contemporary artwork enriches the restaurant, and the tiny hanging lamps add a dramatic touch. The old wood floors have been replaced by light wood. There is a certain charm about this old building with its high ceilings and an old brick wall.

The owners of the Toasted Frog seem pleased with initial response to their business. Both Jon Holth and Shawn Clapp had worked at Sanders 1907 and were involved in operation of the dining room in the restored Hotel Donaldson in downtown Fargo.

The two have created an inviting, very appealing spot that begins with unusual appetizers and winds up with desserts including a pear pie that is served on a pizza crust and includes caramel sauce over cinnamon ice cream.

Customers at Toasted Frog must be 21 and older. Smoking is allowed in the restaurant after 9 P.M. ❡

Dinner at Capone's:
A Rare Seven-Course Production

SEPTEMBER 13, 2006

These days, restaurants are doing more microwaving and less cooking. So it is good once in a while to find a place where you can have a complete meal served in several courses. And this is what we found on a recent Saturday evening at Capone's. I was with my daughter Gail (DG), and we enjoyed a leisurely meal served in unhurried courses. I ordered one of the specials for the evening—a combination of grilled shrimp on skewers and a 6-ounce tenderloin. DG ordered Canadian walleye.

We started with a choice of soups. DG had chicken wild rice soup, which she rated excellent. My sweet potato was some of the best ever. For salads, we had our choice of dressing, with an Italian spring mix salad that was a cut above those usually served. The greens and tomato wedges were fresh. It was not one of those package mixes. And then there was a small loaf of warm rosemary garlic bread served with three dipping sauces. The bread was extra good.

Next came a lemon sorbet served with a mint leaf . . . to cleanse the palate.

We were into the meal and enjoying a chance to visit in an unhurried atmosphere. There were several tables of diners. There were lit candles in Chianti wine bottles on each table. The music was soft, and the lights were low. We had our choice of a glass of house wine or other beverage.

Our main course arrived. DG's walleye was well-seasoned and had a nice golden crust even though it was broiled. My steak arrived on a bed of wild rice and with two skewers of four grilled shrimp on each. With it was a special mango sauce. We shared the shrimp, which were the highlight of the meal. The steak was good.

We were fairly well-sated before

the dessert arrived, but it was one you could not shove aside. It was a small and wonderful wedge of layered chocolate cake, presented with a small chocolate machine gun and Port wine. I learned later the guns are made from a specially designed mold. And the Port is made by the local Vintner's Cellar. Our check for the two dinners was $69.53.

Capone's opened Jan. 17—Al Capone's birthday. The gangster theme is carried out in the decor as well as by the style of service and the wording of the menu. Our server used "gangster speak" when she took our order. She said "youse guys" and things such as that. She was wearing clothing from the Capone era, which servers find in a big wardrobe in a back room. They are dressed in characters such as Dora the Doll, singer Vicki Pipes and Jenny Gams, the dancer. Customers are greeted by roaming gangsters shouldering guns, who also help clear tables.

There was a big bathtub of gurgling "hootch" coming out of a brass still in the entryway. The unusual theme is carried out well and makes Capone's a fun place. It's there. You can enjoy it, but it doesn't overwhelm you.

Capone's also serves lunch with excellent soups and unusual sandwiches. The high noon menu features lunches at $5.95 and less. Dinner begins at 5 P.M. and ends at 8:30 or whenever the last customer arrives. It's closed Sunday and Monday.

Liz Stempinski, owner and executive chef, says business was superslow this summer. She says it's picking up with the opening of schools and UND. While the dinner menu is pricey, she points out the several courses and wine included. The menu also features an air-dried and cured beef bresaola and beer or other beverages for two at $29.99. And for $9.99 during dinner hours, Capone's serves soup, salad and bread with a dipping sauce.

Along with the pluses, there were a few minuses. The wild rice with the main course seemed overcooked and somewhat soft and mushy. However, the carrots with the entree more than made up for that. The service mostly was good, but we were without forks for our dessert for quite a while. The pluses include the extra care in presentation of each course and the sauces that flow from the kitchen, and an adequate and clean restroom. ¶

Capone's closed in 2007 and became the new location of Al's Grill, still currently in business.

Golden Corral Buffet and Grill Offers Endless Selections

MARCH 28, 2007

A man from Red Lake Falls, Minn., sat down at the table next to me in the new Golden Corral Buffet and Grill. He had his plate piled high, and he grinned as he said to his wife, "Too bad I couldn't find anything I liked."

Since the tables are so close together, we struck up a conversation about the seemingly unending array of food in one of the newest and largest eating establishments in Grand Forks. Like the new Texas Roadhouse across 32nd Avenue South, the Golden Corral has been drawing crowds of people wanting to give any new place a try. One day since it opened

in February, there were close to 3,000 people in and out.

The parking lot was almost full when I went in for a late lunch on a Friday. Once inside, I noticed a sign that said, "No checks." Another sign said, "Please, no sharing." As you enter the Golden Corral, you are asked what you want to drink. Then you move along and when you pay, your beverage is added to the cost of the buffet.

After paying, I was seated in one of the four large dining areas and given a card saying Jessica would be serving me. She brought me silverware of decent quality, wrapped in a substantial paper napkin, and a serviceable plastic plate, then turned me loose to visit the huge buffet, which is set up as a market.

There are separate areas of picnics and salads, soup, Pagoda Far East, fresh-carved meat, a steak dinner buffet, a Brass Bell bakery and dessert cafe.

The salad bar was the most extensive I have seen for a long time. The food was fresh and inviting, although at the end of a very busy lunch hour, some of it was a tad messy. I was especially impressed by the freshly cut cantaloupe and the pine nuts among the salad offerings. The cottage cheese was exceptional. And the noodles in the chicken soup were thick and homemade.

After a salad course, which should have been enough, I went back and tried some very tasty pulled pork with a couple of Brussels sprouts, done just right. Since I saw so many children enjoying soft-serve, I went back for a taste of that. And then I couldn't resist tasting some blueberry pie. I think I gained 2 pounds.

It was my good fortune to meet Erin Nagle (EN) in the buffet line. She's a senior at Red River High School and told me it was her third trip to Golden Corral. She likes the variety and the fact that everything is so fresh. EN goes for the barbecued chicken and the mashed potatoes, which are peeled and cooked and mashed on the premises. She says they taste like the ones her grandmother makes. But "breakfast is the best," she said.

Breakfast is $7.39, lunch is $6.99 and dinner is $9.79. You can get buffet to go by the bag for $3.99 a pound. There is a 50-cent lunch and $1 dinner discount for seniors. Kids buffet is $3.97 and $4.99. Seniors who show up for the early bird hours of 1:30 to 3:30 P.M. get a free beverage. ❡

Golden Corral no longer operates in Grand Forks.

North Side Cafe Features More than Everyday Cooking

SEPTEMBER 19, 2007

Hoa Rodriguez, who operates the new North Side Cafe on Gateway Drive, claims she makes the best egg rolls in town. She makes 300 of them Wednesday evenings for the Thursday special of egg rolls and chow mein. In the course of a week, she often makes between 700 and 800 egg rolls to fill special orders and meet the restaurant's needs.

Her plump egg rolls are filled with ground beef, celery, onion, carrots and cabbage that she chops in the cafe's gleaming new kitchen. They are encased in an eggshell wrap and come fresh from the deep fryer. Unlike most egg rolls of today, they have never been frozen.

When Rodriguez told me about her egg rolls, I ordered a couple of them for a trial. I was eating with the Rev. William Sherman (WS) and Delores Hackenberg (DH). Before long, the egg rolls came out of the kitchen accompanied by a serving of a mild plum sauce. DH and I gave an approving nod, and WS said he would vouch for Hoa's claim they are good.

The taste test was on a Wednesday in September. On Thursday, I went back for the luncheon special of egg roll and chicken chow mein ($5.95) and found it to be substantial. The chicken is nice and tender and the celery and cabbage slices large enough to be discernible.

The dish tends to be bland, but you easily can heighten the taste by adding soy sauce that comes along on the side. I also asked for some hot mustard to go with my egg roll. And I quickly found out that a little touch of this mustard is more than enough. It was a good thing Rodriguez warned that it is "hot-hot-hot."

The cafe has a menu similar to other truck stop or travel restaurants near Interstate 29. Breakfast offerings are extensive and are served all day. Dinners include liver and onion ($7.75) and a chicken-fried steak dinner topped with white gravy ($7.95). There are hamburgers and buffalo burgers. The sandwich list includes hot beef, turkey or pork sandwiches served with mashed potatoes and gravy or french fries ($5.95). Nine salads on the menu are served with dinner rolls and butter.

The servers wear crisp white shirts and black trousers, and the staff is the strength of the North Side restaurant. So, too, is the presence of Rodriguez, who greets and talks to customers and keeps an eye on everything. She bakes carrot cake and makes bread pudding once a week along with the pies she turns out almost daily.

The vegetable beef soup is as good as any I've ever eaten. I tried a cup of it on my first of three visits and wished I had ordered a bowl. The beef was lean and tender. There was a nice tomato base to it, and fresh-tasting green beans, corn, celery and carrots.

With all the pluses, there are a few minuses. The napkins wrapped around the tableware are very thin and small. The glasses are plastic. Service is on the slow side at times, although the waitresses work together to keep up. An orange slice or some garnish would add appeal to breakfast plates. ❡

North Side Cafe continues to operate in Grand Forks.

Blue Moose's Creative Menu Changes with the Seasons

SEPTEMBER 26, 2007

Home-style roast beef dinners and sandwiches and cheese fondue will be newcomers to the Blue Moose menu with the changing season. The bar and grill on res-

taurant row in East Grand Forks has a unique menu that seems to consistently draw good business for lunch as well as for dinner, with items such as Norwegian barbecued ribs with a sweet, smoky but mild sauce.

The restaurant was remodeled earlier this year and now is more inviting. Two blue moose grace a nicely landscaped area at the Second Street entrance. On the other side, an outdoor balcony overlooks the Red River. Inside, the decor still is north woods style. The interior is finished with logs and light wood.

Our group of past and present neighbors recently chose the Moose for lunch. The soups for the day were French onion, which always is available, along with beef-barley and pork and bean soup. I chose the beef-barley soup with something called buffalo salad, and fruit. Instead of the buffalo meat I was expecting, it turned out to be buffalo-wings-style chicken. The soup I had was rich in flavor but oily on top.

I was sitting next to Marilyn Lundberg (ML) and Jan Wendell (JW), who were impressed by the coarse Italian ciabatta bread on which JW's walleye sandwich was served. And JW, who doesn't usually eat all the bread, finished every bit of it. ML ordered a Sunset Lime Chicken salad, which she had tried at a previous trip to the Moose. She likes the tangy lime cilantro marinade and the lime tortilla chips that go with it.

All in all, the Moose was a good choice for lunch. Everyone seemed well satisfied. I especially like the way my lunch was presented on a triangle-shaped plate. The place rates an A for coming up with minidesserts as a choice in the lunch combos.

Along with the pluses, there are some minuses. The variety and the creativity are strengths of the new menu, but it is enormous, and hard to figure everything out at first reading. For years, the Moose had a shorter menu, in a newspaper format. Our group of eight was seated in the new lounge area, but unfortunately, we were right next to the door. The breeze was too cool when people came in or out of the balcony. And there were the inevitable flies of September. Before long, the door will be closed for the winter and shouldn't be a problem.

The Moose has become an institution in East Grand Forks, along with Whitey's. The Moose started out on the south side of DeMers Avenue, but it had to move after the

Flood of 1997, closing for 40 days and 40 nights, owner-manager Dave Homstad said. "They were building the dike on the wrong side of us." The whole building—except for the kitchen—then was moved to its present location.

The location along restaurant row has been good for the Blue Moose. Homstad credits some of the good business from the coming of Cabela's to East Grand Forks. He also is looking forward to business that should come from the new theater operation in the nearby mall. ¶

New Bowl Meals Prove to Be Very Popular at KFC

FEBRUARY 13, 2008

I pulled in between two red pickups in the parking lot of KFC, or Kentucky Fried Chicken, on South Washington Street and went inside to eat dinner around 2 P.M. on a recent Sunday. I was thinking of the bowl meals I have seen advertised, but I was drawn to a Value Meal that I could tailor to suit my fancy. I ordered a piece of chicken breast with an extra-crispy crust and sides of mashed potatoes and gravy and coleslaw. Also included was a baking powder biscuit with tiny packets of margarine and honey. I had wa-ter for my beverage. The cost was $4.80 including tax.

Service was quick. I picked up my plastic tableware and napkins and chose one of two tall tables with high-stool chairs in the newly refurbished dining area. People were coming in and out, picking up buckets of chicken and bags of chicken wings. The people eating inside were having full meals. At one table, two young men were sharing a bucket of wings.

My food was good. It was hot. I soon discovered I would rather have plain crust than crispy, so

I peeled the crisp coating away from the chicken. The chicken was moist, tender and very tasty. The mashed potatoes and gravy were perfect, and the portion was adequate. The coleslaw was the best I have run across. The cabbage was finely chopped with a few carrots. The vinegar and oil dressing is made with sugar and a tad of Miracle Whip, and there was a nice taste of celery seed. However, the biscuit was not as good as it looked. While it was golden brown, it still seemed doughy on the inside.

KFC has been in Grand Forks since 1966 and is one of 5,000 in the U.S. And there are KFCs all over the world. Manager Rick Hanson says the relatively new bowl meals are very popular. KFC sells 75 to 80 of them daily. They are meals in a bowl layered with the customer's choice of potatoes, corn, chicken, gravy and cheese. Other popular items are chicken strips and boneless wings, and pot pies sell well in cold weather.

Takeout an is important part of the business. Eight-piece chicken meals are much in demand. The chicken goes out for $10.49, or $17.99 when it includes side orders and biscuits. The side choices are potatoes, veggies, baked beans and coleslaw.

A refurbishing of the Washington Street KFC was completed in September. The exterior is done in earth tones of brown and tan with the bright red and blue accents of KFC now used worldwide. Inside, the brown, beige and gold theme is used, with a few red booths in the corner of the light and bright seating area that is surrounded by large paneled windows.

The local KFC has 34 full- and part-time employees. The people at the counter wear red and blue shirts, and their hair is restrained by caps. Tables were being wiped regularly with a sanitizer solution, helping to create a clean feel in the dining area. Kentucky Fried Chicken was founded by Colonel Harland Sanders in 1952 and has become a well-known institution with headquarters in Louisville, Kentucky. ❡

KFC continues to operate in Grand Forks.

Tavern United Would Make an English Pub Proud

FEBRUARY 20, 2008

It's rather dark inside Tavern United in Grand Forks' new Canad Inn, and there are small, skinny hanging lamps here and there. You can settle in wherever you feel comfortable. So, three of us found a table and looked over the menu recently on a Saturday evening. We wanted to try some of the English pub fare offered in one of three separate restaurants in the big Canad Inn of Grand Forks.

Our waitress, who was wearing a skirt that looked like a kilt, was very helpful. She answered our questions about the English Toasties (toasted sandwiches) and English Classic entrees on the menu and gave us plenty of time to make up our minds.

I toyed with the idea of ordering the Yorkshire Pudding Bowl, but I tried that once on a trip to England and didn't care much for it. So, I figured it might be too English. There also was Molly Malone's Meatloaf and O'Malley's Beef Stew.

I ended up ordering Bailey's Bangers and Mash. This got me a couple of banger sausages on a bed of garlic red-skinned smashed potatoes with a brown onion gravy and the chef's vegetable of the day. That turned out to be a nice serving of broccoli that was done just right. All of this was $8, and it was an ample meal.

My friends tried Beer Battered Halibut and Chips and a Classic Reuben sandwich from the English Toasties section of the menu. The halibut was reminiscent of that served years ago by Mrs. Oliver in the downtown Golden Hour Cafe. The English cut chips that came with it would be called french fries by most of us; but these had a slightly different, wide cut. The halibut was $14, but as suggested on the menu, we got a half-order for $10, and that was a large serving.

The corned beef was piled high, as the menu promised, on the Classic Reuben sandwich, and the marble rye bread was toasted to a golden crisp. It came with English cut chips and a tossed salad ($9).

Tavern United goes an extra step in its presentation of food. My plate of bangers and mashed potatoes was decorated with a sprig of rosemary and a few thin slices of red cabbage to make it more inviting. The chips and halibut came in a basket with a lining of waxed paper that had a newspaper pattern on it, thus carrying out the British tradition of serving fish and chips wrapped in a newspaper.

Dining is informal, and items from the pub snacks menu seem to be popular. Choices on the long list include baby calamari, miniburger stacks, bite-sized morsels of halibut and mussels in a spicy chipotle sauce.

Tavern United is large, with seating around the bar as well as in an area where there are dart and pool games going on in the evening. Background music is classic rock, played through a satellite radio system.

And since it's a pub, the ales and beers are important. Tavern United serves Guinness, Smithwick's and Samuel Adams ales and others in schooners and pints. The establishment also boasts the coldest beer in North Dakota, which was a pilot project of Coors in Canada.

Since its opening last year, the Pub has become a well-known gathering place. In good weather, many customers prefer sitting out in front on the patio area. Along with Tavern United, the Canad Inn also houses Aaltos Family Garden Buffet and 'l Bistro Mediterranean eatery. ❡

Tavern United, a small chain based in Canada,
continues to operate in Grand Forks.

Greater Grand Forks Offers Diners a Variety of Restaurants

MARCH 26, 2008

"What's your favorite restaurant?"

That's the question I get fairly often from readers of the Eatbeat. And I am at a loss to name any one favorite place. It depends on what I am seeking. I like the light breakfast at Perkins. I would go to Al's for meatloaf and to North Side Cafe for egg rolls. I think the liver pâté at Whitey's is very good. I like the waiters at Sanders. Very proper, you know. 'l Bistro at Canad Inn has some very nice items. I could go on and on.

Grand Forks has an eclectic array of eating places. And I try to describe them so that readers can get an idea of the choices. I also describe restaurants in area towns and sometimes in cities I visit on my travels.

In the past, I have said this is not New York City, and I am not a critic. This is Grand Forks, and I am a reporter. I have attended sessions on writing reviews at conventions of newspaper food editors. I regularly read restaurant reviews in major newspapers.

In the beginning, this restaurant column was called Out to Lunch. Then, it branched out into the Eatbeat. It started out in the food section and moved briefly to the entertainment section. And in recent years, it is back on the Wednesday food page.

I visit restaurants at my own personal expense. Sometimes, owners offer to take my check, but I do not accept free meals or free food. When I explain that would not be professional and would not leave me feeling free to write what I think, they say they understand. They usually appreciate that.

First of all, I concentrate on the food. I try to describe the taste and the quality. I take note of the place and describe the ambience and the surroundings. I like to tell of the specials. I often check the restroom because I think it indicates the condition of the establishment. I try to point out the pluses and minuses of a visit to each restaurant.

Then, after I have eaten, I often talk to the manager or call them on the telephone. That way I am sure of my impressions, and I can get the facts about the staff and the business. Sometimes, these visits turn up interesting sidelights on the restaurant or the people involved in it.

Friends and acquaintances often talk of things they like or dislike about restaurants. One friend goes crazy when she sees a restaurant employee wipe the seat of a booth or a chair and then use the same cloth to wipe the table. Some people don't like to be called "you guys." Some people complain about food not being hot enough. At times, it is annoying when diners are asked over and over again if everything is all right. One man I know is put off by servers who

have hair flowing all over with no attempt at restraints. He likes a cap or a ponytail.

Some of my pet peeves are plastic glasses that have grown weary from the dishwasher and napkins that are so skimpy it takes four or five to do the job of one good-quality napkin. I like fairly good quality tableware. It doesn't have to be Royal Danish silver, though.

Most servers are more than considerate. Most of them are quite friendly and go the extra mile. They split orders. They hand out take-home boxes. Servers have their wish lists, too. They would like it if people would pay attention when they describe the specials and not keep asking over and over again. They would like people to order, and not to try to be comedians. They appreciate proper tips. One local restaurateur says the 10 percent tipper is a vanishing breed. Guides talk of 20 percent tips, but 15 percent seems not too shabby around here. ❡

Tasty Smoked Salmon Salad Draws People to Suite 49

OCTOBER 1, 2008

Salmon and avocado salad draws me back to Suite 49, near Ralph Engelstad Arena. This salad is made with tossed greens and laced with artichoke hearts, capers and slices of avocados. Then it's topped with the house smoked salmon and served with a choice of dressing. I like the raspberry vinaigrette, although I notice others choose honey mustard, ranch or French.

The full salad is $9. Half a salad is $6, and I find that just the right amount—especially if you order a side of focaccia bread for 50 cents.

Suite 49 has been part of the Grand Forks restaurant scene for the past four years. It opened around the time of the World Juniors Hockey Tournament in 2005. And this fall, Chef Nathan Sheppard is making seasonal changes in the menu. He is going into comfort food that he thinks most people identify with and appreciate when the days get colder. One

is a Cuban sandwich made with pulled pork and topped with tarragon coleslaw. It's designed to be a balance of crunchy and sweet. He also will bring on a baked macaroni and cheese dish that will be basic but still upscale. He promises it will be "warm and gooey" with a three-cheese sauce tossed with the noodles, and a crisp cheddar and mozzarella topping.

Sheppard also is redoing some Suite 49 classics such as cedar plank roasted salmon, which will have a tarragon dill crème fraiche sauce. He is coming up with totally different desserts, including Kaffir lime panna cotta. And he is testing a chocolate Irish cream cake that will be heavy and dense.

Sheppard has a kitchen staff of 12. A graduate of Le Cordon Bleu in Portland, Ore., he is a native of Grand Forks and returned here for the opening of Suite 49. After two years, he moved to the Canad Inn but came back to Suite 49, where he has fewer administrative duties and can spend more time concentrating on the cuisine.

Suite 49 is long on appetizers, with lettuce wraps ($9) being one of the most popular. They are filling but not heavy appetizers and are a nice snack any time of the day.

Lunch is served from 11 A.M. until 4 P.M., with most of the items available at any time. The regular fare includes beef or bison burgers and lavosh. Sandwiches are served with lettuce, tomato, onion and a pickle spear as well as the restaurant's beer-battered french fries.

Patronage at Suite 49 varies. Jessie Thorson, general manager, said events at Engelstad Arena bring brisk business, and business comes from the area developing around the restaurant. Reservations are taken for parties of 10 or more in the party rooms before events, such as Sioux hockey games. ❡

Suite 49 closed for business in December 2008.

People Know Their Dumplings at Viking, Minn., Restaurant

SEPTEMBER 16, 2009

VIKING, Minn.—My project on the first Friday in September was to find my way here and eat the potato dumplings recommended recently by an Eatbeat reader. It was a beautiful, sunny day, and I had no trouble following state Highway 220 north out of East Grand Forks to Alvarado, Minn., where I turned east on state Highway 1 and made it to Warren, Minn.

And then, I couldn't figure out the little squiggles on the map. So I stopped in a gas station and learned that you go about 10 miles east of Warren on Marshall

County Road 10, and then you see a green sign that points to Viking. You take this winding stretch of road a couple of miles and find yourself in a village of maybe 100 people.

Welcome to Viking!

Viking Diner and Antiques was ringed with cars by 11 A.M. on a Friday morning. I knew I was in the right place. There were people at a dozen tables, serious about eating dumplings. I found a place at a long table where four people were sitting. I nodded. They nodded. Then, Ray and Joyce Olson (RO and JO) from Thief River Falls came and sat across from me.

The Olsons know their dumplings. They come here every other week or so, JO said. "It's something to do." She suggested the dumpling tastes better if you use butter that comes in a 1-inch cube in a little cup. She also uses salt and pepper.

That made a difference. The dumplings were good. I guess they are sort of like soul food for those who have roots in this Norwegian community. Some order side pork with it, others bacon. The dumplings are good-sized—bigger than a tennis ball but smaller than a softball.

A dumpling costs $2. Side pork, ham or bacon is $2. Eat one with meat, and you should be set for the day. But I ended up trying one of three desserts, just for good measure. I decided on a piece of raspberry cheesecake. I was just going to taste it, but it was so good, I ate the whole thing.

The dumplings have a nice, earthy potato taste and a pleasing texture. I visited with Marge Olson (no relation to RO and JO) about them. She has developed her own recipe and said she is amazed at the number of people who come for dumplings on Fridays. They serve about 100. She uses 20 pounds of flour and 150 pounds of red potatoes. She and her husband, Mike, start peeling Tuesday. She perfected her recipe by trial and error and gathered tips from area cookbooks. She said the key is to have the water boiling before you put in the dumplings.

Waitresses Cindy Ellingson and Ardell Anderson, former mayor of Viking, say the diner is the gathering place for people all around. The place closes in the early afternoon, and about 10 A.M. Saturdays because—as one of them said—"Everybody goes to town."

The diner serves a full breakfast until 11 A.M., and has sandwiches and burgers with fries for lunch. It serves Schwan's ice-cream sundaes for $1.50 or $2 and waffle cones for $1.25 and $1.50.

Viking Diner also serves area groups. It is unique because it is in a spacious new building and is an antique store as well as a cafe. The antiques are the business of Jerome and Cheryl Peters. And the walls are lined with showcases with vases, china, crystal and rows of plates that have become collector's items. The curios extend around the walls of the two rooms of the diner. Whether a visitor is just eating, the chance to browse makes a trip to Viking Diner an interesting adventure. ❡

Viking Diner and Antiques still operates in Viking, Minnesota, and still serves dumplings on Fridays.

Pumpkin Figures Into Fall Menu at 'l Bistro Canad Inn

OCTOBER 7, 2009

Baked seafood penne is a signature item at 'l Bistro in the Canad Inn, and I could see why after ordering it there on a Saturday in late September. You can order the $10 petite size for lunch, or go all out with the bistro size for $14.

The $10 size is just right. It comes with a nice warm bread-stick. The pasta is moist but not sloppy wet. It has shrimp, scallops and crab tossed in asiago sauce. It was recommended to me by several in a group of friends I joined for lunch. And I would probably order the same thing on my next trip.

Because of its classy decor and

convenient location in the Canad Inn, I am pleased when someone suggests meeting there. Our group chose mainly from a half-dozen classic pasta dishes. And then, of course, we had to share the ice-cream sampler ($5) that is too good to be true. As one of the friends said, "You can't beat ice cream."

'l Bistro is one of three restaurants in Canad Inn. The others are a pub, Tavern United, and a buffet restaurant called Aaltos. 'l Bistro has a complete menu with starters and share plates, soups and salads, entrees, pizza and pasta and sandwiches. Lunch is served from 11 A.M. to 2:30 P.M. The menu is inviting and fairly easy to follow.

And with the cooler days of October, the seasonal fall menu is available. It is heavy on pumpkin, with a roasted pumpkin and white bean bisque and a pecan-crusted pumpkin pastry. There is also a pumpkin divine martini for $6, which I can do without. The creations are by Bobby Garcia, who has been chef of 'l Bistro since it opened more than two years ago. He works on dishes with Robert Parks, executive chef for Canad Inn.

For those who have their own ideas, there is a section on the menu for creating pasta your way. There is choice of pasta (linguine, spaghetti, farfalle or penne), sauce (Alfredo, meat, pesto cream, marinara or tomato cream) and topping (meatballs, Italian sausage, spicy chicken, baby shrimp or oven-roasted vegetables).

On weekends, the chef comes up with specials such as blue marlin and Angus flat-iron steak. On Mondays, it's half-price pizza and Tuesdays, it's Bistro-size pasta for a petite price. On Wednesdays, it's two meals for $30 that include entrees, wine and dessert. On Sundays, it's all the spaghetti you can eat for $9, or $10 with meatballs.

The service was good for our group of 12. An 18 percent tip was added to each of our checks, because of the group service. There was one fly driving me crazy. I do hope it soon will freeze or go south. ❡

'l Bistro continues to operate at the Canad Inn in Grand Forks.

Toasted Frog Brings High Energy to Downtown Scene

NOVEMBER 25, 2009

A couple of recent visits to the Toasted Frog on North Fourth Street substantiate my impression that this may be the liveliest dining place in town. The restaurant, in an old, high-ceilinged building, is jumping with customers from the time it opens late afternoon and on into the evening.

The reason is the unique menu, which offers appetizers that are interesting, sandwiches you don't find anywhere else and a full dinner menu. Then there's the inviting aroma that comes from the wood-fired ovens.

Sweet potato fries, a signature item at the Frog, are served crisp with chipotle aioli sauce that makes you sit up and take notice. Then there are frog legs and fried cheesy pickles—dill pickles wrapped in Havarti cheese and fried. They are a favorite of many customers.

For some, it's the appetizers to go along with something from the wine room or bar that bring them to the Frog. There are salads and soup. The seafood lavosh comes with shrimp, scallops, crab, artichokes, roasted red peppers, sundried tomatoes, red onion and Havarti cheese. It was plenty for three and rated very good by some discerning friends the other night. Wood-fired pizza comes in various versions, including spinach and wild mushroom and barbecued pork.

Dinner prices are medium to high, with the most expensive item, lobster, at $32.

The appeal of the Frog is that you can spend $10 or $15 or you can have a sandwich or pizza for a midrange outlay. Or you can have a fine dinner of something like Asian spare ribs, fish and chips made with breaded walleye strips or brown-butter mahi-mahi served with a potato and vegetable.

At the heart of the kitchen is Chef Scott Franz, a local person who is imaginative and creative, according to Shawn Clapp, who owns and operates the Frog with Jon Holth. There are a dozen kitchen employees and a dozen on the serving staff.

The owners are hometown products and enjoy being part of the downtown scene. They grew up here and learned about restaurants working for Kim Holmes, the owner of Sanders restaurant. It was Holmes who encouraged them when they went to Fargo to head up the staff when the HoDo restaurant opened in Hotel Donaldson downtown. And it was Holmes who encouraged them to return and do something with the building that stood empty on Third Street.

Over the years, the place has been home to a furniture store and an auto dealership. Some remember when it was Lola's, the Green Stamp Store or the Pink Hanger. Now a second Frog is being opened in downtown Bismarck. People say they like the Frog because it is trendy and full of energy. ❡

Toasted Frog continues to operate in Grand Forks and Bismarck, North Dakota.

Eclectic Menu Keeps EGF Applebee's Up with the Times

DECEMBER 30, 2009

When it's cold, you want soup—and you want it hot. We found it that way at Applebee's on the Boardwalk in East Grand Forks when our Meet and Eat group met there recently.

With help from my neighbors, I found the place on the menu where you order from something called Pick 'n Pair. Starting at $5.99, it says you get a choice of two items. I had a cup of tomato basil soup and a grilled shrimp and spinach salad. The soup was thick with plenty of basil flakes and chunks of tomato. It was a very nice, very satisfying lunch, especially with the toasted focaccia bread that comes with the salad.

My neighbor, Jan Wendell, proclaimed the broccoli soup as the best she ever tasted. And that's high praise from a good cook. Ruth Barney ordered a Reuben sandwich in a basket, and got a box to take half of it home. The portions are generous. The Reuben features a pile of corned beef brisket sliced thin with sauerkraut and Russian dressing along with melted Swiss cheese on rye bread. It's topped with dill pickle slices and served with fries.

We nodded our approval of the "Sweet Finish" dessert, called "shooters" of ice cream creations, for $1.99.

The menu is in keeping with a trend to serve smaller items that you can pair. There are a dozen or more appetizers to choose in lieu of ordering a full meal.

They are called "Killer Apps" and include boneless buffalo wings and sliders—three burgers with cheese, onion and sauce on toasted mini-buns. They are served with fries for $7.99.

Manager Greg Remz says customers like the "2 for $20" offerings of two full-size entrees and an appetizer for $20. He says people like to know how much they're spending, especially with the stressed economy. A couple can eat for $10 apiece.

While some Applebee's have been updated, the EGF location still sports the original design—hanging lamps of colored glass and an eclectic decor including sports banners from local high schools and colleges. And there is the traditional barber pole. During the holidays, it has been bright and inviting, with a multitude of cheery white lights.

Service was very good. Our waitress was pleasant and able to keep everything, including separate checks, in her stride. ❡

The Applebee's in East Grand Forks closed in 2011, but there is currently a franchise operating in Grand Forks.

Pear Tree Menu Takes On an Appealing Italian Flavor

MARCH 3, 2010

The Clarion Inn still is remembered as the Holiday Inn by many, and the new owners have been building up the Sunday brunch buffet that was popular in years gone by.

Served from 10 A.M. to 2 P.M., the Sunday buffet had more than 200 people on President's Day, which was also a Canadian holiday. There were so many staying over Monday that the buffet was continued. I had a chance to sample it when I joined a group of friends for brunch.

I was especially impressed by the quality of the scrambled eggs, but the bacon was not crisp as I like it. So I moved on to the sausage patty, which was quite good. There were pastries, including a very nice bran muffin. A medley of fruit went well with the buffet.

On Sundays, the buffet has a cart on which omelets are made to order, and there are free mimosa drinks for adults. The cost is $10.95 for adults, $6.95 for children and free for those younger than 5.

Alan Kargbo, food and beverage manager, came here six months ago from the Clarion Inn in Gillette, Wyo. He said there will be more menu changes with the change of seasons. Since his arrival, the Pear Tree has gone Italian with its dinner menu. The a la carte menu offers appetizers, or antipasti, along with salads and combinations for $6.95 to $9.95. The restaurant has five lasagnas and other pasta entrees are available for $6.95 to $9.95.

My check was $11.72 including tax when I ordered baked stuffed ravioli with cheese one evening. It was a perfect meal with a cold, crisp salad served first along with a wedge of fresh focaccia bread. The ravioli dish had an excellent flavor with a sun-dried tomato sauce. The serving was so large that I took half of it home.

The Pear Tree specialties are Italian steaks served with Italian salad and homemade focaccia. They include a Grilled Italian 16-ounce Black Angus sirloin and a 16-ounce New York Angus strip steak, both for $18.95, as well as a 12-ounce Tuscany sirloin for $16.95.

Employees have changed their shirts from white to black with the new ownership. Joan Omdahl, a server there for eight years, is an experienced worker who makes customers feel welcome. She is especially proud of the Italian wedding house soup that is served with tiny dumplings, or acini de pepe.

Karen Smith, dining room manager, said servers have eaten the food on the menu and are able to describe it to customers. "We ask customers how their food is tasting after the first few bites. If there is a problem, we make it right." ❡

The Clarion Inn is now a Howard Johnson's;
Pear Tree restaurant has been closed.

Wendy's Shows Low-Cost Fast Food Is More than Burgers

MARCH 24, 2010

There are so many choices at Wendy's that it makes your head swirl. When I went there recently with friends, we decided that the combos were by far the best deal. One of us ordered a burger and sides separately, and another who chose the $2.99 deluxe value meal was money ahead.

Unless you go there regularly or make a thorough study of the offerings, you don't know. One thing I have found is that for $2.97 I can get a good meal at Wendy's. That is when I order a baked potato and a small serving of chili. I drink water.

When I want a quick meal, I stop and pick up a chicken mandarin salad ($3.19). It is crisp and so large that you could split it or take some home. I am more likely to eat the whole thing. After all, it's only 180 calories. That's before adding the dressing and toppings. With these, you have as many as 370 more calories. Still, I like this salad because it has personality with little packets of sliced almonds and Chinese noodles for topping. A couple of times, however, the salad has been too watery.

My third choice at Wendy's is a burger. I am not sure why, but I like the distinctive square shape of Wendy's burgers. And I notice they advertise their beef has never been frozen. All too often on the fast-food circuit, burgers have a heavy composition and taste like they have been heated up rather than freshly cooked on a grill.

I often visit Wendy's on South Washington Street, where Brent Moen is the manager. He says the fish fillet sandwiches have been bestsellers during Lent. They are made with cod from the north Pacific. Fillets are crisp and dusted with Japanese panko breading before frying. Sandwiches come in combos or alone.

While both Wendy's have similar menus, there is a difference in their customers. On South Washington, the customers seem to come from the local area. On 32nd Avenue South, patrons are from the business area, and many are travelers off Interstate 29. The Wendy's dining rooms close at 10 P.M., but the drive-throughs are open until midnight.

Frostys are worthy as an afternoon or evening treat. And they cap off a quick meal in fine fashion. The very small chocolate or vanilla Frosty is 70 calories. But the coffee toffee twisted Frosty will add 540 to your calorie count.

You can rack up a lot of calories at Wendy's. A bacon deluxe single is 640 calories. And that's probably OK if you are shoveling snow or running marathons. The good news is that you can get a junior hamburger with standard toppings for 230 calories or order a naked junior hamburger for only 90 calories.

Ken Towers, whose family also operates Italian Moon, has owned Wendy's on South Washington for 26 years. He has had the second Wendy's for almost five years. Under Towers' direction, the Wendy's have excelled in outdoor landscaping. And the store on South Washington has been a meeting place for a cross section of the community. ⸮

Both Wendy's outlets continue to operate in Grand Forks.

Mashed Potatoes, Gravy Go Over Well at Kitty's Cafe

MAY 5, 2010

OSLO, Minn.—People have to eat, whether or not their town is surrounded by water. For two years in a row, Kitty Stromberg has been faced with running a restaurant where people come in and out of town by boat during end-of-spring flooding.

Kitty laughs about it now. The 2010 flood is over. This year, only nine days did she have to sleep in makeshift surroundings. A year ago, right after she took over the cafe, she was marooned in Oslo for 16 nights with only a mattress to sleep on.

Kitty lives in Argyle, Minn., and commutes to work. She was asked to run the restaurant in this town of 274 by businessmen who want to be sure there is a place to eat. So far, things have gone well. Kitty knows how to serve meat and potatoes. She does an especially good job of making potato salad. And she has kitchen help who know how to bake. She calls Krista Marciniak a "lifesaver."

The coffee is always hot and ready. People serve themselves and take a seat at the counter or in one of the booths. Some go into the side room, where there's a big fireplace, tables and chairs. Kitty and her staff—which includes two dependable waitresses, Jean Corradi and Shannon Bakken—keep folks happy.

The midday special was a pork chop dinner ($6.95) when I dropped in recently with a friend, Sue Huus (SH). We sat in a booth near the counter and looked over the menu. I ordered a cup of ham and bean soup and a hamburger. SH had a BLT sandwich with macaroni salad.

The soup was great—nice and hot. The serving of macaroni salad was ample. My burger was for real, although I would have liked it better if the bun was toasted. We took home some potato salad, made with red spuds that stay nice and firm and a nice sharp-tasting dressing.

When the lunch rush slowed, we visited with Kitty, who's been working in restaurants since she was in high school—first in Kennedy, Minn., then in Argyle. But she finds it is far different running a restaurant than just being an employee. Before, she would just forget about work when she got through with a shift. Now she must think of the cost and profit margin, a challenge that keeps her hopping.

She feels good about business. In the morning, one group of men comes in early. Later, another group from Dahlstrom's car dealership shows up. They all have coffee. Some have pastries. They shake dice to see who pays. If someone is getting a car serviced at the dealership and has to wait, it is a good omen for Kitty. The customers get a coupon for a meal at the cafe.

The place is the heartbeat of the town. A bulletin board has notices and messages to let people know what's going on. The news of the day is exchanged over coffee. Daily specials with mashed potatoes and gravy go over well. For people in a hurry, the cafe handles takeouts.

Kitty's is rather plain, but inviting. The counter has five comfortable seats with backs. Walls are light, and windows to the street large. Carpeting is dark green with a pattern. The side room is comfortable.

Reach Oslo by going north on Interstate 29 about 16 miles and then east on state Highway 54. Or take state Highway 220 north of East Grand Forks until you hit Highway 1. It's an easy and worthwhile drive. ❡

Kitty's continues to operate in Oslo, Minnesota.

Fosston, Minn., Cafe Serves Unique German Hamburger

MAY 12, 2010

FOSSTON, Minn.—If you want to find the best restaurant in town, just stop one of the local people on the street and ask them where to go. That's what we did when four of us were in this gateway to the Minnesota lake country a week or so ago. We asked a woman who was shopping for flowers. She pointed out Maple Ridge Cafe on Johnson Street. And away we went to a place where we found unusual taste combinations and wholesome homemade food.

This is an ordinary-looking cafe in an older building at the corner of Johnson and U.S. Highway 2 in the business district. It's a cafe where there are people peeling potatoes and mashing them in the kitchen, and where they roast their own beef and make their own soup.

We arrived before noon and found a table near the back of the restaurant, not far from the kitchen. The specials for the day included tortilla chip taco salad with homemade salsa and sour cream ($6.29). The soup of the day was smoked sausage and cheddar. There was an Asian noodle salad with bread ($5.99). And, of course, there was a hot beef sandwich ($5.99). "That is what we stick by," owner Linda Nelson told me later.

We were especially interested in the promotion for German hamburgers. What on Earth could that be? So a couple of us ordered them and found it to be a burger topped with sauerkraut. It was served on a very good bun that had been toasted. It was close to perfection, one of the best hamburgers I have eaten in ages. It was served with a garnish of parsley atop dill pickle rings. It was grade AA in my book.

On another trip, I will plan my day to eat breakfast or lunch, which is known here as dinner, at Maple Ridge Cafe.

Lunch companions that day

were Laurie L. Bakke (LLB), Merri-lee Brown (MB), and their mother, Donna McEnroe (DM). We tasted the biscuits and gravy that chef Bob Pawlitschek brought out from the kitchen. He was wearing a white jacket and chef hat. Then, we decided we could not leave without tasting the lime pie. This version was white and creamy with a sharp, inviting dimension to it.

Nelson, who owns and operates the cafe, is proud of the chef, who has attended culinary school. On weekends, she said the cooking duties often go to her husband, Bruce Nelson. He actually is an engineer, a UND graduate, who supervises the Team Industries plant in Bagley, Minn. They have two sons, Justin, 14, and Jack, 11, who help out in the cafe.

There are five part-time waitresses. One of the crew, Joyce Olson, has worked under four owners in the cafe. "When they sell it, I go along as a fixture," she said. Before leaving, we checked out the ladies' room, which is important when you're on the road, concluding it was small, but clean and adequate. ❡

Maple Ridge Cafe continues to operate in Fosston, Minnesota.

Mexican Fare Draws Crowd to Forest River on Wednesdays

SEPTEMBER 8, 2010

FOREST RIVER, N.D.—Walk into Tom's Lounge here on a Wednesday evening and you don't have to ask if this is where you find the action. You know it is because the slightly dark, slightly musty bar is alive with people from all over the area.

This is Mexican Food Night, and it's served by a crew called Jeanette's Kitchen, who also serve fish fries Friday evenings.

Jeanette Irwin is a local woman who is a whiz at cooking Mexican and other food. Lately, she has been drawing a full house. She's been in the cooking mode since 1985.

I went to Forest River on a Wednesday evening in August with a friend, Bernie Goodman (BG), to meet another friend, Rhonda Tibert (RT), who lives in the area, and her sister, Robin Feltman (RF) of Warsaw, N.D. The tables were so crowded that it didn't matter who you were meeting. You were just one in the crowd. Everyone was talking to everyone else, eating the Mexican fare and having a good time.

Some Wednesdays, Jeanette draws 150 to 160 from 5:30 to 9:30 P.M. But her repertoire goes far beyond Mexican food. She cooks lunch every weekday at Cliff's Lounge in nearby Gilby, N.D., with the help of Linda Paschke. And she caters parties and weddings. This time of the year, she cooks for the Forest River Bean Plant, and she bakes cookies and bars for Forest River Elevator.

Jeanette is a middle-aged woman who wears diamond ear-rings and a cap to hold her hair back. She was born in Ardoch, N.D., and has a son, Chris Irwin, who lives near Gilby. She also has three grandchildren.

We also met Jill Nelson, who helps out on Mexican night at Forest River, and her sister, Sara Nelson, who was in training. On their advice, before RT and RF arrived, I decided to order the combination plate, which is $7.50 for a small one and $9 for the large. I got a deluxe burrito, a side of beans and rice and a homemade corn taco.

My order was enough to hold a person for a couple of days. It was good. I brought some of it home, though. BG was more restrained in her order. She had a deluxe tostada without the beans.

We talked about summer food and harvest food with Jeanette. She makes a salsa and cheese sauce that is pleasantly hot. Her helpers said that Jeanette's sauce is what attracts people. It is nice, warm and mild—not hot. And it is velvety smooth.

Jeanette has a way with salads and beans. She uses eggs, celery, pickles, relish and a little sugar along with mustard in her potato salad. She uses a bit of whipping cream in the dressing.

Her Mexican Food Menu is complete with chicken, salads, nachos, tostadas, burritos, tacos and more. And then, just to top things off, the reverse side of the menu says in part: "Hello and welcome to our kitchen. Sit down, shut up, and quit your bitchin. What's on the menu is all we've got. Stop with the questions so you get it while it's hot. We serve chicken, beef, and seafood. A few bucks in the jar puts us in a good mood. Snowcats, farmers, bikers—we serve 'em all. Once the dishes are done we have a ball. Just place your order and take a seat. Cause you know our tacos can't be beat." ¶

Jeanette's Kitchen continues to serve Mexican food on Wednesdays at Tom's Lounge.

Del's Ushers In Holidays with Lutefisk, Lefse, Dumplings

DECEMBER 15, 2010

When Del Kresl occasionally comes back to town, he stops at his former restaurant every day. He loves to "chew the fat" with old friends.

Meanwhile, Laura Hanson, one of the new owners, is in the kitchen looking at what she needs to cook next from the wheel where waitresses place orders. She keeps turning out good, plain food for which the small cafe in the Grand Cities Mall is noted.

Laura used to run the Third Street Cafe downtown before she went to work as a cook for Kresl. She asked him one day if he was thinking of selling the cafe. Del said yes, and when he told her how much he wanted, she said it was too much.

He then said, "Well, don't buy it." She said, "I will buy it."

That was two years ago, and these days she is wearing a happy smile as she cooks and manages the restaurant with help from her sister, Becky, who also teaches at Winship Elementary School.

Del's is one of the few restaurants still serving lutefisk and lefse, the traditional holiday fare for people of Norwegian descent and other people with curiosity. People can order plates of the codfish soaked in lye and then boiled and served on a plate with drawn butter, lefse and potatoes for $9.29. Del's also is serving potato dumplings and side pork ($6.49).

When Laura isn't serving all of Del's specialties, she is turning out his ever-popular burgers made from meat that is ground and hand-pattied daily. She has a Monday–Friday breakfast special of two eggs, toast or cakes and hash browns for $2.29 that includes a small glass of orange juice or coffee.

Del's is noted for old-fashioned food such as liver and onions ($6.69) and meatloaf ($6.79). The menu still lists the Winnipeg Gas Station Special among its sandwiches. It is a toasted, triple-decker sandwich with bacon, lettuce, tomato, fried egg, baked ham and American cheese ($7.79).

The food is good, not fancy. The service is very friendly, and nobody comes around repeatedly asking if everything is all right. The place is small enough so you can catch the attention of the waitress.

Laura has a background in business here. She started working at age 15 at Miller's Cafe on South Washington Street and 17th Avenue South. She sold cars at Eide's for 10 years. She and her sister own the Kegs Drive-In and run it from April through September. ❡

Del's Coffee Shop continues to operate in Grand Forks.

Little Bangkok Strikes Chord with Sushi, Traditional Thai

FEBRUARY 9, 2011

A new Asian restaurant in East Grand Forks has come up with a dish called "DeMers Avenue." It's made of spicy tuna, salmon, shrimp, tomato, asparagus and avocado.

It was one of many Asian foods we sampled when I spent 2½ hours over lunch on a Friday afternoon at Little Bangkok. The restaurant, with its sushi and traditional Thai foods, has struck a chord with many area residents. Since opening in November, it has drawn customers who occasionally have to wait to be served. The menu is the same for lunch or dinner, and there is a tendency for people to linger over their meals.

Owner Keng Deckawuth is in a partnership with other family members who operate three sushi places in Fargo. He is the chef and relies on a Thai chef he calls Sheng to run the sushi bar with Dan Olson, whom they've trained.

The sushi bar is a popular place where people sit along a low counter with a full view of items that vary but are listed on the a la carte menu, including shrimp, egg, flying fish roe, octopus, red snapper, salmon, scallops, seared tuna, squid, super white tuna, surf clam, tuna, cooked eel and albacore.

Joel Elvrum (JE), who operates the Ranch House and has interest in the Cove restaurant in Devils Lake, was waiting for a table with his daughter, Maddy (ME), when Katie David (KD) and I were also in line. We shared a table for four and had a delightful experience because JE is knowledgeable and loves Asian food. He said he would travel to Winnipeg or Fargo to find sushi but now seems pleased to have found a place in East Grand Forks.

JE ordered a Large Boat ($40), an amazing array of sushi served on a wooden boat and decorated with tiny parasols. There was eel, red tuna, salmon, green cucumber pickles and red snapper.

I chose a mixed seafood curry dish ($15). That in itself is a more than adequate meal. We started with a salad that had a thin, nicely flavored dressing. The red curried rice was recommended by our waitress, Dom. She said it was not too spicy. This was tasty and just right.

I also enjoyed the steamed eda-mame (soybeans) we had as an appetizer. The shells were covered with sea salt, and the inside of the beans were tender and tasty.

The decor of the restaurant is inviting with tones of gray and black and red and gold accents. There is Asian art. The floor is gray. Keng plans to work with Kimberly Hess, Halstad, Minn., to develop prairie flowers that can be used on the tables in East Grand Forks as well as the Fargo locations. ❡

Little Bangkok continues to operate in East Grand Forks.

Winnipeg Woman Finds Loss of Whitey's Devastating

MARCH 9, 2011

When Pam, a businesswoman from Winnipeg, comes to Grand Forks, she wonders where to go now that Whitey's is closed.

She sent me an e-mail saying:

I am a Winnipeger, who is a longtime frequent visitor to both Grand Forks and

East Grand Forks. I spent my childhood visiting all the time. I just found out that Whitey's has closed and am devastated!!!!! After many years I tried the lobster bisque soup there and fell in love with it, of course.

While planning my visit this year, I was checking out old

and new restaurants around Grand Forks. I was checking out restaurants to visit and the hours of business and menus. I decided to check on the price of lobster bisque from Whitey's. I was planning to take some soup back home with me, only to find it closed.

So, I am still in shock, to say the least. However, I did see a lack of patrons over the years. Our visits will never be the same.

In closing, Pam said, "I am e-mailing you in a desperate hope to find a comparable restaurant that makes lobster bisque, at least close to Whitey's. Can you help?"

Well, I thought about it for a while. Then, I told Pam that I have had pretty good lobster bisque at Red Lobster on 32nd Avenue South and Columbia Road.

As I considered her question later, I decided I should tell her about the new restaurants that have opened here in the past year. These include Little Bangkok, the Thai restaurant in East Grand Forks, and Babylon in downtown Grand Forks.

I should remind her there is a cluster of restaurants around the theaters in East Grand Forks. Mamma Maria's in the theater mall has very good Italian food, and the Blue Moose across the way is a full-service restaurant with plenty of incentives.

The Boardwalk, Mike's Pizza and Applebee's add to the variety of food on the east side of the Red River. I thought, of course, of Sanders fine restaurant in the heart of downtown Grand Forks and the Toasted Frog, also on North Third Street. Bonzer's is noted for its soups.

When I posed the question to some bridge players of where Pam should go, there was a variety of suggestions. We agreed that Texas Roadhouse is a great place for steaks, and lots of people still prefer the Bronze Boot on U.S. Highway 81.

On a recent visit to Qdoba Mexican Grill, I noticed a bus from Canada pull up. We talked with the driver, and he said they were returning from a trip to Fargo and that they stopped there because they don't have Qdoba in Winnipeg.

We know Canadians are attracted to the English pub and the Bistro in the Canad Inn.

Now, I am wondering what readers would suggest to Pam from Winnipeg. For one thing, she wonders if she could find a good old-fashioned milkshake in Grand Forks.

Oh yes, and I am wondering where Pam likes to eat in Winnipeg. You can scout Winnipeg for places to eat. You can consult the guidebooks and go online for clues. But nothing beats getting advice from someone who lives there and goes out to eat often.

That person is Pam. She doesn't want me to use her last name, but she is a businesswoman. ❡

Babylon Offers a Chance to Experience Old World Cuisine

MARCH 23, 2011

Presentation is everything, and I was delighted when Thamir Khadim placed an entree called Gyro (Shawirma) Beef before me at Babylon.

The Middle Eastern restaurant that opened at Christmastime in downtown Grand Forks is doing well, according to the owner. And it offers a chance to eat a different style of food. You find lamb and falafel on the menu, as well as stuffed grape leaves called dolma, which are made with rice and meat.

When I ordered the gyro beef dish, I had no idea what I was getting for $8.99. The menu said only, "Tender slices of beef and lamb in spices." It was served on a square black plate with thinly sliced lean meat and hummus along with a light cucumber sauce, a tomato slice in one corner and cucumber slice in the other. There was a small cup of salad on the plate along with a pleasing cucumber sauce for dressing. The meat was tender and tasty, though a little too salty. The combination of tastes was nice.

It was a complete meal. With it, I had a cup of Arabic tea (99 cents) and, for dessert, a Ladies Arm, described as "curled dough with cream and pistachio." On the menu, it says $7.50, but Thamir said that was a mistake. Well, whatever.

The Ladies Arm turned out to be three small rolls of very nice mild flavored pastry—not too sweet and not too much. I finished the meal thinking I would certainly go back. If for nothing else, I would go there for Arabic tea and Ladies Arm in the afternoon. The tea was exceptionally good and so inviting, served in an ornate teacup with a tiny sugar bowl on the side.

I was having lunch with Maggie McDermott (MM), who enjoyed gyro chicken ($6.99). And MM found the pressed, thinly sliced chicken to be some of the best ever. She ordered Arabic coffee (99 cents) and found it very good. We wondered where else you can find coffee at that price.

Babylon is a small family business run by Thamir and Waffa Khadim with help from some of their five children. It's the same facility that has been the site of other restaurants in recent years—most recently Bella Vino. Some people remember the location as the lounge of the Dacotah Hotel.

There is a high back table with chairs down the center with three tables on one side and six roomy black wooden booths on the other side. The new owners have enriched the decor with artwork from their homeland.

The family, originally from Iraq, came here by way of Turkey two years ago with help from the United Nations. They have been learning English, and Thamir, who had graduated from college in Iraq, said his family feels safe in Grand Forks. ❡

Babylon continues to operate, in a new location, in Grand Forks.

Kon Nechi Wa's Japanese Cuisine Goes Well Beyond Sushi

MAY 4, 2011

They started out 10 years ago in Grand Forks selling egg rolls, fried rice and Japanese doughnuts at the downtown Farmers Market. They moved on to a little takeout place in Grand Cities Mall. And five years ago, Sadako (Sachi) and Lester MacGregor opened Kon Nechi Wa's at 3750 32nd Ave. S.

Today, they offer a daily special of chicken- or beef-fried rice, egg roll and beverage for $4.95. And they go far beyond the special, with Japanese cuisine concepts such as sushi, sashimi, edamame and harumaki. Their menu offers smoked salmon sushi, eel sushi with cucumber and avocado and items such as orange masago sushi crab meat.

The whole restaurant is tastefully decorated with Japanese art. Many of the pieces were brought by Sadako MacGregor, who came to the U.S. after she met her husband, a U.S. serviceman, on duty in Japan.

Their restaurant has quietly grown and flourished with the help of family members over the years. Twin daughters—Cathy Haines and Sandy MacGregor—are on the serving staff along with a grandson, Steven Haines, 15, who is starting out as a busboy and hopes someday to take over the business.

Cathy Haines was our waitress when I went with a group for lunch. She explained the choice of chicken- or beef-fried rice with egg roll and beverage choice on the special. She told us of the gluten-free meals served at Kon Nechi Wa's. She explained the series of sauces so we could decide how sweet or how hot we wanted to make our rice.

The menu draws diners who seek out appetizers such as calamari, coconut-breaded shrimp skewers and yaki-tori. There are several tempura offerings among the appetizers. There is a teriyaki stir-fry section, which comes in several versions. Some of the dinners feature steamed red snapper, walleye, chicken or crab legs. Entrees are in the $14 to $16 price range.

With the coming of spring and summer, Kon Nechi Wa's will add more sushi. Sushi platters, which start at $14.95, are made up in a wide variety of choices. The most expensive on the menu is Platter 9, with a half rainbow roll, Caterpillar roll, California roll, Philly Smoked Salmon roll, spicy tuna roll and hamachi, tuna, sake, ika and shrimp nigiri for $49.95.

The entire menu is there to meet the fancy of diners who want to explore the cuisine. ❡

Kon Nechi Wa's continues to operate in Grand Forks.

Cajun Cooking, Hot Wings Draw Diners to Parrot's Cay

MAY 11, 2011

Curiosity led me to an amazingly interesting adventure in eating at Parrot's Cay, just east of South Washington Street on 36th Avenue South.

Actually, it's an eating and drinking establishment that seems away from the crowds. But when I drove up to it around 6:30 P.M. on a Wednesday evening, I had a hard time finding a place to park within a block.

Once inside, I was looking around for a friend. Before I knew it, a man came over and asked if I wanted a seat. There were no empty places in the booths or tables. The man stood by his friend, Dawn Acker. They made sure we had a place to sit. And Dawn told us about the hot stuff on the menu.

At Parrot's Cay, they talk in numbers of heat you get in food items. Although the wings run from 3 to 15 in heat level, I decided on a 7 for my wings. The menu says 13 will make you sweat. All I wanted to do was eat. I ordered some fried dill pickles and a bottle of light beer to go with the wings.

My friend, who loves Cajun-style food, ordered a pasta with crawdads that comes with green peppers, onions, mushrooms and black olives sautéed in Parrot Cay sauce. This is served over a bed of angel hair pasta and topped with Parmesan cheese. You can get this for $11.99 or a half-size version (which is plenty) for $6.49.

I found the people friendly and helpful. They told me about the hot-wing eating contests held there, and pointed to the pictures on the far wall of those who had survived the wing contest.

Rob Drahovzal, who has owned Parrot's Cay for the past nine years, is around most of the time, mingling with the customers. A friendly man, he was wearing a colorful Cajun-style shirt. He said his chef, Geoffrey Stallard, comes up with more recipes than they can put on the menu. And the assistant chefs are full of ideas for wings, pasta and lavosh. He's proud of winning a wing competition at a creative barbecue contest last year in Buffalo, N.Y. The big menu at Parrot's Cay claims this is the "home of the best damn hot wings in town."

On the menu, which says a cay is a small, low island composed largely of coral and sand, there are appetizers, house specialties including salads, poor-boy sandwiches, lavosh and burgers. The Phat Guy Burger is described as a half-pound beef patty with Canadian bacon, pepperoni, fried onions, American and Swiss cheese and topped with the special Phat Guy sauce. All for $8.99.

The menu also lists red beans and rice served with Andouille sausage, bell peppers, onions, celery and spices. The Cay also serves a bowl of corn covered in Cajun butter for $1.

Food is served with utensils wrapped in a napkin. But on the table where we sat, there were a couple of rolls of paper towels that came in most handy. You need something like that when you are eating wings. ❡

Parrot's Cay continues to operate in Grand Forks.

Diners Find the New and Old Appealing at Mexican Village

SEPTEMBER 7, 2011

Mexican Village is one of those places that's always there. It's been around for decades and is always a good place to meet and eat. Mexican Village is the offshoot of the first Mexican restaurant opened downtown in Grand Forks in the 1960s by Bob Mora, who stayed in this area after retiring from the U.S. Air Force.

It's the home of the Norwegian taco ($5.59), a lightly deep-fried pita bread topped with beef, lettuce, cheese, tomatoes and sour cream. It has a steady following here since it was introduced by Mae and Ray Gordon, who operated the restaurant before selling it to Angie Green 10 years ago. She had worked for them, and with her partner, Joe Egstad, carries on the same traditions as the Gordons.

My order recently for a late lunch was for a small beef quesadilla ($5.09) and a diet cola in a bottle—not one of those hu-mongous glasses—($1.89). As I waited, I demolished a half basket full of chips with some very, very mild salsa. The quesadilla also was mildly flavored with a pleasing combination of lettuce, green pepper, beef, olives and tomato.

The menu said, "Real Mexican foods are not overly hot, just seasoned well enough to satisfy the taste for something very exciting." That is why many people enjoy the food at Mexican Village. And it also has been the subject of criticism from some who prefer more hot and spicy fare.

Among the specialties is a Mexican pizza. This is a crisp flour tortilla topped with beef, cheese, onions, green peppers, tomatoes and black olives. The small version is $5.49, and the large is $6.49.

Desserts are there for those who want a sweet finish to a meal. They include Mexican fried ice cream, apple cinnamon delight and sopapilla, which is fried bread dough sprinkled with cinnamon and sugar and served with warm maple or chocolate syrup for dipping ($3.19). And then there's cinnamon ice cream.

Mexican Village has daily lunch specials ranging from $4.09 for a flour tortilla with cheese to a medium burrito for $5.19. A small Mexican pizza is featured for $4.89. Kids eat free off the children's menu Sundays.

Mexican Village stays pretty much the same from year to year. However, the new chicken pepper gravy has taken off on burritos, according to Green. ❡

Mexican Village continues to operate in Grand Forks.

Ruby Tuesday's Vast Menu Offers Many Healthy Choices

DECEMBER 21, 2011

My yearning for lobster was satisfied on a recent visit to the new Ruby Tuesday restaurant. I don't need a huge amount, and the small lobster tail served with the Shellfish Trio was perfect. It was served with a lump crab cake and three jumbo shrimp.

The cost for the shellfish trio dinner is $17.99, and with it, you have a choice of two fresh sides. I chose steamed broccoli that was done just right—not that mushy stuff that often shows up in restaurants. And I had another side of grilled green beans. There was a tiny biscuit served with the meal.

The decor is warm and inviting, with dark wood and brown tones throughout. Soft lamplight provides a cozy feeling. Servers look professional in all-black shirts and trousers.

Ruby Tuesday features lobster specials on weekends, including a lobster tail served with petite sirloin steak ($17.99). Other specials include lobster mac and cheese and garden bar ($14.99). The "shareables"—or appetizers— include Asian dumplings and Southwestern spring rolls. There are chicken tenders and quesadillas.

I would go back and order the grilled salmon salad ($13.99) that comes with fresh greens, peas, grated Parmesan cheese and croutons—a person would become familiar with them after a few visits.

I chose a late-afternoon time on a Saturday in December to try out Ruby Tuesday, one of five in North Dakota and 1,200 around the country. And even at 4:15 P.M.,

the parking spots in front of the new restaurant were filling up. It has received a warm welcome here. The menu at Ruby Tuesday is vast, varied and full of healthful choices. At the same time, it is mind-boggling at first.

There was little to criticize in this beautiful new restaurant. The only thing I noticed was watermarks on the steak knife that came wrapped with a fork and spoon in a nice clothlike paper napkin.

One plus for the restaurant was found on the menu saying, "We don't add automatic gratuity for groups. We believe the amount you reward your server should be your choice." ❡

Ruby Tuesday continues to operate in Grand Forks.

Positive Vibes Permeate in Newly Refurbished Whitey's

DECEMBER 28, 2011

The newly remodeled version of Whitey's in East Grand Forks is

up and running. And sometime in January, there will be a grand opening, according to Tim Bjerk, the new owner.

He lists such house specialties as braised beef short ribs, Italian roasted chicken and pasta dishes. And the new menu offers a series of dinner choices including salmon, walleye, shrimp, lobster tail, steaks, prime rib, pan-fried chicken, stuffed pork chop and baby back ribs.

When asked how things are going, Bjerk shook his head and said, "I've got a lot to learn."

When I went there for lunch Dec. 17 with my daughter Gail (DG), from Bismarck, we agreed Whitey's is back on track.

We remember the days long ago when Whitey's was a wide-open place full of people from all ranks and ages. The old horse-shoe bar is still the center of activity. A game room sports a Schwinn bicycle hanging by the entry. A formal dining room with white cloths and desirable round tables is an important part of the new Whitey's.

But it's the food that matters. DG and I found our lunch visit quite good. Chef Michael Rude is turning out appetizers, including chicken liver pâté, long a trademark of Whitey's. When I found the Riverboat sandwich on the menu, I had to have it—for old time's sake. I found this version very satisfactory, served with onions and mushrooms on crunchy grilled ciabatta bread for $11.99.

I was especially pleased with the coleslaw as a side. I had, in fact, inquired about it since I don't believe it should be cabbage swimming in sloppy dressings. Our waitress offered to bring me a sample in a tiny cup before I made my choice.

The Whitey's coleslaw is great—crisp, with a light dressing. And often I think that as the coleslaw goes, so goes the menu.

The luncheon special of beef tips, onions, mushrooms, pepper and red wine gravy on mashed potatoes ($9.99) was DG's choice. She was pleased with the basic, good taste and commented, "The idea here is we won't eat for the rest of the day."

We decided to share dessert and chose the chef's own version of tiramisu. The traditional layered dessert with sponge cake soaked in espresso syrup and a whipped Mascarpone mousse was $6.99. It was heavenly to taste and beautifully presented, with tiny puffs of whipped cream and a tiny mint leaf.

There is a positive feeling about the food, the kitchen, the service. There is a general hope that the restaurant—one of the oldest in this region—will succeed.

Recently added is a large, new black-and-white painting by Patty Kobetsky that is a study of the history surrounding the Wonderbar of days gone by. It stirs memories for some customers. ❡

Marilyn reports, "Whitey's is still open and doing OK as far as I can tell. It has lots of competition but the advantage, too, of being in what we call the Boardwalk, or 'restaurant row,' above the Red River in East Grand Forks. With its long history, it is a place people go to when they come back for visits or reunions."

Southgate Serves Up Tasty Food, Fun at Bargain Prices

JANUARY 11, 2012

Southgate Casino Bar and Grill has entrenched itself as a place where people go for good food as well as bingo and games. On the first day of January, I joined a group of friends to visit and eat at Southgate, a laid-back type of place where people go for good times and good food at bargain prices. Our server was Rachel, and she did a very good job of keeping a large group with varied orders happy.

When I ordered the clubhouse sandwich with fries, I feared it would be too much for one person. The sandwich was nicely presented, and the fries were as good as they get—light golden in color and lightly salted. My idea of a club sandwich is turkey, bacon, tomato and lettuce in a toasted double-decker format. The Southgate version has all of that, plus some bland cheese that seems unnecessary. But it is good, and it is excessive. Half of it went home to join other leftovers in the refrigerator. My check was $8.49.

Others in the group were eating Walleye Chunks ($9.99) and Walleye Subs ($10.99). After a discussion, they decided the walleye fillets were preferable to the chunks, which had a heavy coating. In fact, the fillets were rated quite high.

The Southgate soup stood up to its standards in the potato dumpling version available.

Customers seem to find their favorites at Southgate. And they wait for the specials that show up—such as the French dip and fries Wednesdays, which is sometimes offered for $1.99. That is, if you also purchase a drink from the bar.

The No. 1 seller is the sirloin tips with mushrooms, onions and peppers. The deluxe version is $11.49 for a small order or $16.99 for a large one. These come with garlic toast and creamy red potatoes. Otherwise, you can get the tips and reds for $9.99.

If it's a dessert you seek, forget it. Southgate doesn't list any on the menu. Otherwise, the Southgate menu is fairly complete, with burgers, Mexican food, soups and salads, chicken, wraps and appetizers and lavosh—along with Southgate specialties. These include the steak sandwich, Reuben, Southgate Philly and a steak or chicken chipotle melt. There is also a "Poutine" item on the lavosh menu. It is described as fries and cheese curds topped with gravy ($16.99). ❡

Creativity Helps Blue Moose Stay Ahead of the Game

JANUARY 18, 2012

The concept of tapas (small plates dining), which originated in Spain, is doing quite well at the Blue Moose in East Grand Forks. The current tapas menu promotes sharing, and provides different tastes to a meal.

New on the tapas menu are an olive-and-cheese platter ($8) and chicken pâté served with butter crackers and garnished with red onions ($5). Then, there's a barbecue rib taster ($8) that has "Blue Moose Norwegian barbecue sauce." The menu claims that sticky fingers never tasted so good. Also among the tapas choices is a Mini Mac classic ($4).

The Blue Moose keeps switching and offering changes. In March, Chef Nate Sheppard promises a new section of the menu offering beer pairing choices.

Sheppard, who has become well-known as a chef in the Greater Grand Forks area, is one of the new owners of the Moose.

With Patrick Boppre, the front house manager, he is in the process of buying the restaurant from manager Dave Homstad, Lyle Gerszewski and Greg Stennes.

Boppre is a native of East Grand Forks and has worked his way up at the Moose, starting as a busboy. Sheppard, who grew up in Grand Forks, is a graduate of Le Cordon Bleu in Portland, Ore. He has been featured in healthful cooking classes in the area. He stresses use of fresh ingredients and a minimum of salt and fat. He employs about 30 in the kitchen at Blue Moose.

The Moose moved to its present location along the East Grand Forks "boardwalk" of restaurants after the Flood of 1997. Before, it was on DeMers Avenue.

The Blue Moose fares well as an independent restaurant, one of several non-franchise operations in East Grand Forks. While it misses out on the national advertising for chain restaurants, its owners believe they fare well because of their creativity.

While several restaurants run buses to UND hockey games on weekends, the Blue Moose has no bus. Owners said they wouldn't know where to put the extra people, since 6:30 to 7:30 P.M. Fridays is already a rush.

The restaurant was pleasantly busy Jan. 9 when I stopped for lunch to savor their soup, advertised for $4. I chose chicken fajita

($4), and it was almost a meal in itself. It was piping hot, very rich. It came with just the right amount of crackers.

Because its menu is so varied, people stop for quick lunches, afternoon repasts and dinner. The menu features New York Strip Steak ($22), a flat-iron steak ($14) and a bone-in ribeye ($27). They offer chicken and seafood.

The menu is folksy and fun in a newspaper format, although it's a little hard for the occasional diner to follow. ❡

The Blue Moose continues to operate in East Grand Forks.

Long-Awaited Olive Garden Receives a Warm Welcome

MARCH 7, 2012

After a lengthy wait for Olive Garden to open in Grand Forks, the lines were long in February. The novelty is slowly wearing off, but the steady following attests the warm welcome.

My first visit to Olive Garden

was during mid-afternoon, so I could be sure to get in. After a late breakfast, I figured a late lunch would be fashionable.

The place is impressive. It's fashioned in Tuscan farmhouse style with a welcoming entryway.

There is seating for those who are waiting. My booth was near the kitchen, and I watched the waiters in white shirts, ties, black trousers and aprons adorned with gold-colored towels. They were busy at midday, punching in orders and carrying out bread and pasta.

It had been a few years since I ate at the older Olive Garden in Fargo, so I studied the two manageable menus offering appetizers, soups and salads, grilled sandwiches, pizza, classic dishes, chicken and seafood and filled pastas.

At length, I asked my server what she would recommend. She suggested chicken Alfredo, and I went with that. Instead of the raspberry lemonade she suggested, I drank water.

She first brought me the familiar Olive Garden salad bowl with crisp greens, peppers, onion rings and yes—several black olives. Along with it came a plate with two long, warm breadsticks.

The chicken Alfredo ($10.95) was warm and comforting on a cold day. The portion was generous. My server was ready with Parmesan cheese. As I ate, I noticed the vases and planters with permanent flower displays on the ledges. There are several dining areas with arched doorways. And there is a fireplace that adds warmth to the decor.

Olive Garden has an attractive bar area to the right of the entryway. The restaurant has a full liquor license and a wine list offering a wide selection to complement Italian meals. Nonalcoholic beverages include coolers, specialty coffees and hot teas. On a hot summer day, I will try the raspberry lemonade that was recommended.

There's a homemade soup, salad and breadstick lunch available until 4 P.M. daily for $6.95.

An olive branch on menu items signified low-fat entrees. There is a Garden Fare Nutrition Guide available for customers seeking gluten-free food. And for those with food allergies, Olive Garden has an Allergen Information Guide.

All in all, it is the largest and

most beautiful restaurant now operating in Grand Forks. It attracts visitors from out of town as well as people who live here. Olive Garden is part of the Darden chain of restaurants, which also operates Red Lobster. There are about 700 restaurants, including four Olive Gardens in North Dakota's major cities.

Olive Garden has gained a following since 1982 with its ample portions and relaxed ambience. It's known for its classic lasagna, fettuccine Alfredo and chicken Parmigiana. ❡

The Olive Garden continues to operate in Grand Forks.

Elegant Food, Impeccable Service Define Le Bernardin

MARCH 21, 2012

We had dined at Dovetail—one of New York City's finest restaurants—the first evening we were in the city. With friends, we had a wonderful time visiting and tasting. We went to Shake Shack in Times Square the second evening. Ryan Babb of Forum Communications, who accompanied me on our whirlwind tour, thought we should see where real, down-to-earth people eat.

We took a Shake Shack menu handed out on the sidewalk and stood in line about 20 minutes before we could even get inside. We enjoyed the experience. And actually the burgers were very tasty. They had that good flavor that only comes with a little fat. We are not sure if they contained the pink slime that has hit the news waves of late. And we didn't ask.

Then, there was a lunch at the

exclusive Crown, on Madison Avenue. There, the food seems unexcelled and the ambience both warm and sedate.

We approached Le Bernardin with awe because of its reputation as THE top restaurant in the city. It is a longtime holder of the top star ratings by the Michelin Guide. We spent almost four hours in this famous restaurant, which has its origins in France.

It was an unforgettable experience because of the elegant food and impeccable service. We came away marveling at the highly professional serving staff, the sommelier who described the wines he paired with each course, and the chefs in the kitchen. We were surprised when Eric Ripert, chef-owner of Le Bernardin, invited us into the kitchen.

This was a dazzling scene, with pastry chefs and sous chefs in stiffly starched bright white uniforms, busily engaged in their work.

On Thursday, we were treated to the chef's tasting menu. Servings were light and inviting. First course: caviar wagyu. Second course: octopus. Ryan said he had never eaten it before. I nodded and said, "Neither have I. Dig in."

The sommelier, Aldo Sohm, stayed with us, describing in a delightful witty way of how he paired each course with the right wine. It was a leisurely meal with small, very dainty servings. We were comfortable.

Sohm really made the meal an enjoyable adventure. He has been voted best sommelier in America—and indeed the world. He is wise about wines and explained how each wine blends with the food. He poured sipping-sized portions. The wine did not overwhelm the tastes we experienced.

Waiters were on hand with a variety of breads, and there was softened butter with a dash of sea salt in small metal containers.

The courses kept coming. There was a sea medley, then codfish. We ate monkfish with Brussels sprouts. Then there was a Seville orange sorbet with olive oil and basil.

The final course was called chocolate peanut. This was a Madagascar chocolate ganache, peanut mousse and salted caramel ice cream. Each was bite-sized—a medley of wonderful tastes. When the salted caramel ice cream drooped a little, the waiter took it away and replaced it.

While we came ready to be served and pay the cost, we realized the staff was aware of our mission of testing, tasting and writing. We received special attention, but I think the experience would be as good for all customers.

The diners were middle-aged and older, dressed in fine cloth-ing and enjoying their conversations over fine food. We found it all quite appealing.

There were special touches I liked about Le Bernardin. At the beginning of the meal, the waiter asked if we had any food allergies. We noticed small tables where women can place their purses. No need to sit there wrestling with a bag all evening.

There are not many minuses at Le Bernardin. That, obviously, is why it is considered tops in the Big Apple. ❡

Le Bernardin continues to operate in New York.

Sleek, Large New Fuji Offers Japanese Cuisine with Flair

APRIL 4, 2012

Nick Zak (NZ) said he had a Philadelphia roll for lunch at the relatively new Fuji Japanese Seafood and Steakhouse on South Washington Street. His friend, Wayne Bakke (WB), had just finished a Feija lunch box.

"My gosh," he said. "It was plenty."

Both NZ and WB paid $8.95 for lunch. They like checking out restaurants around town. Next time, they said, they would bring their wives.

After talking with NZ and WB as they were leaving the restaurant, which opened Feb. 1, I sauntered inside the sleek and large new facility. I figured I was in luck when I ran across a 10-year-old named Ben Christoferson (BC), a fourth-grader at Century Elementary School.

He watches food shows on TV and is well-acquainted with the likes of Anthony Bourdain. BC was having a late lunch afternoon—free of school—with his mother, Kim Cowden (KC). We proceeded to explore the restaurant together. For me, it was a mystery, but BC was quick to explain the offerings at the sushi bar, where chefs in white uniforms artfully prepare specialties—many of which feature raw fish. (Diners also can choose seating at hibachi tables, in booths or at a long, attractive bar.)

Here's where a child's knowledge came in handy. He told me they call the drinks something else, but they are really made from Coca-Cola. After ordering sweetened iced Nestea, I thought green tea would have been a better fit with my meal.

My sushi lunch platter was a beautiful creation of a tuna roll and California roll, which were artistically arranged with spikes of crisp cucumber and leaves of thinly sliced cucumber. And we tasted a marvelous king crab crunch roll. With it, I took a dab of wasabi, and BC giggled as he reminded me it was "hothot." The pickled ginger was a great palate cleanser.

BC was saving himself for one of the four hibachi tables, where patrons—young and old—can sit and watch Japanese chefs prepare their food. He loves to order steak and shrimp.

A chef named Johnny put on a wonderful show for us. He appeared in a red hat and prepared food with a flair. At one point, he cracked an egg and managed to gather the yolk with a spatula and toss it in the air. He returned it to the table intact. He was—in a word—fantastic. And the food was excellent—the steak, shrimp, rice, vegetables so crisp and tasty. We were pleasantly filled and generally pleased.

Fuji is spacious with a clean, uncluttered design. Tiny hanging lamps add to the ambience. The restaurant is one of three under the same management in North Dakota. Others are in Fargo and Bismarck.

This style of restaurant is rare in our area. For those familiar with Japanese restaurants, it is a delight. For others, it is an experience. The menus at Fuji are long and detailed. It seems it would take several visits to figure out what you want. Those who wish to stay away from raw fish will find plenty of choices. And the menu is full of pictures of the various dishes to help diners make decisions. ¶

Fuji Japanese Seafood and Steakhouse continues to operate in Grand Forks.